SPIRITUAL EVOLUTION

ALSO BY GEORGE E. VAILLANT

Aging Well

The Wisdom of the Ego

Adaptation to Life

The Natural History of Alcoholism

How Fathers Care for the Next Generation

SPIRITUAL
EVOLUTION

A Scientific Defense of Faith

GEORGE E. VAILLANT, M.D.

BROADWAY BOOKS

New York

PUBLISHED BY BROADWAY BOOKS

Published in the United States by Broadway Books, an imprint of The Doubleday Broadway Publishing Group, a division of Random House, Inc., New York.
www.broadwaybooks.com

BROADWAY BOOKS and its logo, a letter B bisected on the diagonal, are trademarks of Random House, Inc.

Permissions appear following the notes.

Illustrations on pp. 28 and 33 by Jackie Aher.

Library of Congress Cataloging-in-Publication Data
Vaillant, George E., 1934–
Spiritual evolution : a scientific defense of faith / George E. Vaillant.—1st ed.
 p.   cm.
Includes bibliographical references.
1. Psychology, Religious. 2. Psychology and religion. 3. Emotions—Religious aspects.
4. Positive psychology. 5. Faith. 6. Spirituality. I. Title.

BL53.V25 2008
200.1'9—dc22
2007043278

ISBN 978-0-7679-2658-4

First Edition
146086900

For

S.B.V. (1908–1995)

In filial gratitude and love

I believe that I can see a direction and a kind of progress for life. . . . If my hypothesis is correct . . . with their cyclical development horse, stag and tiger became like the insect, to some extent prisoners of the instruments of their swift moving or predatory ways. . . . In the case of the primates, on the other hand, evolution went straight to work on the brain, neglecting everything else, which accordingly remained malleable.

PIERRE TEILHARD DE CHARDIN, *The Phenomenon of Man* (London: Collins, 1959), pp. 142–60

CONTENTS

❧

ACKNOWLEDGMENTS

This book has been twelve years in the writing and there are many to thank. James Lomax, MD, the wise and generative Baylor College of Medicine training director, provided the initial impetus for this book when he invited me to give five talks between 1994 and 2004 at the annual Psychotherapy and Faith Conference of the Institute for Religion and Health at the Baylor College of Medicine. The conference topics he assigned me were hope, love, faith, joy, and forgiveness, topics on which at that point I had not yet written a single word. Sometimes called the theological virtues, the topics were a gift, but for a psychiatrist they were a challenge. A generous and imaginative Texas philanthropist, Loise Wessendorff, underwrote the support for these psychiatric conferences.

During the same period I served as a Class A (nonalcoholic) trustee of Alcoholics Anonymous. For six years, AA members, too many to list, gently educated me in the fact that spirituality was about the "language of the heart" and not about the language of written words. After leaving AA, I passed into the equally generative hands of Martin Seligman in order to join the steering committee of the Center for Positive Psychology at the University of Pennsylvania, from 2001 to 2007.

I wish to acknowledge the generous support during the past twelve years of the National Institute of Mental Health, and also of the John Templeton Foundation. During the preparation of this book, from 2005 to 2007, the foundation underwrote six weeks a year at the Center for Positive Psychology and provided the resources to invite exciting guests such as Melvin Konner, Greg Fricchione, Stephen Post, and Robert Cloninger to ponder with me the relationship between mammalian evolution and human spirituality. The foundation also stimulated the book's creation by inviting me to give the Templeton Research Lectures in Religion and Science at the University of Pennsylvania (2005–2006).

Along the way, many individuals critiqued the book's eleven chapters. Among the particularly helpful readers were: Monika Ardelt, Dan Blazer, Maren Batalden, Brock Brower, Sara Coakley, William Clark, Debbie Cohen, Kirsten Cronlund, Mike Csikszentmihalyi, Greg Fricchione, Emily Greenfield, Diane Highum, Christine Howard, Kahlil Kahlil, Melvin Konner, Ernest Kurtz, Sue and Ilan Kutz, Irene Kontje, Ronald Lee, William Miller, Sue Mancie, Jenni Mariano, Mary McCarthy, Michael Morton, Jill Niemark, John Peteet, James Pritchard, Paulding Phelps, Stephen Post, Frank Robertson, Howard Spiro, Carolyn Spiro, Debbie Swick, Kathy Sanders, Martin Seligman, Janice Templeton, Anne Vaillant, Joanna Vaillant, and Phyllis Zagano.

Caroline Vaillant, Joanna Settle, Montgomery Brower, and Tom Kinder read drafts of the entire book. Their help was enormous.

Perhaps the greatest challenge was getting the book out of my brain and into readers' hands. For this daunting task of translation I had four very gifted editors. The first agent to whom I showed the book, Jill Kneerim, read it carefully and then took me to lunch and the woodshed, for which I am very grateful. A year later, Laura Yorke, both editor and agent, generously provided me her orderly mind to help me outline and organize the text. Of equal importance, she placed the book with a mainstream New York publishing house and with a gifted editor, Amy Hertz. Amy passed along the book, which still needed clarity, to Kris Puopolo at Doubleday Broadway. Kris, a no-nonsense taskmaster, provided real focus by completing what Laura had begun. At last, coherent words were attached to my music.

Two other women were also essential to this book but in rather different ways. The first was Robin Western, who, when she was not protecting my writing time by looking after the Study of Adult Development (my "day" job) at Brigham and Women's Hospital, was generously retyping the drafts of this slowly evolving book. My deepest thanks go also to my wife, Caroline. For almost forty years she has been my model for the positive emotions of trust, love, hope, forgiveness, and compassion. If that were not enough, she has induced in me the reciprocal positive emotions of joy, love, and gratitude.

SPIRITUAL EVOLUTION

1

Positive Emotions

※

Lord, make me an instrument of your peace.

Where there is hatred, let me sow love.

Where there is injury, let me sow forgiveness; . . .

Where there is doubt, let me sow faith;

Where there is despair, let me give hope. . . .

Where there is sadness, let me give joy;

O Master, grant that I may not so much to seek

compassion but to give compassion.

—*"The Peace Prayer of St. Francis"*
ATTRIBUTED TO FATHER ESTHER BECQUEREL (1912)

※

Just as a prism separates white light into a spectrum of discrete colors, so this book separates spirituality into a broad spectrum of positive emotions. By focusing on the positive emotions, I wish to perform for spirituality what the science of nutrition has performed for the world's discordant diets. Just as nutrition identifies the vitamins and the four basic food groups that make other people's peculiar ethnic diets nourishing, so neuroscience, cultural anthropology, and ethology identify the love, community building, and positive emotions that enduring religions have in common.

Here's a true story told by Jack Kornfield, a clinical psychologist. Traveling by train from Washington to Philadelphia, Dr. Kornfield found himself seated next to the director of a rehabilitation program for juvenile offenders, particularly gang members who had committed homicide.

One fourteen-year-old boy in the program had shot and killed an innocent teenager to prove himself to his gang. At the trial, the victim's mother sat impassively silent until the end, when the youth was convicted of the killing. After the verdict was announced, she stood up slowly and stared directly at him and stated, "I'm going to kill you." Then the youth was taken away to serve several years in the juvenile facility.

After the first half year the mother of the slain child went to visit his killer. He had been living on the streets before the killing, and she was the only visitor [in jail] he'd had. For a time they talked, and when she left she gave him some money for cigarettes. Then she started step by step to visit him more regularly, bringing food and small gifts. Near the end of his three-year sentence, she asked him what he would be doing when he got out. He was confused and very uncertain, so she offered to help set him up with a job at a friend's company. Then she inquired about where he would live, and since he had no family to return to, she offered him temporary use of the spare room in her home. For eight months he lived there, ate her food, and worked at the job. Then one evening she called him into the living room to talk. She sat down opposite him and waited. Then she started, "Do you remember in the courtroom when I said I was going to kill you?" "I sure do," he replied. "I'll never forget that moment." "Well, I did," she went on. "I did not want the boy who could kill my son for no reason to remain alive on this earth. I wanted him to die. That's why I started to visit you and bring you things. That's why I got you the job and let you live here in my house. That's how I set about changing you. And that old boy, he's gone. So now I want to ask you, since my son is gone, and that killer is gone, if you'll stay here. I've got room, and I'd like to adopt you if you let me."[1] And she became the mother he never had.

Her compassion! Her forgiveness! Where did they come from? We can all identify with the woman's primal growl of "I'm going to kill you." And when, in her living room, she reminded her boarder of what she had said in court, I feared what would come next. But then I was surprised. For Hindu and Jew, for Buddhist and Christian, that moment would have been equally moving, but this story lacked even a hint of "religion." What had happened? Unselfish love had conquered both Darwinian "selfish" genes and Kantian pure reason. The transformative power of positive emotion had interceded.

Positive emotions—not only compassion, forgiveness, love, and hope but also joy, faith/trust, awe, and gratitude—arise from our inborn mammalian capacity for unselfish parental love. They emanate from our feeling, limbic mammalian brain and thus are grounded in our evolutionary heritage. All human beings are hardwired for positive emotions, and these positive emotions are a common denominator of all major faiths and of all human beings.

Thus, this is, in some respects, a revolutionary book. I shall argue that the positive emotions are not just nice to have; they are essential to the survival of Homo sapiens as a species. In Descartes' Error, Antonio Damasio, a sensitive clinical neurologist and arguably the wisest student of emotions on the planet, convincingly argues that the mind and the body are one. However, he concludes, "it is difficult to imagine that individuals and societies governed by the seeking of pleasure, as much as or more than by the avoidance of pain, can survive at all."[2] If readers will permit me to define pleasure as the result of positive emotion rather than mere hedonism, then Damasio is in error. This book summarizes scientific evidence—gathered over the fourteen years that have elapsed since Damasio made his assertion—suggesting that positive emotions are very important indeed. As noted in chapter 6, by the year 2003 Damasio too had softened his position.

As the twenty-first century begins, a great many people—especially in the English-speaking world—are in search of some kind of common spiritual ground. On the one hand, increasing education and intolerance for patriarchal dogma have led to steady erosion in membership in most mainstream religions. On the other hand, this shift toward secularism has been offset by an equally steady increase in fundamentalist religions that isolate their believers from the rest of the world. As a result, contemporary culture holds no universally accepted view of human nature. If the world is going to function as one small planet, the development of some kind of consensus regarding human nature is essential. That consensus should include the recognition that human nature is more than a bunch of "selfish" genes.

و۶۶

Recently, I tentatively began to discuss spirituality with a close friend of mine, a brilliant woman and a devout Episcopalian to boot. "When I hear the word 'spirituality,'" she exploded, "I break out in spots!" I was surprised to hear her voice her sentiment so strongly, but to her spirituality was no more than illusion. The problem, of course, is that the word "spirituality" has many meanings. While spirituality is both the source and the outgrowth of faith for many people, for just as many others it is considered suspect. For them, spirituality is equated with the occult and with bogus faith healers; it brings to mind reincarnation, telepathy, crystals, angels, and tarot cards. To others, spirituality can appear as nothing more than covert narcissism and a new-age mandate to follow your bliss. I believe these mind-sets to be terribly mistaken.

True, we may have trouble defining spirituality, but we all know and admire it when we see it. Let me mention three men who would be on most people's list of spiritual exemplars. For reasons embedded in our evolving genes, it is likely that the behaviors of three forgiving and compassionate leaders, Nelson Mandela, Martin Luther King Jr., and Mohandas Gandhi, will remain in memory and continue to shape human behavior.

This book defines spirituality as the amalgam of the positive emotions that bind us to other human beings—and to our experience of "God" as we may understand Her/Him. Love, hope, joy, forgiveness, compassion, faith, awe,[3] and gratitude[4] are the spiritually important positive emotions addressed here. I have omitted from the list four other positive emotions—excitement, contentment, hilarity, and a sense of mastery—because we can feel these latter four emotions alone on a desert island. In sharp contrast, the eight positive emotions that I have selected all involve human connection. None of the eight are "all about me."

Negative emotions such as fear and anger are also inborn and are of tremendous importance. Dedicated to individual survival, the negative emotions are "all about me." In contrast, positive emotions have the potential to free the self from the self. We feel both the emotions of vengeance and of forgiveness deeply, but the long-term results of these two emotions are very different. Negative emotions are often crucial for survival—but only in time present. The positive emotions are more expansive and help us to broaden and build.[5] They widen our tolerance, expand our moral compass, and enhance our creativity. They help us to survive in time future. Careful experiments document that while negative emotions narrow attention and miss the forest for the trees,[6] positive emotions, especially joy, make thought patterns more flexible, creative, integrative, and efficient.[7] In the example of the mother and her son's killer, positive emotion led to a remarkable expansion in the lives of each. In contrast, negative emotions like disgust and despair freeze us in our tracks. When we are frightened, angry, or depressed, it is hard to create or to learn new things.

The effect of positive emotion on the autonomic (visceral) nervous system has much in common with the relaxation response to meditation popularized by Harvard professor of medicine Herbert Benson.[8] In contrast to the metabolic and cardiac arousal that the fight-or-flight response of negative emotion induces in our *sympathetic* autonomic nervous system, positive emotion via our *parasympathetic* nervous system reduces basal metabolism, blood pressure, heart rate, respiratory rate, and muscle tension. Indeed, if sleep slowly lowers our basal metabolism by 8 percent, meditative states lower our metabolism 10 to 17 percent. Functional imaging (fMRI) studies of Kundalini yoga meditation by Andrew Newberg and associates at the

University of Pennsylvania Medical School have documented such increased parasympathetic activity producing relaxation, followed by a profound sense of quiescence.[9]

California psychology professor Robert Emmons has spent his career
studying gratitude and notes that ingratitude shrinks the self; gratitude
expands the self. "First, gratitude is the acknowledgement of goodness in
one's life . . . second, gratitude is recognizing that the source(s) of the goodness lie at least partially outside of the self."[10] The wonder of an American
Thanksgiving Day celebration need not be religious, but I would like to
submit that it is more spiritual than humanist. If the universe were just
about humans, it would be a terrible waste of space.

Positive emotion, meditation, and spiritual experience cannot be dis-
entangled. One report noted that 45 percent of people sensed the sacred
during meditation and 68 percent experience a sense of the sacred after
childbirth.[11] Benson reports that 80 percent of his meditators chose a sacred
symbol as a mantra for meditation.[12]

Spirituality, then, is not just about following your bliss. Spirituality has
a deep psychobiological basis—a reality rooted in the positive human emotions that needs to be better understood. Today many fear or mock religion
because of its association with "holy terror" and "assault on reason." In contrast, I believe that by taking the science of positive emotions seriously, we
can make spirituality palatable, even useful, to the critics of religions. Simultaneously, we can help those enthralled by their own faith traditions to
appreciate what they have in common with the faith traditions of others.

Positive emotion is a brain activity that all humans share because they
are born with it. Richard Davidson is a University of Wisconsin neuropsychologist who has built his distinguished career on clarifying that in people
with gloomy, introverted personalities the right prefrontal brain (above
your right eye socket) is biologically more active than the left prefrontal
brain. In people with sunny, outgoing personalities, the left prefrontal brain
is more active than the right. In studying the brain activity of a devout Tibetan monk with decades of loving-kindness meditation behind him,
Davidson found that the monk's left prefrontal brain activity was higher
than in any of 175 normative Westerners he had tested.[13]

Once we recognize that spirituality has a biological basis, we realize that we must have evolved toward spirituality. It is not too great a leap to hope that as natural selection continues, if we don't denude or blow up our planet first, human beings may become still more spiritual.

⁂

Spiritual Evolution builds on the relatively new scientific disciplines of ethology (animal behavior) and neuroscience—both of which have enabled the scientific study of positive emotions such as love, joy, awe, and compassion. Each of these emotions has a neurobiological basis and an evolutionary architecture that will be explored in individual chapters. The exact mechanism by which such evolution takes place is a subject of speculation, but over the last fifteen years it has become clearer. The mechanism undoubtedly has something to do with the fact that "emotions are curious adaptations that are part and parcel of the machinery with which organisms regulate survival."[14] You see, evolution has the daunting task of organizing 100 billion neurons into an adaptive brain, using only 45,000 genes. All the genes can do is to provide the means by which environment can do the heavy lifting in sculpting our brains.

Over the past fifteen years, four scientists have suggested the means by which natural selection could lead to prosocial behavior. In 1992 Gerald Edelman began with his concept of "neural Darwinism": the sculpting of the brain by individual and cultural environments, outlined in an influential book, *Bright Air, Brilliant Fire*.[15] A few years later, Antonio Damasio with *Descartes' Error*, and Jaak Panksepp, with his magisterial but less well known book *Affective Neuroscience*, marshaled evidence that the genetically hardwired mammalian emotional system might provide the value system by which our prosocial behaviors and "seeking" systems evolved.[16] Finally, David Sloan Wilson with *Darwin's Cathedral* provided convincing evidence for positive group selection.[17]

This architecture, and the evolution of the title, do not, however, refer just to genetic natural selection. There are actually three forms of evolution that are relevant here: genetic, cultural, and individual. For selfish reptiles to evolve into loving mammals took genetic evolution that led to the development of the limbic system, the brain region underlying our positive emotions. For loving, playful, passionate mammals to become creative scientists and intellectual theologians took genetic evolution that led to the development of our huge human neocortex, the brain region underlying both our science and our religious dogma. Although these two very different brain regions are neurologically rich in their connections, they sometimes treat each other like strangers. Emotion and reason, spirituality and religious dogma often fail to understand each other.

For human beings to have evolved into Samaritans who often place compassion, forgiveness, and unselfish love above a mentality of might-makes-right has required cultural evolution, for cultural evolution is more rapid and more flexible than genetic evolution. True, evil probably still occurs at the same per capita rate as it did in the Iron Age. However, with each passing century, cultural awareness, if not always scientific understanding, of the positive emotions gains ground and contributes to community survival. Positive emotions have been experimentally shown to help humans behave more communally and more creatively and to learn more quickly.[18]

The third kind of evolution is the evolution of the individual over the human life span. Drawing on my thirty-five years as director of Harvard's Study of Adult Development, I explore the brain maturation and increasing social awareness that takes place in all of us as we mature from self-absorbed teenagers to generative grandparents.

Evolution toward spirituality takes place not only in the genetic and cultural arenas but also in the lives of every one of us as we mature our focus from caterpillar "me" to community butterfly. This is illustrated in a quote from a forty-five-year-old member of my research study who wrote, "At twenty to thirty I think I learned how to get along with my wife. From thirty to forty I learned how to be a success in my job. And from forty to fifty I worried less about myself and more about the children."

Adult development, however, does not stop at midlife. Consider the life of the Australian Donald Bradman, who began life as an isolated, self-absorbed youth teaching himself cricket. At age twenty-five, he was the Babe Ruth and superstar of Test cricket. At forty, he became the generative captain of arguably the greatest cricket team ever assembled. In old age, his talents belonged to the world, not to himself, and he was called "the Greatest Living Australian." From sixty to seventy in the international cricket world, he fought apartheid, and at home, instead of captaining elite players, he promoted cricket for Australian Aboriginals and won the admiration of Nelson Mandela. But Bradman had begun life, like the rest of us, as a self-centered, not very useful, adolescent.

৯৶

My focus on positive emotion, however, does not mean that I intend to ignore evil. The Holocaust, murder, addiction, torture, and child abuse are all mentioned. Nor will I deny that "selfish" genes and negative emotions like pain, rage, and grief are extremely valuable. For example, grief draws others to the side of the bereaved. Lepers become disfigured only because the pain fibers to their extremities are destroyed. Anger protects us all from trespass. However, while pain, rage, and grief provide short-term benefits, positive emotions provide benefits over the long term. On the one hand, we are a challenged and embattled species. Global warming, nuclear bombs, urban decay, overpopulation, selfish capitalism gone berserk, and the destruction of natural resources threaten our planet. On the other hand, astonishing as it may seem, we are learning to live peaceably with each other in greater and greater numbers.

The genetic evolution that led to the positive emotions took 200 million years, but consider the cultural evolution of Europe's relationship to Africa over just 500 years. In the fourteenth and fifteenth centuries, the highly cultured Jews and African Moors were slaughtered or expelled by the Spanish Inquisition. Selfish genes make *Homo sapiens* xenophobic. Intellectually, Spain has never completely recovered from this ruthless ethnic cleansing.

In the seventeenth and eighteenth centuries, the lives of Africans were spared; instead, the dominant European powers profitably sold them into slavery in the Americas. Selfish genes render *Homo sapiens* hierarchical and exploitative of strangers. America is still recovering from such ruthless use of power.

In the eighteenth and nineteenth centuries, realizing that slavery was a spiritual disaster for everyone, devout European Christians fought for the abolition of slavery, only to assert that the superiority of their Christian religion and science gave them the moral right to claim all the land in Africa for their own. Selfish genes make human nature territorial and in love with certainty. Once again, instead of leading to Darwinian success, European colonialism contributed heavily to the onset of World War I, which in turn led to the extinction of the very European emperors who had promoted empire building. Perhaps for successful human natural selection a mode of communitarian evolution more adaptive than only selfish genes is necessary.

What next? In his tiny 1913 hospital in Equatorial Africa, physician and Bach master Albert Schweitzer provided all Europe with an inspirational example of the genetically enabled, other-oriented emotions of compassion, love, and hope. By 2008, Schweitzer's example, unlike that of the emperors (who had gone the way of the dodo), has multiplied a thousand times. At first so-called enlightened France had snatched "enemy" Dr. Schweitzer—who in fact would not even kill a mosquito—from his hospital and interned him in 1917 as a prisoner of war. Later, Schweitzer's example helped inspire France to found Médecins Sans Frontières (Doctors Without Borders). The organization was founded in 1971 because France was the first major Western country to appreciate fully the human tragedy taking place in distant Biafra during the Nigerian civil war. Human beings learn from their mistakes, albeit slowly. That is what cultural evolution is all about. For the survival of humanity, genetic evolution and cultural evolution are both important.

Over the last century, with its tyrants disappearing and its state religions hobbled, Europe has—with ever-evolving unanimity—agreed that Africa belongs to Africans and that Europe needs to ask for African forgiveness. With every African famine and epidemic, Europe has responded with increasing, if imperfect, compassion. And I believe that the difference is made by cultural evolution. Just as the genetically derived limbic system with its positive emotions facilitated the survival of mammals over dinosaurs, so has evolving cultural focus on positive emotions contributed to the communal survival and success of *Homo sapiens*. Since the beginning of recorded history, sixty years (from 1945 to the present) is the longest period of time in which one European nation has failed to declare war on another.

Religion has played a very uneven role in such cultural evolution. On the one hand, religious beliefs have provided cultural justification for some of the most heinous and selfish human behavior ever committed. On the other hand, for all their intolerant dogma, religions have provided communities with a unifying view of the human condition and have often provided the portal through which positive emotions are brought to conscious attention. While neither Freud nor psychiatric textbooks ever mention emotions like joy and gratitude, religious hymns and psalms give these emotions pride of place.

Thus, my intent is that *Spiritual Evolution* will create a middle ground for readers seeking to have both their spiritual hearts and their scientific intellects taken seriously. Science and the "left brain" are correct in asserting that my brief history of Europe has been rhetorical rather than dispassionate and that the evolution of human love and compassion has been an arduous process of natural selection, good luck, and trial and error lasting more than 100 million years. Meanwhile, the limbic and the "right brain" are correct in singing:

> *My life flows on in endless song,*
> *Above earth's lamentation.*
> *I hear the clear, though far-off hymn*
> *That hails a new creation.*
>
> *No storm can shake my inmost calm*
> *While to that Rock I'm clinging.*
> *Since love is Lord of heaven and earth,*
> *How can I keep from singing?*
>
> —ROBERT LOWRY (1860)

Or as Albert Schweitzer, a both passionate and thoughtful scientist, maintained, "Man can no longer live for himself alone. We realize that all life is valuable, and that we are united to this life. From this knowledge comes our spiritual relationship to the universe."[19]

⟨⟨⟩⟩

At this point, even tolerant readers may ask what right have I—a septuagenarian "Western" research psychiatrist studying adult development—to presume to write a book about spirituality. Perhaps my best answer is that by virtue of being for thirty-five years the director of Harvard's seven-decade-old Study of Adult Development, I have been profoundly privileged to watch teenagers mature into great-grandparents. I have been able to watch prospectively what Gail Sheehy and Erik Erikson only speculated about—adult evolution as it unfolds. By watching adolescent caterpillars evolve into great-grandfather butterflies, I have been impressed by how unimportant parental social class, religious denomination, and even our conventional conception of IQ are to human development. Instead, human relationships and the positive emotions seemed critical to adaptation; best-selling author Daniel Goleman and Yale psychology professor Peter Salovey call it "emotional intelligence." In addition, by studying lifetimes, I have learned to pay attention to how people behave, not to what they say—and to how they behave over decades, not just during last week.

When I was ten years old, I wrote my first "term paper" on the origin of the universe. I imagined that I would grow up to be an astrophysicist. In college, impressed by the devastation of the Great Depression, I gave up astrophysics for economics and then gave up economics too, because neither science had a heart. Next, I debated becoming a minister, but I abandoned that because the ministry tried to help people without science. Instead, I chose medicine, where I hoped that science and the heart were inseparable, where limbic compassion and left-brain reason worked in synchrony.

In medical school I began to realize that Western medicine was often more spiritual than it acknowledged. When I began school in 1955, the best available "scientific" treatment for schizophrenia was insulin coma. The research literature included 700 papers showing that insulin coma—a dangerous but care-intensive treatment—helped schizophrenics. The scientific papers did not always acknowledge that the patients receiving insulin coma treatments were also viewed by hospital staff as having the best chance of recovery. Not only were they regarded with hope rather than despair, but also, since insulin coma was dangerous, they were looked after by the most competent nurses and were the focus of special attention and care in otherwise barren and loveless public institutions.

However, once modern medicine obtained Thorazine—a medicine that chemically alleviated schizophrenia—a series of scientific papers emerged proving that insulin coma was no more than a form of active placebo therapy.[20] Thorazine and its more effective pharmacological descendants now dominate schizophrenia treatment. Insulin coma as a therapy for schizophrenia has essentially vanished. We must never forget, however, that the efficacy of the faith, hope, and love with which insulin coma was administered was initially attributed to medical intervention in 700 scientific papers! Patients who received the care-intensive treatment recovered faster than those who did not receive it. While no medical journal would call the treatment spiritual, such caring behavior, involving as it did the three "theological virtues" of faith, hope, and love, would be regarded as spiritual by most religious denominations.

From 1960 to 1966, in residency and in subsequent fellowships, I was exposed to the zeitgeist around the birth of neuroscience. A fellow psychiatric resident and friend, Eric Kandel, who four decades later went on to win the Nobel Prize, was already at work on his groundbreaking research on the neurobiology of memory. After residency, I did research in pharmacology in the Harvard Medical School basic science quadrangle, which was suffused with the generative spirit of Stephen Kuffler, one of the fathers of modern neuroscience. My own mentor, Peter Dews, the Stanley Cobb Professor of Psychiatry, used to consult, with me tagging along, to two future Nobel Laureates in neuroscience, Thorsten Wiesel and David Hubel, who were studying the neurobiology of vision in the laboratory below us. Although I was to spend the rest of my life as a clinician and a clinical researcher, the scientific inspiration of those years never left me. My wonder about the origin of the universe was replaced by my wonder about the origins of the human brain.

Years later I became codirector of an alcohol detoxification center and a professor of psychiatry at Harvard Medical School. As a condition of employment, for ten years I had to attend one Alcoholics Anonymous meeting a month. I was surprised to find that these monthly, nonsectarian AA meetings met my spiritual needs and my alcoholic clients' medical needs better than either of the faith traditions in which I was raised—the Episcopal Church and the Boston Psychoanalytic Institute.

In 1998 I was fortunate enough to be chosen as a non-alcoholic trustee of Alcoholics Anonymous. After a year, a fellow non-alcoholic trustee, a bishop, confided to me that there was more "spirituality" in our trustees' meetings than in his diocesan conventions. I believed him. For six years I tried to understand how one could have a medically effective spiritual program that served 150 countries and that was *not* a religion. Those six years of reflection led to the ideas that started this book. What is the difference between spirituality and religion? Why does the former provide only comfort while the latter causes so much pain as well as comfort? Why should the emphasis of AA on positive emotions work as well or better than the exploration of negative emotions in which I engaged as a psychotherapist? In order to understand this paradox, for the last seven years I have been on the steering committee of Martin Seligman's Positive Psychology Center at the University of Pennsylvania.

Certainly, I am no theologian. By studying human behavior over a lifetime, I have perhaps become more a psychobiologist than a psychiatrist. My research has more in common with ethologists like Jane Goodall and Konrad Lorenz than with psychoanalysts like Sigmund Freud. Over the past four decades I have been tracking shifts in the evolving spiritual beliefs of the men in my study. It has all proven very instructive. With maturity, religious belief does not increase, yet we develop a more nuanced emotional life and a deepening spiritual appreciation.[21] In the first thirty years leading the study, I learned that positive emotions were intimately connected to mental health. In the last ten years, I have come to appreciate that positive emotions cannot be distinguished from what people understand as spirituality.

&&

Does the link between positive emotion and spirituality mean that people with the most halcyon childhoods, with the most fulfilling adult family lives, and with the most reason for positive emotion are the most spiritual? No, quite the opposite. Often the most broken individuals, with a little help from their friends, become the most spiritual. In the words of playwright Eugene O'Neill, whose early life was filled with lovelessness and negative emotion, "Man is born broken, he lives by healing, and the grace of God is glue."[22] For research psychiatrist Gail Ironson, one of the most unexpected and moving experiences of working with fatally ill AIDS victims was witnessing the increased salience of spirituality and positive emotion in their lives.[23] Among the hundreds of men I have followed for many decades, the men with initially the most traumatic lives often became the most spiritual.[24]

In order to illustrate the transmutation of pain into positive emotion, I intend to show and not tell. Life histories will follow in later chapters. For now, let me provide a statistically convincing example of the power of emergent positive emotion. In an ongoing web-based survey of 24 positive character "strengths," two well-known psychologists, Christopher Peterson and Martin Seligman, charted the effect of the September 11, 2001, terrorist attacks. They compared the self-reported character strengths of 529 web respondents in the two months before the event with the self-reported character strengths of 490 web respondents in the two months after the 9/11 World Trade Center bombing. Cognitive strengths, like prudence, curiosity, bravery, self-control, and wisdom, did not change significantly. Six strengths more emotional in nature went up the most—all significantly. These strengths were gratitude, hope, kindness, love, spirituality, and teamwork.[25] Work from several other investigators has confirmed the strong causal association between positive emotions and post-crisis resilience.

Barbara Fredrickson and her colleagues also undertook a study of University of Michigan students during the months before and the month after the World Trade Center bombing. The awareness of positive emotions after the crisis appeared to be a core ingredient in buffering students against depression by broadening their post-crisis resources.[26] As I have already pointed out, negative emotions help us to survive in time present, while positive emotions help us to survive in time future.

Certainly, violence, tantrums, cruelty, dishonesty, exploitation of the weak, and the madness of crowds are also important to write about. Theological historian Karen Armstrong wisely reminds us, "Unless we allow the sorrow that presses in on all sides to invade our consciousness, we cannot begin our spiritual quest. In our era of international terror, it is hard for any of us to imagine that we live in Buddha's pleasure park."[27] But there are already thousands of books on negative emotions.

This book follows a less traveled path. First, in contrast to popular science, which places spirituality in our huge, reasoning *Homo sapiens* neocortex, I concede that religious dogma might live there, but I place the spiritual impulse in our mammalian, emotional brain—the limbic system. I argue that spirituality is not rooted in ideas, sacred texts, and theology. Rather, spirituality comprises positive emotion and social connection. *Love* is the shortest definition of spirituality I know. Both spirituality and love result in conscious feelings of respect, appreciation, acceptance, sympathy, empathy, compassion, involvement, tenderness, and gratitude. Like the prayer that serves as epigraph for this chapter, these unsimplistic words are not the worst place to seek what is important in life.

Second, I argue that spirituality reflects humanity's biological press for connection and community building as much as it reflects the individual's need for sacred revelation. Spirituality is more about *us* than *me*. Thus, I would suggest that our spirituality is made manifest not as much by our inner enlightenment and our prayers as by our outward behavior. For example, Jesus Christ and Karl Marx are not usually paired, but both men were revolutionaries who mistrusted organized religion because religion talked about, without actually creating, loving communities. Physical fitness, after all, is not about the regularity with which you follow your exercise regimen or, worse yet, talk about it. Physical fitness is defined by how well you function in the real world. The Buddhist ideal is that of the bodhisattva, one who elects voluntarily to stay in this world and to help others rather than entering directly into Nirvana.

Third, I hold that we do not have to be taught positive emotions. Our brain is hardwired to generate them. Humanity's task is to pay attention to them, for they are the source of our spiritual being and the key to our cultural evolutionary progress. For the last three thousand years, organized religions, for all their limitations, have been the best means that humanity has found for bringing the positive emotions into conscious reflection. Only by noting the long-term consequences of competing faith traditions can we separate evolutionary truth from scriptural superstition.

We need to bring our positive emotions to conscious attention, and we must not disdain to study them with our science. If my purpose as an author can be oversimplified into a single wish, it would be this: to restore our faith in spirituality as an essential human striving.

2

The Prose and the Passion

જી

*Natural selection built the brain to survive in the
world and only incidentally to understand it. . . .
The proper task of scientists is to diagnose and correct the misalignment.*

—Edward O. Wilson, *Consilience* (1998), p. 61

ઈરિ

Only recently have scientists rediscovered that the compassion, joy, and
unselfish love so important to religion and to the Neolithic mind are not ir-
relevant to science. You see, the Neolithic (hunter-gatherer) mind that
"natural selection built" was more like that of a four-year-old—all images,
animism, magic, and emotion—than like that of a modern, highly educated
adult. Dependence on the written word and the use of the scientific experiment to verify imagined cause and effect were still far in the future by the
time that natural selection had completed the "hardware" of the *Homo sapiens* brain. Moreover, ever since our invention of new "software" like the
printing press and the scientific method, we have had less and less respect
for the superstitious, mystical brain that natural selection built.

The task of a thoughtful future humanity must be to correct the "misalignment" between our scientific and our emotional brains. Only in the last few decades have ethology and brain imaging rendered the positive emotions and spirituality of the Neolithic mind "visible" to the scientists, who, until recently, thought that they could do without it.

Since the emergence of first Greek and then Renaissance science, humanity has rushed to understand the world. The one-sidedness of this effort was exemplified by the French and then the Bolshevik Revolution, which tried to abolish all traces of the awestruck fables of the hunter-gatherer brain. Churches were converted to "temples of science," but man's inhumanity to man was not ameliorated. A psychiatrist friend of mine, Professor Russell D'Souza, characterized the dichotomy between the spiritual and scientific mind: "The Buddha's enlightenment was considered too good to be true, but now Western enlightenment is being seen as too true to be good."[1]

Primitive drumming and emotion are not better than prose and ideas; they simply arise in different parts of the brain. Only connect the prose and the passion; only connect the limbic and the neocortical brain! That is what twenty-first-century neuroscience is all about. The danger of scientists' ignoring the Neolithic brain built to survive in the world can be revealed by prolonged observation. At the end of the day, neither the French nor the Bolshevik revolutionaries were successful. Within decades the temples of science were reconsecrated back into churches. Ideologue Ralph Nader's bestseller *Unsafe at Any Speed* raised consciousness about the very real dangers of the automobile; ideologue Richard Dawkins's bestseller *The God Delusion* raises our consciousness about the very real dangers of religious dogma. Religion, like the automobile, may lead to tens of thousands of pointless deaths every year. Religions, however, are even more valuable than the automobile to humanity. At the price of the "smog" of sometimes misleading superstition, religions keep the prosocial emotions in consciousness. Society ignores the emotional brain at its peril, and both science and society need to work to make automobiles and religions safer.

In the last seven decades there has been a scientific revolution that achieved what the Enlightenment, Freudian psychology, and Darwin's evolutionary biology failed to do—to render our emotional life tangible. This new science has liberated the positive emotions from the realm of mysticism—and from religious dogma.

These newer sciences—neuroscience, cultural anthropology that is not ethnocentric, and the scientific study of animal behavior (ethology)—are all more recent than atomic physics. Each of these new sciences has tempered our highly evolved neocortical human preference for culture, for language, and for creating dogmatic, intolerant "religious" memes. These new sciences have accomplished this by teaching us about our inarticulate, subcortical, limbic, mammalian capacity for positive emotion and for altruistic action. These capacities are inarticulate because they are not directly connected to our neocortical language centers. Human stroke victims, rendered dumb (aphasic) from damaged left neocortices, cannot voluntarily speak a word. Nevertheless, if their limbic systems are intact, they can swear like top sergeants if you step on their toes or give them a painful injection.

These new sciences offer hope that our brains are constructed for loving cultural evolution and not just for heartless scientific progress and brute instinct, red in tooth and claw. For example, cultural anthropology has demonstrated the universality of the positive emotions. Awe, faith, hope, love, and reliance on a power greater than ourselves are found to be universal in cultures around the world.[2] Nonetheless, until very recently, emotion has been an unwelcome guest at the academic table, for passion often unsettles reason and emotion seems to threaten Enlightenment science.

In their lengthy and influential nineteenth-century textbooks, which founded scientific psychology, Wilhelm Wundt and William James each allotted a single chapter—and a somewhat disdainful one at that—to the emotions.[3] By the time modern physics had discovered quantum mechanics, biology still knew very little about human emotional life. In 1933, psychologist Max Meyer, founder of the psychology department at the University of Missouri and a former mentee of theoretical physicist Max Planck, had prophesied, "Why introduce into science an unneeded term, such as emotion, when there are already scientific terms for everything we have to describe?... In 1950 American psychologists will smile at both these terms [will and emotion] as curiosities of the past."[4]

As he predicted in 1953—a decade after the invention of the atomic bomb—Burrhus F. Skinner, a brilliant and most rational psychologist, still could dismissively proclaim, "The 'emotions' are excellent examples of the fictional causes to which we commonly attribute behavior."[5] All three of the respected graduate psychology programs with which I have been associated—Stanford, Dartmouth, and Harvard—have for decades been careful to exclude clinical psychology from their graduate psychology curricula. I presume this is because as soon as psychology becomes too concerned with healing, its science becomes entangled with emotion, superstition, and passionate belief. Yet we cannot ignore that we have evolved to be compassionate parents and clinicians as well as dispassionate scientists.

Medical psychiatry has been a little—but only a little—more tolerant of emotion than academic psychology. Beginning with Sigmund Freud, psychiatry has taught clinicians much about negative emotion while rendering clinicians wary, even phobic, of positive emotion. In the 1890s, deprived of any way to study living brains, Freud, arguably the most brilliant psychologist of his day, proved an imaginative pioneer. He introduced to medicine the clinical importance of emotion—emotion that half a century later B. F. Skinner still deemed too poetic to be true.

Unfortunately, Freud ignored positive emotions. The human nature that Freud reported was gloomy, and he often dismissed as infantile the adult passions of his "id." As a way of holding human attachment at dispassionate arm's length, Freud talked about love with the frigid, intellectualized concept of "libido." I suspect he would have regarded the term "cuddle"—and I know that he regarded singing—as beneath his dignity. Freud relegated mothers and positive emotions to the backseat, while fathers, guilt, and lust drove the car. To keep tender passion at bay, psychoanalysis is still often conducted without eye contact.

As an example of how recent our understanding of human emotion is, consider the phenomenon of infantile autism, less severe forms of which are called Asperger's syndrome. Infantile autism, a not uncommon genetic disorder of emotional attachment, was not discovered until 1943 by a Johns Hopkins child psychiatrist, Leo Kanner—in his own son. Twenty years later, when I was a psychiatric resident in 1963, autism, discovered in Baltimore, was still diagnosed by that name only rarely in Boston and New York. Medical science was still limited in its capacity to articulate a positive emotion as basic as attachment. Today the congenital lack of empathy and difficulties of attachment in childhood autism can be recognized by any competent pediatrician.

It was in the years 1945 to 1950 that psychoanalyst John Bowlby's ethological studies first convinced physicians that orphans needed affection as much as food. It was in the 1950s that Harry Harlow's objective findings of attachment behavior in rhesus monkeys rendered nonsexual love a tangible biologic reality for psychologists.[6] Jane Goodall's observations on attachment behavior in chimpanzees made the importance of primate love a suitable topic for scientists.[7] Two decades later, Paul Ekman, a California neuropsychologist, and his colleagues rendered emotions still more tangible by linking specific facial expressions and their underlying musculature not only with subjective emotional report but also with behavioral follow-up.[8] Through careful study of facial expression, Ekman could demonstrate that the flight attendant's voluntary smile differed from her involuntary smile of mirth and emotional welcome. Doubting Margaret Mead's assertion that emotions and their facial expression were culturally based, Ekman traveled as far afield as the New Guinea highlands to demonstrate that the expressive facial musculature used to communicate affects was the same around the globe and that our social emotions were biological not cultural.

By 1990 modern science fully accepted the reality of emotion, but to many, positive emotions remained unmentionable. Consider that in 2004 the leading American text the *Comprehensive Textbook of Psychiatry*, half a million lines in length, devotes 100 to 600 lines each to shame, guilt, terrorism, anger, hate, and sin, thousands of lines to depression and anxiety, but only five lines to hope, one line to joy, and not a single line to faith, compassion, forgiveness, or love.[9]

By contrast, organized religions—so mistrusted by the French and Bolshevik revolutionaries and by twentieth-century social scientists—focus intently on the positive emotions. By way of illustration, consider the seventh blessing of a traditional Jewish wedding ceremony:

Blessed art thou, O Lord, who has created joy and gladness,
bridegroom and bride, mirth and exaltation, pleasure and delight,
love, brotherhood, peace and fellowship.

Ten years after writing his influential textbook of psychology, William
James, a less dogmatic scientist than Skinner, was to embrace emotion of
all kinds. In his seminal work, *The Varieties of Religious Experience*, James
noted, "In re-reading my manuscript, I am almost appalled at the amount
of emotionality which I find in it." He continued, "It is the terror and
beauty of phenomena, the 'promise' of the dawn and the rainbow, the
'voice' of the thunder, the 'gentleness' of the summer rain, the 'sublimity' of
the stars and not the physical laws which these things follow, by which
the religious mind still continues to be most impressed. . . . You see now
why . . . I have seemed so bent on rehabilitating the element of feeling in
religion and subordinating its intellectual part."[10] Despite himself, William
James found himself appreciating the Neolithic mind.

Similarly, modern neuroscience has also allowed us to appreciate that
we have more than one brain. If there are important differences between
ideas and emotions, there are differences in the parts of the brain most important to their appreciation. If there are important differences between
lyrics and music, there are differences in the parts of the brain important to
their creation. To oversimplify, the left-brain hemisphere specializes in de-
tails and articulates and understands ideas, words, and component parts.
The right brain specializes in inarticulate music, visual images, and wholes
(gestalts). The limbic brain specializes in emotion.

Cognitive ideas can be expressed in words and controlled voluntarily,
and for their expression ideas are powerfully dependent on the *Homo sapiens'* cerebral hemispheres—the neocortex. Emotional feelings are equally
dependent on our more mammalian subcortical brain—the limbic system
and the hypothalamus.

I shall discuss the difference between the right and left hemispheres
first, and then I shall discuss the "mammalian" subcortical limbic system
and finally the "reptilian" hypothalamus. Not until the 1960s did "split

brain" studies establish the distinction between the right- and left-brain hemispheres—a discovery for which Roger Sperry received the Nobel Prize. Sperry and his coworkers at the California Institute of Technology had taken advantage of the fact that sometimes the right- and left-brain hemispheres are separated from each other by congenital malformations, and sometimes by the surgical treatment of epilepsy. Sperry's research, and later the research of his student Michael Gazzaniga, gave proof to the proverb: the right hand knows not what the left hand doeth.

The nonverbal right brain pays attention to integration of space and time, to context, empathy, and the minds of others, and to the gestalt of facial recognition.[11] The verbal left brain is all about detail, the certainty of cause and effect (confabulated or true), exegesis, and verbal communication. Neither the seemingly spiritual right brain nor the seemingly religious left brain is a trustworthy arbiter of truth, but like Gilbert and Sullivan, like Rodgers and Hammerstein, the left and right brain work well together.

Modern neuroscience, exemplified by brain imaging and neurochemistry, has shown us that our brain's most recently evolved centers, especially in our left neocortex, mediate language, ideas, theology, scientific analysis—and idiosyncratic religious belief. In contrast, our right neocortex mediates music, emotion, symbols, and a sense of spiritual wholes.[12] The same small area of our brain that on the left interprets words, on the right interprets music. Just as the musical score is linked to the verbal lyrics, just so is emotion linked to science.

Let me provide a concrete example of the differences between the two brain hemispheres. If sodium amytal, a brain anesthetic, is injected into one brain hemisphere but not the other, the left brain can talk while the right brain is asleep, but it cannot sing. The right hemisphere can sing when the left is asleep, but cannot talk.[13] Without knowing Italian, we can make no sense of the great Italian poet Dante. Without knowing Italian, we can be moved to tears by the songs of Giuseppe Verdi. Throughout this book, I quote evocative verses from songs to make points that I could not make if I confined myself to prose—or even to rhetoric and poetry.

The difference between our "human" cerebral hemispheres (our neocortex) and our mammalian limbic system is just as great as the differences between our two neocortical hemispheres. Just as a pianist's fingers governed by striated voluntary muscle are under the conscious control of his human neocortex, so the thrust of one idea can be voluntarily replaced by another idea. Consider our serial (one-at-a-time) responses to a grocery list. Like the smooth muscles of our viscera, however, emotions are powerfully controlled by the nonverbal subcortical brain structures that humans share with other mammals. Emotions, like the smooth muscle of our viscera, cannot be controlled by conscious will. They may emerge suddenly, but they fade slowly and may become muddled with other emotions.

Homo sapiens' ideas are neutral, "colorless," and valueless. They elicit no conscious sensation. In contrast, emotions are felt physically in the body, and like visceral smooth muscle, they cannot be rapidly turned off. Emotions are almost always either "good" or "bad" and almost always elicit approach or avoidance. Emotions are associated with activity in our involuntary autonomic nervous system. Negative emotions are associated with our alerting sympathetic nervous system; positive emotions are associated with activity in our calming parasympathetic nervous system. In addition to being value-laden, emotions have color; for example, we are green with envy, blue from grief, yellow from fear, and red from rage. To survive we need both ideas and emotions, be the latter positive or negative.

৳৳

The *cultural* evolution of the Neolithic mind into that of the twenty-first-century mind has come after the *biologic* evolution of the mammalian brain into that of *Homo sapiens*. Over time ideas have become increasingly prominent in human life. To understand the world rather than just survive in it, about 150,000 years ago humans developed abstract language.[14] Four thousand years ago humans discovered writing, and finally, 900 years ago the Chinese and 560 years ago a European, Johannes Gutenberg, discovered printing. The results of such cultural evolution were spectacular. Planting times no longer needed to be remembered in the mystical immanence of some Stonehenge solar observatory or in magical, sacred Bohemian fertility trees fruited in anticipation at springtime with lovingly decorated eggs. With the advent of printing, spring planting times could be relegated to the aesthetically bland, but meticulously accurate, pages of farmers' almanacs.

When science focused only on the lexical brain, devoid of emotion, however, there were problems. The brain that Neolithic humans had evolved in order to survive was designed to regard human attachment as more useful than calculus, and emotional intelligence (EQ) was more adaptive than a high IQ. Skinner was wrong. Emotions were not "fictional"; they were essential to survival.

You experience (feel) an affect. You communicate (emote) an emotion. Descartes, who in 1649 first formulated the concept of emotion, could count six: wonder, love, hatred, desire, joy, and sadness. A generation later, Spinoza could count only three emotions: desire, pleasure, pain. By 1893 William James could acknowledge four: grief, fear, love, and rage.

Charles Darwin, one of the first scientists to study emotion scientifically, could count nine emotions.[15] Influenced by Sir Charles Bell (for whom Bell's palsy was named), an anatomist and student of facial expressions, Darwin listed rage, terror, excitement, astonishment, grief, contempt, joy, disgust, and affection as important in humans. In addition, it was Darwin who demonstrated that most human emotions and the facial expressions of them are shared by dogs and primates. Perhaps one reason that science ignores emotion is that emotions do not set us apart from other mammals. After all, only humans can do calculus, while most dogs are paragons of positive emotion. I suspect that is why dogs are "man's best friends." Over the short term, negative emotions are particularly necessary to survival. But over the longer term, positive emotions are also here to stay—even if currently they are given airtime only by religion and art.

As an antidote to the supremacy of the modern, word-dominated left brain, for centuries the Buddhists have devised meditation techniques and shamans have used psychoactive drugs to access the emotion- and image-dominated Neolithic brain. For centuries the Catholic Church, a little like modern lawyers, resisted translation of the Bible from Latin into vernacular languages for fear that increased cognitive understanding would weaken the "spiritual" awe produced by incomprehensible, sonorous Latin scripture.

For millennia artists have circumvented the lexical brain with music, paint-
ing, poetry, and rhetoric, but of course many scientists have protested that
such emotionally colored right-brain experiences are misleading. To oversimplify, in order to survive, the human brain chants communal songs; in
order to understand, the human brain writes scientific treatises. Sometimes
each is true; sometimes each is illusion.

෫ඁ

There is a brain region serving the positive emotions that is far more potent
than the right-brain hemisphere's music and its unarticulated images of
beautiful wholes. This brain region is called the limbic system.

The late-twentieth-century sea change that validated positive emotion
actually began in 1878 when a French anatomist, a contemporary of Freud
and the father of neurosurgery, Paul Broca, announced to the world his important anatomical finding that the brains of all mammals contained a set
of structures that he christened "le grand lobe limbique." These limbic
structures were absent from the brains of reptiles.[16] (In fact, two hundred
years before Broca, the same structures had been noted and christened the
cerebri limbus by the pioneer neuroanatomist Thomas Willis, but his discovery was all but forgotten for two centuries.) Broca also noted that the neural arrangement of the limbic cortex differed from, and seemed more
"primitive" than, the cortex of the surrounding cerebral hemispheres. However, it was to take another seventy years before behavioral scientists, especially Paul MacLean, a physician and pioneer neuroscientist at the National
Institute of Mental Health, started to suspect that positive emotion and approach (as contrasted to avoidant) behaviors depended not just upon the
hypothalamic "instincts" that we equate with the Freudian "id" but also
upon the limbic system. The tender, nuanced human emotions like compassion, joy, and maternal attachment were mediated by mammalian structures
in the inner recesses of the brain beneath the neocortex but outside of the
still more primitive brain stem and its hypothalamus.

Just for a moment, imagine the human brain divided into three con-

centric parts (figure 1). At the center are the midbrain and the hypothalamus; these structures, which have evolved relatively little in the last 200
million years, serve both scientists and crocodiles equally well. This most
primitive, instinctive, or "reptilian" brain coordinates most autonomic
functions (such as heart rate, breathing, muscle reflexes, and wakefulness).
When stimulated, these structures, particularly the hypothalamus, result in
primitive responses, sometimes called instincts, that are selfish and that,
unlike the social emotions, are relevant only to the self. These primitive
emotions are sometimes summarized as the four Fs: fight, fright, feeding, and
fornication. In humans the hypothalamus is about the size of the tip of your
little finger. Neither you nor crocodiles could survive without it. When I
was in medical school in the 1950s, this is where I was taught emotions
came from.

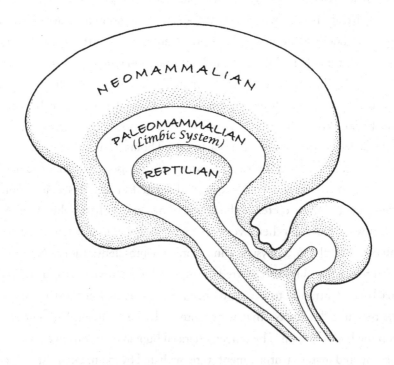

FIGURE 1: Paul MacLean's "Triune" Brain

This reptilian midbrain is embraced by Broca's "le grand lobe limbique" (MacLean's paleomammalian limbic system), which for 200 million years has evolved steadily in our mammalian ancestors alone. The limbic system is where both positive emotions and the more nuanced negative emotions arise, and it consists of several different anatomic structures, which I shall outline later. The limbic system synthesizes information from the body, links emotions to past memories, and passes this now valenced information on to the neocortex to be processed as thought and motivation.

More than just mediating our emotions, our limbic brain provides our human connection. In his brilliant fable *The Little Prince*, Antoine de Saint-Exupéry, the French poet-aviator, explained the difference between the neocortical and limbic systems when his fox observed, "It is only with the heart that one can see rightly; what is essential is invisible to the eye."[17] In more scientific language, a cascade of sensory input passes through our brains every second; the limbic system, poetically referred to by most of us as the "heart," selects and provides affective coloration for the experiences that we treat as important. The limbic system helps humans to appreciate the difference between people and inanimate objects. Think how differently you feel touching an attractive person and touching a cinder block. Destroy the limbic system and we destroy our ability to desire selectively.

Covering the limbic system like a helmet is the neocortex, which in our human ancestors (but not in golden retrievers) evolved most spectacularly—more than doubling its weight—over the last two million years. Put simply, the neocortex generates our science, our culture, our ideas, our beliefs, and our religions. Equally important, our neocortex creatively elaborates our limbic positive emotions into awareness.

The neocortex is the most recently evolved part of our brain, and its size relative to our bodies distinguishes us from the other mammals. Anthropocentric vanity has led us to place our more noble emotions within its huge, conscious, reasoning embrace. But our vanity has misled us. Many dogs, admittedly having been selectively bred by humans for these qualities, radiate trust, hope, forgiveness, and love, and some very brilliant scientists and theologians do not. When a beloved woman is weeping, both golden retrievers and two-year-old children will rush thoughtlessly, speechlessly, but empathically to her side to provide comfort. In contrast, her highly educated physician may piously suggest over the phone, "Take two aspirin and call back in the morning." The blind faith of the kitten's or the human infant's separation cry evokes unselfish love in almost all of us. Unconditional love may be no more than mammalian parental love transformed by maturity and cultural evolution to encompass more creatures than our own babies. Advocates of the "selfish" gene often bridle at what they regard as a Panglossian notion that unselfish social behavior could be inherited. Recent work with baboons, however, shows that females with the widest social networks have the most surviving offspring.[18] Altruistic communal behavior is favored by natural selection.

Human limbic systems differ from those of other mammals only in that human limbic systems are larger and better integrated with our much larger neocortices. Thus, by combining both words and emotions, our mothers and best friends are often more comforting than either undereducated two-year-olds or overeducated physicians.

To locate positive emotion in the mammalian limbic system has been a slow, arduous process. Not until 1955 was the neurobiology of positive emotions born. James Olds, an innovative neuropsychologist, discovered that rats would work harder to receive electric stimulation of their brain than starved rats would work to receive food. Of more lasting importance was Olds' finding that thirty-five out of forty-one electrode placements within the limbic system of rats but only two out of thirty-five placements outside of the limbic system proved sufficiently rewarding to lead to self-stimulation.[19]

Beginning in the 1950s also, neurobiologist Paul MacLean devoted his life to the study of what he named first the "visceral brain" and then the "limbic system." MacLean pointed out that the limbic structures govern our mammalian capacity not only to remember (cognition) but also to play (joy), to cry out at separation (faith/trust), and to take care of our own (love).[20] Except for rudimentary memory, reptiles express none of these qualities. Virtually all mammals do. Since 1995, modern brain imaging studies have also been critical in confirming Olds's initial finding that emotion is located in the limbic system rather than the neocortex.[21]

Despite MacLean's research, it remained difficult for some scientists to accept that positive emotions are more than figments of the theological mind. It remained difficult for laypeople to believe that positive emotion could exist anywhere in the brain but the human neocortex. Only in the last decade have MacLean's intellectual successors, pioneering neurobiologist Jaak Panksepp and his colleague Jeffrey Burgdorf, rendered ineffable love and joy scientifically tangible to empirical study.[22] Only in the last decade has Jon-Kar Zubietta demonstrated low opioid tone in limbic circuits during self-reports of sadness.[23]

When through personal reminiscence individuals subjectively experience existential states of either fear and sadness or happiness, blood flow increases in limbic areas and decreases in many higher brain areas. Various studies have located human pleasurable experiences (tasting chocolate, winning money, admiring pretty faces, enjoying music, and orgasmic ecstasy) in limbic areas—especially in the orbitofrontal region, anterior cingulate, and insula, all of which I shall discuss shortly.[24]

&

I begin my travel guide through the limbic system with a caveat. Since 1990, modern neuroscience has demonstrated that the neuroanatomy of emotion is complex and that the boundaries of the limbic system are far more ambiguous than Broca and MacLean imagined. Moreover, just as each investigator has a different list of basic emotions, just so investigators have different lists of structures that do and do not belong in the limbic system. But everyone's definitions show enormous overlap. For example, Joseph LeDoux, a sophisticated investigator of the neurobiology of emotion, can declare, "I have to say that it [the limbic system] does not exist."[25] On the same page, however, he can grudgingly admit that the limbic system "is a useful anatomical shorthand for areas in the no-man's land between the hypothalamus and the neocortex." No-man's-land it may be, but if the limbic system did not exist, none of us would have loving mothers.

Scientists have to be careful with lack of precision. To the general public, however, the concept of the limbic system is still very handy. The term "limbic system" is as useful, say, as the romantic concept of "Broadway" to a visitor to New York City. To the geographer, Broadway is a specific street, while the boundaries of New York's theater district (Broadway) are impossible to define with precision. Most visitors to Manhattan, however, care little about abstract street maps. Instead, they care passionately about the vibrant humanity of the theater district and know perfectly well that the metaphorical term "Broadway" is not about a macadam road. That is the spirit with which this book shall continue to use words like "limbic," "music," "love," and "spirituality"—words that defy the lexical precision of scrupulous lawyers, philosophers, and neuroscientists.

Nevertheless, the brain works as an integrated whole, and assigning anthropomorphic functions to specific brain regions would be oversimplification. For example, the limbic emotion of joy catalyzes all sorts of neocortically mediated behaviors like bursting into song, public demonstrations of affection, and conscious cognitions of the state of joy. Again, the hippocampus, universally accepted as a limbic structure, is just as essential to conscious, declarative neocortical memory as it is to emotional memory. Perhaps, then, it is more cautious to note that the limbic system is very much at the center of our emotional life, but is neither its beginning nor its end.

Nevertheless, human evolution has created a brain that is really two brains: a mammalian brain that can feel and emote and cry in a Broadway theater and a *Homo sapiens* brain that can speak, think, analyze, and chart the path of Broadway as it runs diagonally across Manhattan. Paul MacLean understood this very well when he wrote, "The visceral brain is not at all unconscious . . . but rather eludes the grasp of the intellect because its animalistic and primitive structure makes it impossible to communicate in verbal terms."[26] As a result, passionate writers, beginning with Martin Luther, have been as contemptuous of reason as B. F. Skinner was of emotion. Luther could assert, "Reason is the greatest enemy that faith has; it never comes to the aid of spiritual things, but—more frequently than not—struggles against the divine Word, treating with contempt all that emanates from God."[27]

But the whole brain cannot work properly if it is divided against itself—whether by Luther or by Skinner. The brain will not be "aligned" unless science and passion walk hand in hand. "Only connect! . . ." E. M. Forster pleads in his novel *Howard's End*. "Only connect the prose and the passion and both will be exalted, and human love will be seen at its height."[28] The brilliant Princeton psychologist Sylvan Tomkins translates Forster's poetry for the academic mind: "Out of the marriage of reason with affect there issues clarity with passion. Reason without affect would be impotent; affect without reason would be blind."[29] One has to wonder whether Tomkins was paraphrasing Albert Einstein's famous quote about science and religion.

Having acknowledged that the brain's functions are nuanced and integrated to a degree that defies precise scientific description, let me continue to define the major limbic structures within the admittedly oversimplified format of a travel guide.

Among the more important and familiar limbic structures are the amygdala and the hippocampus. The insula, the anterior cingulate gyrus, the ventromedial prefrontal cortex, and the septal area will all also be important to this book's discussion of positive emotions (see figure 2). These diverse structures are closely integrated and organized to help us to seek and to recognize all that falls under the rubric of mammalian love and human spirituality.[30]

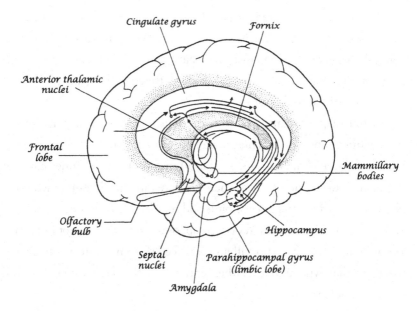

FIGURE 2: Major Components of the Limbic System

The *hippocampus* serves visual as well as verbal memory, and its removal can make our closest friends appear as strangers. The *amygdala* gives passion and importance to emotional experiences—both past and present, both positive and, more often, negative. Remove the brain area surrounding the amygdala and male monkeys will try to copulate with any creature that walks. In humans the amygdala is eight times as large as in primates and one hundred times its size in primitive mammals.[31] FMRI studies of Kundalini yoga demonstrate that meditation increases activity of the hippocampus and the right lateral amygdala, which in turn leads to parasympathetic stimulation and the sensation of deep peacefulness.[32]

Equally important is the less familiar *anterior cingulate gyrus*, which is also part of the limbic system. In metaphor (and probably in neuroanatomic fact), the cingulate gyrus links valence and memory to create attachment and along with the hippocampus is the brain region most responsible for making the past meaningful. The anterior cingulate is crucial in directing whom we should approach and whom we should avoid. Maternal touch, body warmth, and odor via the limbic system, and especially via the anterior cingulate, regulate a rat pup's behavior, neurochemistry, endocrine release, and circadian rhythm.[33]

For example, mediated in part by the anterior cingulate gyrus, the infant's separation cry advertises vulnerability and distinguishes mammals from fish and reptiles. The last thing a baby crocodile wants to do is to advertise its vulnerability to its own kind, but kittens, puppies, and human babies are hardwired to do just that.

In rodents, attachment is primarily olfactory, but in humans love is more auditory and visual. Thus, mammalian evolution has led to an intricate three-boned (malleus, incus, stapes) apparatus in the inner ear that permits rodent mothers to hear their separated infants' high-pitched cries, which are inaudible to predator birds and reptiles with a less evolved hearing apparatus. The separation cry presupposes a hardwired emotional trust in a maternal protector who will find you, feed you, and protect you—a maternal guardian who, unlike a father reptile or mother fish, will not just find you and gobble you up.

Because of its early evolutionary association with olfactory attachment,

the limbic system was initially called the rhinencephalon, the "smell brain."
But without eye or auditory contact, attachment in humans becomes difficult. For example, fMRI studies reveal that the anterior cingulate gyrus is
aroused neither by facial recognition of friends per se nor by sexual arousal
per se. Rather, the cingulate gyrus fMRI image lights up when a lover gazes
at a picture of a partner's face or when a new mother hears her own infant's
cry. In one study the biological activity of the anterior cingulate cortex was
highest in individuals with the highest levels of social awareness (based on
objectively scored tests).[34] Congenitally blind infants manifest many of the
same symptoms as autistic children, who are denied (by an as yet unknown
brain pathology) a full capacity for human attachment. Autistic and blind
infants both receive loving breast-feeding—but to no avail. Love comes in
through our eyes, our skin, and, ultimately, our limbic systems, not through
our stomachs.

There is good evidence that the anterior cingulate gyrus has a more
"primitive" laminar structure and preceded the neocortex in evolution.[35]
The anterior cingulate gyrus regulates the blending of thoughts and feelings. Without it, a ticket to La Scala, the World Series, or a Rolling Stones
concert becomes just an oblong, insignificant piece of cardboard. In terms
of attachment, the anterior cingulate receives one of the richest dopaminergic innervations of any cortical area. Thus, the cingulate gyrus provides
motivational salience not only for lovers but also for drug addicts.

To offer another example, damage the anterior cingulate gyrus and we
lose our capacity for spontaneous smiling, but we can still voluntarily produce inauthentic "flight attendant" smiles that fool only a few. Damage the
motor neocortex and the face of the flight attendant is frozen to free will,
but she can still authentically smile from joy and from laughter when boring passengers are replaced with beloved friends.[36] In inarticulate monkeys,
the anterior cingulate gyrus also affects emotional vocalizations and communication through facial expression.[37]

Perhaps no area of the brain is more ambiguous in its evolutionary heritage than our *prefrontal cortex*. Whether the prefrontal cortex belongs to
the limbic system[38] or the most recently evolved portion of the neocortical
brain[39] is still debated. What is certain is that the ventromedial (or orbito-

frontal) prefrontal cortex (the part of the brain nearest to our noses) is closely connected to all the other limbic structures. The prefrontal cortex is in charge of estimating rewards and punishments and plays a critical role in adapting and regulating our emotional response to new situations. Thus, our prefrontal lobes are deeply involved in our emotional, "moral," and "spiritual" lives. Or, in the words of the brilliant Emory University anthropologist Melvin Konner, the orbitofrontal cortex is "the crossroads of emotion and thought, one place where the ancient limbic brain meets the great human computer of the neocortex."[40]

Our morality exists both in the realm of ideas and in the realm of emotion. Neuroimaging and lesion studies reveal that the ventromedial prefrontal cortex is affected more by the emotional facets of "moral" decisions and that the more recently evolved lateral prefrontal cortex is more affected by the cognitive facets of morality.[41]

From an evolutionary standpoint, the human frontal lobes are no different from those of chimpanzees in terms of number of neurons. Rather, it is the frontal lobe white matter, the connectivity between neurons through myelinated fibers, that accounts for the larger frontal lobes of humans.[42] This connectivity to the limbic system underscores its "executive" function, which includes the ability to delay gratification, comprehend symbolic language, and, most important, establish temporal sequencing. By being able to connect memory of the past to "memory of the future," the frontal lobes establish cause and effect.

Destroy the medial prefrontal lobes of the neocortex, as was done by the tamping rod that penetrated the skull of the legendary nineteenth-century railroad worker Phineas Gage, and you destroy our capacity for obedience to social mores.[43] Phineas Gage had been a responsible foreman until an explosion drove the tamping rod that he was using to place a dynamite charge through the orbit of his left eye and out through the top of his skull. Although he survived, his medial frontal lobes were destroyed, as was his capacity for socially appropriate and empathic behavior. His intellect remained intact.

Like the amygdala, the prefrontal cortex uses the past memories from the hippocampus to modulate reflexive responses from the brain stem, but this function depends heavily upon maturity. An infant is alarmed by everything sudden and new, but by age thirty a woman may respond to the unexpected appearance of an engagement ring with alarm, or with joy, or with tears, or, depending on the circumstances, all three. It is through the lifelong maturation of the brain, through both experience and brain development, that we learn to discriminate our emotions. Ablate the frontal lobes, however, and the ring might become as boring as a plumber's washer. For example, touch the human hand with a block of wood and the somatosensory gyrus of the neocortex lights up; stroke the human hand with velvet and the limbic orbitofrontal cortex lights up.[44]

Surgical or traumatic ablation of the ventromedial prefrontal cortex can turn a conscientious, responsible adult into a moral imbecile without any other evidence of intellectual impairment.[45] A normal response to guilt and social anxiety is thought by many to be absent in the true psychopath.[46] Unlike the rest of us, psychopaths when presented with loss or disaster claim to "feel" nothing viscerally. The elevated galvanic skin response reflecting social anxiety in most of us is used on the forensic polygraph to detect lying, but is useless in the case of some psychopaths.

The work of University of Wisconsin psychologist Richard Davidson and his colleagues has done much to support the importance of the lateral prefrontal (more recently evolved) neocortex to our emotional lives. One of Davidson's contributions has been to confirm and expand prior work showing that excitation of a small area in the left prefrontal cortex leads to enhancing positive emotion and to perceiving cups as half-full. Excitation of the corresponding area of the right prefrontal cortex leads to depressed mood and perceiving cups as half-empty. Ablate the right frontal area by experiment or stroke, and humor, hope, and extroversion are all increased. Ablate the left and despair predominates.[47]

Another contribution of Davidson and his colleagues has been to show that deep Buddhist meditation increases left-brain activity and decreases anxiety.[48] In contrast, showing spiders to spider-phobic individuals increases activity in the right prefrontal areas.[49] As a result of this work, there is now

abundant evidence that meditation techniques are perhaps the most powerful means that humans have—besides opiates and other people—of in-
ducing relaxation and positive emotion.[50]

The *insula* is another part of the limbic system that is only beginning to
be understood. It is left out of the illustration in figure 2 and, until the last
decade, left out of most discussions of the limbic system. The insula is a medial cortical gyrus located between the amygdala and the frontal lobe. Our
brain has no sensation; we feel emotion only in our bodies. The insula helps
to bring these visceral feelings into consciousness: the pain in our heart of
grief, the warmth in our heart of love, and the tightness in our gut from fear,
all make their way into consciousness through the insula.

Both the limbic anterior cingulate and insula appear active in the positive emotions of humor, trust, and empathy. The higher apes are set apart
from other mammals by a unique neural component called the spindle cell.
Humans have twenty times more spindle cells than either chimps or goril-
las. (Adult chimpanzees average about 7,000 spindle cells. Human newborns have four times more, and human adults have almost 200,000 spindle
cells.) Monkeys and other mammals, with the possible exception of whales
and elephants, are totally lacking in these special cells. These large, cigar-
shaped spindle or "Von Economo" neurons appear to be central to the gov-
ernance of social emotions and moral judgment.[51] Spindle cells, associated
with limbic vocalizations in primates, may help us to feel human connection and indirectly to reflect upon and act on that feeling. In brain imaging
studies, the insula lights up "when people look at romantic partners, perceive unfairness . . . experience embarrassment, or if they are mothers, hear
infants cry."[52] Spindle cells may have helped the great apes and humans integrate their mammalian limbic system with their expanding neocortices.
Spindle cells are concentrated in the anterior cingulate cortex, the prefrontal cortex, and the insula.

More recently, scientists have discovered a special group of "mirror
neurons" that reside in the insula.[53] These neurons are more highly developed in humans than in primates and appear to mediate empathy—the experience of "feeling" the emotions of another. These specialized cells are
discussed more fully in the chapter on compassion (chapter 9). Buddhist

"insight" meditation by experienced meditators (for example, six hours a week of meditation for nine years) not only resulted in apparent thickening of the prefrontal cortex but also increased thickening in the right insular cortex.[54]

A final limbic region of interest is the septal region. This region is best known because electrodes placed in the mammalian septal area can produce self-stimulation until the animal is exhausted. But the septum is not just about hedonistic pleasure. The seemingly "moral" motivational behaviors mediated by the prefrontal cortex are modulated by input from the septal nuclei—especially as we grow older.[55]

It is fitting that we end our tour of the many-brains-in-one here, for my next task is to outline how we became what we are: creatures whose pleasure centers are connected to their centers for moral behavior. This process required three separate evolutions—a natural selection of genes that led us from reptiles to Homo sapiens, a cultural evolution that led us from Homo sapiens to men like the forty-year-old Albert Schweitzer, and finally, evolution over the life span that leads most of us to generative maturity.

3

Three Evolutions

ॐ

Suprainstinctual survival strategies generate some-
thing probably unique to humans: a moral point of
view that, on occasion, can transcend the interest of
the immediate group and even the species.

—Antonio Damasio, *Descartes' Error* (1994), p. 126

ॐ

In a letter dated November 24, 1859, Adam Sedgwick, Charles Darwin's former professor of geology at Cambridge, dismissed his former student's gracious gift of a first edition of *On the Origin of Species* with the stinging rebuke that the "gift caused more pain than pleasure. . . . Tis the crown and glory of organic science that it does thro' final cause link material to moral. You have ignored this link. If I do not mistake your meaning in one or two pregnant cases, you do break it."[1] Born a hundred years too soon to benefit from the new late-twentieth-century sciences, Professor Sedgwick could not comprehend how really very "moral" human natural selection has been. Current evolutionary evidence suggests that neither a "final cause" nor an "intelligent design" is needed to explain how very moral are the positive emotions and their evolution.

Ironically, Darwin's outspoken intellectual descendant, Richard Dawkins, called into question the morality of Professor Sedgwick and his ilk when he wrote, "I think a case can be made that faith is one of the world's great evils, comparable to the smallpox virus but harder to eradicate."[2] Nevertheless, however bitter the debate between the creationists and the Darwinians, the new disciplines of neuroscience and ethology do not cast stones. Instead, they have created a unifying and scientific vision of human evolution that is remarkably decent and unselfish.

The evolution of positive emotions is not something recent. It all began more than 200 million years ago when faithless, walnut-brained, untrusting, humorless, cold-blooded reptiles slowly evolved into warm-blooded, child-nurturing, faithful, hopeful, large-brained mammals capable of play, joy, attachment, and trust in their parents to care for them rather than do them for lunch.

Mammalian evolution had begun in the dark to protect little furry insectivores from hungry, sun-loving carnivorous reptiles. At first their sense of smell was as important as, or more important than, sight. Thus, these early nocturnal mammals possessed a highly developed limbic olfactory system, the rhinencephalon, or smell brain. In order to find food and to remain connected to each other in the dark, a good sense of smell was a necessity. Some scientists have called this smell brain the "seeking system."[3] The seeking, however, was about connection to one's fellow insectivores as much as to food or sexual procreation per se. The brains of mammals, relative to their body size, began to grow. Unlike in the case of dinosaurs and fish, increasing brain complexity, instead of traits like size, teeth, and bright colors, began to be selected for.

Sixty-five million years ago a meteor probably struck the earth, and the mighty dinosaurs, whose brains had not grown in 100 million years, vanished forever, thereby facilitating further mammalian evolution. In time, some of these early mammals evolved into light-loving creatures for whom a stereoscopic visual system and improved hearing reshaped the responsiveness of their smell brain. Primates and many other mammals now use their former smell brain to stay in touch with their mates vocally and visually rather than by odor, but the limbic language of attachment still defies easy translation into spoken language. Instead, humans become quite inarticulate when they try to describe what they smell or whom they love and why. Attachment depends upon mammalian body language, scents, vocal timbre, and lullabies, not the language of the human left neocortex. We confabulate when we try to put the scent of an orchid, the nose of a great burgundy wine, or a life-altering spiritual experience into words.

Indeed, language, like too articulate religions, often separates human beings. We try to put the experience of God into words and then squabble with each other over our competing definitions. In contrast, emotions, body language, facial recognition, touch, pheromones, and the spirituality of a limbic smell brain often bind us together. We give another person a loving hug and feel at peace with the world. Through discriminating audition, the kitten's mew or the human infant's separation cry evokes an unselfish response in almost all of us. Thus, from the limbic system and the temporal (behind the temple) neocortex that it serves comes the sort of information provided in hymns, psalms, and love letters—emotional, musical, mystically important information. Such information is very different from that contained in almanacs, science journals, and theological treatises.

As mammals evolved into primates, another transformative change took place. The ratio of brain size to body weight—relatively constant throughout the mammalian kingdom—began to increase further. At first, as ancestral chimpanzee brains evolved into those of *Australopithecus*, the relative increase was slow. This brain expansion, however, soon led to a magnificent (not vicious) cycle. To pass through the birth canal, primates with relatively large brains needed to be born prematurely. This necessitated a nurturing community. The brain complexity necessary for the continuing evolution of unselfish love required a still larger brain that prolonged childhood still further. And the longer the childhood, the larger and more unselfish was the brain required not only by the child's parents but also by the child's surrounding clan.

Thus, our ancestral primate brains began to expand at an accelerating rate—two tablespoons of gray matter were added every 100,000 years. "By the time the cerebral topping off had finished the human cortex had more than doubled in volume."[4] Arguably, no organ in the history of life has evolved faster.

⟨⟩

The evolution of human brain function rests as much on the complexity and specificity of its biochemistry as it does on sheer neuroanatomic size or specialization. Tinkering with a few microchips in two seemingly identical computers, after all, can lead either to quintupling processing speed or to rapid obsolescence.

For example, specific genes are known to affect the neuronal migration of brain cells during development—i.e., the wiring. In monkeys that are proficient in displays of cooperation and of social grooming, the density of serotonin-2 receptors is elevated in the ventromedial frontal lobes and in the amygdala; in antagonistic, less affectionate monkeys of the same species, fewer serotonin receptors are found.[5] The addition of a single brain peptide, oxytocin, can transform a promiscuous, asocial, pup-neglecting montane vole into a communal, monogamous, nurturant prairie vole.[6]

For the first million and a half years of their existence, tool-making Homo habilis, then Homo erectus, and then Homo sapiens, managed to increase the cutting edge of a kilogram of worked stone only from 10 to 40 centimeters. During this time their brain size almost doubled. Over the last 600,000 years, perhaps stimulated by dramatic fluctuations in global climate or by the need for still greater social cooperation, Homo sapiens' brain size again almost doubled, from 835 grams to 1,460 grams.[7] More important, by the end of the Neolithic era our ancestors could produce 2,000 centimeters of cutting edge out of a kilogram of stone.[8] In short, brain size doubled, and tool-making efficiency grew 5,000 percent. From the scanty evidence available, however, it seemed that until very recently the evolution of human social organization lagged behind the evolution of tool making.

· Only 170,000 to 200,000 years ago, a dramatic change occurred that is sometimes referred to as the "creative explosion."[9] The tool-making, large-brained Neanderthals *Homo neanderthalensis* were well established in Europe about 400,000 years ago, and until comparatively recently, their unchanging tool-making skills had been as good as any in the world. Then, abruptly, less than 200,000 years ago, a new subspecies, *Homo sapiens sapiens*, from whom all human beings are descended, evolved in what is now Kenya and Ethiopia.[10] Both fossil and mitochondrial evidence date this transformation at 170,000 BCE.[11] Suddenly, the tool kit of the Neanderthals' African cousins became increasingly complex. Instead of just stone axes, spearheads, and scrapers, there appeared spear throwers, needles of bone, barbed fishhooks, decorative beads, and vastly more efficient ways of manufacturing stone tools. Between 40,000 and 60,000 years ago, these modern humans reached Europe to stay. These changes facilitated not only more effective, more cooperative hunting but also the exponential growth of the modern human population relative to the Neanderthal.

The most likely explanation for the creative explosion in modern humans was the development of better language as a product of both genetic and cultural evolution. Let me address the genetic evolution first. Modern linguistic ability is perhaps due to a fortuitous mutation in genes like FOXP2, a gene that contributes to facial muscle control. It differs from the chimpanzee's FOXP2 by only two amino acids but has been positively selected for in all humans currently living.[12] The mutation is estimated to have occurred 100,000 to 200,000 years ago, coincident with the emergence of modern humans.[13] Congenital defects in the FOXP2 gene in humans lead to impairment of tongue muscles.

The mutation of the gene microcephalin (MCPA1), which regulates brain size, appears to have increased rapidly in human populations roughly 40,000 years ago.[14] The mutation of another human gene, ASPM, also thought to regulate brain growth, emerged about 6,000 years ago and since then has spread through human populations under strong positive selection.[15] Only time will reveal whether these latter alleged evolutionary mutations have made a meaningful contribution to the development of humankind.

Cultural evolution, mediated by language, has been as important for human survival as brain complexity mediated by genetic evolution has been for mammalian survival. Cultural evolution, after all, is faster and more flexible than genetic evolution. With effective cultural communication, knowledge, accumulated over a lifetime, no longer had to die with the individual. Knowledge started to expand, and thus, analogous to compounding interest, the store of human knowledge began to increase exponentially. The capacity for cultural development gave modern humans a tremendous evolutionary advantage over the Neanderthal. It was as if the hardware of the human brain now permitted the addition of software.

As a result of their physical vulnerability to predators, Homo sapiens became the most social of fauna on the African savanna. For protection, modern humans survived not just through "selfish" genes and survival of the fittest, but also by transcending self-interest in the service of others.[16] Not only does it take a village to raise a hunter-gatherer or a twenty-first-century urban child, but the evolution of food-sharing relationships requires that in good times individuals share so that in leaner times they will be the recipients of the generosity of others.

For the last 50,000 years the evolution of human strength and ferocity began to contribute less and less to survival. Instead, there is good evidence that improved communication facilitated larger and more complex social organizations.[17] These changes led to increased communal sharing of large animal kills and to an increased willingness to care for the crippled and ill. The creative and more gracile Homo sapiens sapiens traveled to, traded with, learned from, and mated with unrelated peers hundreds of miles away. The muscular, big-brained Neanderthal, not built for long-distance walking, remained rooted to their mountain hollows, to their old-fashioned ways, and perhaps became genetic prisoners of exclusive kinship networks.

૮ઙ

The highly regarded linguist Derek Bickerton has speculated that the evo-lution of modern language may also have facilitated cultural evolution by allowing mastery of past and future tenses.[18] As long as you live from day to day, life is pretty mundane. If you have a past, however, you begin to ask, where did I come from? If you have a future, you begin to wonder, what will happen after I die? Reality becomes replaced by awe. Reflective spiritual life begins. Constrained by only a present tense, it is hard to discuss the bene-fits of kindness. A past tense helps you to discuss the past kindnesses you have received, and a future tense helps you suggest to others that bread cast upon the waters might return with interest. The consequences of limbic gratitude, love, and compassion can be brought into conscious awareness by a language that includes a past and a future tense.

In any case, along with cultural evolution and a more sophisticated tool kit, another evolutionary change took place thirty to forty thousand years ago in places as far apart as the Kimberley Range in Australia and the Dor-dogne limestone caves in France.[19] Homo sapiens began to decorate caves in ways that still induce a unifying spiritual gasp of awe and recognition of beauty in their twenty-first-century descendants. For reasons we still do not understand, the capacity to create beauty and spiritual awe go hand in hand.

Another corollary of cultural evolution in humans was an increasing capacity for focused consciousness. True, an eagle's sharp eye can instinc-tively distinguish a distant stone from a distant mouse better than a human eye. A dog's nose is more discriminating than the nose of its master. But hu-mans can reflect upon the distinction and can bring the question of feelings (Am I hungry? Am I loved?) up into reflective consciousness and into the consciousness of others.

Armchair critics of cultural evolution may wonder if there has been any progress at all. They can scoff at the inconsistencies of modern judicial pun-ishments, but for the last thirty centuries, through the conscious cultural reflection upon the long-term consequences of angry retaliation, the deterrence of criminal behavior has become progressively more pragmatic and more compassionate. The postmodern pessimist can point to the appalling handgun-fueled homicide rate in American cities, but the fact-driven longitudinal evidence is more hopeful. For example, in the thirteenth century the European homicide rate was about 40 per 100,000 persons. By the seventeenth century, it had been cut in half. By the eighteenth century, the rate again was halved, and by the end of the twentieth century the European homicide rate had fallen to roughly 2 percent of the rate seven centuries earlier.[20] Admittedly, in Detroit and in many Third World countries the homicide rate is still what Europe's rate was in the eighteenth century.

In the thirteenth century King Louis IX of France ordered the massacres of hundreds of alleged French heretics and later, while crusading, genocidally killed countless Jews and Muslims. Nevertheless, he was still canonized and made Saint Louis by an admiring Europe.[21] Yes, massacres still happen today, but in the twentieth century they are universally condemned and the culprits usually punished, not canonized. Admittedly, there is still much room for improvement.

Over the millennia, through cultural evolution, religions too have evolved. Evidence of organized religion accompanied evidence of stable settlements seven to twelve millennia ago. The growth of religion paralleled the growth of towns and then cities. Nevertheless, until two thousand years ago great cities arose only to disappear. Religions based on power, guilt, retaliation, and hierarchy could not sustain the world's great cities. Ur, Babylon, Mohenjo-Daro, Carthage, Thebes, Machu Picchu, the Mayan metropolis of Tikal, and the early Chinese and Egyptian capitals all have vanished forever beneath sand, fields, and jungle creepers.

Not until a transformative millennium, a millennium extending from 600 BCE to 700 CE, did Buddhism, Confucianism, Christianity, and Islam become established. Although it may sound incongruous to some modern ears, these newer organized religions emphasized love and compassion rather than fear and dominance. It was this transformative millennium that may have permitted great cities to endure. Unlike early cities of history that

self-destructed, the more modern communities that have survived successfully transformed the city from a concatenation of competing tribes into a
more egalitarian hive. For example, Jerusalem is arguably the oldest contin-
uously important city in the world. It may not have been coincidence that
about 600 BCE the black-and-white retaliatory Mosaic Jewish "law" gave
way to the loving suggestions of a gentler prophet:

> *Cease to do evil,*
> *Learn to do good;*
> *Search for justice,*
> *Help the oppressed;*
> *Defend the orphan,*
> *Plead for the widow.*
>
> —ISAIAH 1:16–17

During the twelve centuries between 600 BCE and 700 CE, the spiritual
sages and prophets developed cognitive insights and emotional rituals that uti-
lized inborn positive limbic emotions to counter aggression. The empathic
practices of the world's great religions served to mitigate the equally hardwired
xenophobia and territoriality that is largely responsible for tribal violence.

Karen Armstrong, a former nun and a master of autobiography, is one
of the foremost teachers of comparative religion alive today. In her magisterial *The Great Transformation*, following the 1948 lead of German philosopher Karl Jaspers, Armstrong has titled this period the Axial Age. She sets
its dates a little earlier (900–200 BCE) than I do, but her melody is the same.
In Armstrong's words, "The Axial Age pushed forward the frontiers of human consciousness and discovered a transcendent dimension in the core of
their being, but they did not necessarily regard this as supernatural. . . . If
the Buddha or Confucius had been asked whether he believed in God, he
would probably have winced slightly and explained—with great courtesy—
that this was not an appropriate question."[22] What mattered to Confucius,
Socrates, Christ, and Isaiah was not what you believed but how you behaved. Show me, don't tell me. "God" was the experience of loving compassion, not an all-powerful, judgmental, and often angry patriarch.

For evolving humanity, the Axial Age also reflected what the Swiss-French developmentalist Jean Piaget was later to call "formal operations." Without formal operations (defined as the capacity to abstract general principles from concrete observations), neither science nor mature morality would be possible. Religions needed to look beyond the letter of the law and to distinguish between metaphor and myth. In addition, through disciplined introspection humanity was awakened to the vast reaches of selfhood that lay beneath the surface of their minds. Humanity became fully "self-conscious."[23] The tragedy of fundamentalist religion of all shades and stripes is that it reasons concretely like a third-grader, not a tenth-grader.

In his 1990 book *The Origin of Consciousness in the Breakdown of the Bicameral Mind*, Princeton psychologist Julian Jaynes observed, perhaps too romantically, that the fifth century BCE brought a shift from humans depending upon moral comments from without—the burning bush of Moses and the hallucination of gods' voices in Homer's *Iliad*—to a world in which morality and responsibility came from within, owing to responsible introspection.[24] Instead of being consigned to Mount Olympus and to Heaven, God could reside within us all.

Instead of conceptualizing gods like the Greek and the Aztec deities who, like reptiles, devoured their young (consider Cronus), the culturally evolved fifth-century BCE humans conceived of models like Socrates, the Buddha, and later Christ, who epitomized unselfish love and inspired us to emulate them. During that transformative millennium, the range of people whom a given person felt compelled to regard as equally human greatly expanded. "Tribes" became integrated into empires—a process culminating in both Roman Europe and Chinese Asia. Once the xenophobic, tribal Romans learned to regard millions of "barbarians" as "citizens," not only cities but empires became viable. Today the challenge still remains for Jews, Christians, Hindus, and Muslims to learn to regard one another as fully human. The cultural invention of the Internet may be a step forward.

It was perhaps no accident that Saint Paul put Christ's teachings on the map, as it were, in the same Greek cities that had first conceived of intertribal empathy. The Athenian Aeschylus wrote his tragedy *The Persians* just eight years after he had personally fought in the great battle of Salamis, a battle in which the Persians had tried to destroy Athens. Fortunately for Aeschylus, the Greeks won, but the Greek playwright did not gloat. In his play about the war, Aeschylus, unlike Homer, mentions no Greek heroes at all. Instead, he wishes his audience to feel pity for the Persians.

> . . . From her sweet couch up starts the widow'd bride,
> Her lord's loved image rushing on her soul,
> Throws the rich ornaments of youth aside,
> And gives her griefs to flow without control.[25]

Anticipating a unity of nations that was not to become even a tentative reality until the birth of the United Nations in 1944 in San Francisco, Aeschylus describes the mortal enemies, Greece and Persia, as "sisters of one race . . . flawless in beauty and in grace."[26]

In a China torn to pieces by tribal strife, Kong Qiu (551–479 BCE)—whose name in the West is Confucius—worked out the moral principles of the New Testament 500 years before Christ and 2,500 years before Schweitzer and Gandhi. The "Way" of Confucius led neither to Heaven nor to Yahweh's favor, but rather to a "condition of transcendent goodness."[27] It also undoubtedly helped catalyze the unification of China. If people could only subordinate egocentricity to empathy, then that was the meaning of holiness. In the West we sometimes think of Confucius as only insisting that sons yield to fathers and daughters to mother-in-laws, but in the *Analects of Confucius* warriors are instructed to "yield" to enemies and kings to their retainers. "In order to establish oneself, one should try to establish others. In order to enlarge oneself, one should try to enlarge others."[28]

As a young man, the Buddha tried to learn compassion through intense meditative practices and obedient submission to severe physical deprivation administered by authoritarian yogi teachers. Then the Buddha experienced, at least in legend, a sudden insight. He recalled a memory from his early childhood when he had focused on a furrow torn up by ceremonial spring plowing. The young sensitive boy noted the uprooted shoots of grass and the insects wantonly killed by the ritual. He felt a deep pang of grief, followed by a moment of spiritual release, and then he felt a moment of pure joy. "Could this," the young Siddhartha asked himself, "possibly be the way to enlightenment?" Perhaps, instead of following the negative self-mortification of the yogi, Nirvana could be achieved by behaving gently and kindly toward every living creature. "From now on he was going to work *with* his human nature and not fight against it."[29]

Shortly before Armstrong's "Great Transformation" had come another great transformation that transformed the Neolithic mind—the invention of writing. Step by step, the evolution of first language, then writing, and then printing has led to the ascendancy of left-brain cognition over right-brain musicality and intuition. While the cultural memes of compassionate religions spread throughout the globe, the simultaneous spread of literacy over the last two thousand years made possible the gradual evolution of science at the expense of spirituality. As already noted, the increasing subordination of limbic positive emotion to neocortical left-brain science has continued until the last half-century.

Admittedly, the cultural invention of writing and then the invention of printing five hundred years ago were truly giant steps for mankind. The tools for understanding the world were created. No longer would cultural information important to survival need to be suffused with Neolithic awe and emotion in order to be passed on. Important but neutral memories could be encoded and shared. In preliterate cultures all knowledge had to be passed down verbally from generation to generation. Thus, in hunter-gatherer societies technological advance, while more rapid than for the Neanderthals, was still very gradual. Writing speeded up the whole process. Until the invention of writing, the *Iliad* could exist only in the mind's eye of a few brilliant, dramatically gifted storytellers. Today the *Iliad* and its lessons can exist in cheap, passionless printed pamphlets available to all willing high school students from Alabama to Zanzibar. However, Homer's "music" is sometimes lost in translation.

The downside, of course, was that writing created dogma as well as technological advance. Over the last two thousand years literate humans "forgot" how to think with the brain with which they were born. The more humankind learned to think rationally, the more estranged they became from their innate emotional spirituality. Since the Enlightenment, this divorce between emotion and reason has become complete for many in the West. As I have already noted, until the penetration of neuroscience, cultural anthropology, and ethology into the culture over the past fifty years, the positive emotions were virtually abandoned as a focus for respectable scientific research.

Since the Enlightenment, humanists like Carl Rogers and Richard Dawkins have forgotten that awe and religious rituals often help humanity remember important verities. For example, when literate, scientific, mapmaking English settlers arrived in Australia, they had nothing but contempt for the Neolithic Aboriginals. They viewed the Aboriginals as dirty, intellectually challenged subhumans with the silliest religion imaginable. If the English did not regard the Aboriginal "dreaming" spirituality as actually dangerous, in no way did they regard it as healthy or as based on anything but childish superstition.

In 1800 the "enlightened" English could never have dreamed that this "inferior" race, in terms of DNA, intellect, and ancestry—as recently as 100,000 years ago—was identical to themselves. They could have never imagined that the Aboriginals' ancestors created evocative cave art at least as early as the paler-skinned ancestors of the English painted the limestone walls at Lascaux and Altamira.[30] The culturally punctilious English still have trouble appreciating that there is no word in some Aboriginal languages for "time," and only slowly and grudgingly did the English admit wonder at the Aboriginals' intuitive "right-brain" skill at tracking. Unaware of modern cognitive neuroscience, the English had not yet learned the wisdom of the bumper sticker "Don't believe everything you think."

Eventually, the English learned to marvel that although the settlers, even with maps and compasses, died of thirst in the outback, the Aboriginals could find water. A mystery. The English understood the sweet reason of Enlightenment science, but died of thirst; the Aboriginals could not even read or keep time, but they survived. Only very recently have anthropologists deduced that the animistic, fancy-ridden, superstitious "dreaming" world of the Australian Aboriginals provided them with an awe-filled, if not always conscious, map for survival. Without written language or rational map-making skills (which evolved in parallel with humanity's acquisition of "left-brain" writing), the Aboriginals had developed emotionally and spiritually significant stories in order to remember every rock, rill, and water source in their environment. Such seemingly irrational, but affectively significant, fables allowed the Aboriginals to find life-giving water in the desert generation after generation. Put more provocatively, the Aboriginal "dreaming" spirituality actually delivered what the white man's printed Holy Bible and scientific maps only promised. "The Lord is my shepherd. I shall not want. . . . He leadeth me beside still waters" (Psalm 23).

Arguably, the publication of Charles Darwin's *On the Origin of Species* in 1859 rivaled the invention of printing as a catalyst to human cultural evolution. Charles Darwin and Alfred Wallace recognized that, just as the earth was not the center of the universe, *Homo sapiens* was not the center either. Humans are just another mammal that is a work in progress. Like Christ, Darwin reflected a step forward in modeling spiritual wisdom and humility.

A century after Darwin, but before the scientific elucidation of positive emotions, two evolutionary biologists set forth a bold outline for the possible future collective evolution of humankind. The first biologist was Pierre Teilhard de Chardin. He was a French Jesuit priest and a distinguished paleontologist who helped discover Peking Man. On the one hand, the Catholic Church barred him from teaching because as an evolutionist he was too outspoken; on the other hand, he was condemned by other evolutionary biologists, like Stephen Jay Gould, for being a theist. Teilhard's visionary colleague was Sir Julian Huxley, the atheist brother of Aldous Huxley and the grandson of T. H. Huxley, sometimes known as "Darwin's bulldog." Julian Huxley may have been an atheist, but he was the very spiritual cofounder of the World Wildlife Fund and the first director-general of UNESCO. Julian Huxley wrote the introduction to Teilhard's most famous book, *The Phenomenon of Man*, written between 1938 and 1940 but not published until 1955.[31] (Teilhard, like Galileo, has been rehabilitated by the Catholic Church only in the last fifty years.)

Both atheist Huxley and theist Teilhard believed that human awareness of evolution would make possible further evolution and that future evolution, if it took place, would be organized into the increasingly cooperative organization of social units. Teilhard's neologism, the "noosphere," suggested that "man is nothing else than evolution become conscious of itself." The highest levels of consciousness in the universe could then be coupled with the higher levels of psychosocial organization.[32] A dream perhaps, but for the last fifty years UNESCO and the World Wildlife Fund—unimaginable in Darwin's day—have both flourished. In the twenty-first century, both the unifying effects of the Internet and the terrifying decoding of the human genome reflect additions to Huxley's and Teilhard's vision of the potential self-sponsored collective evolution of humanity.

The world is still a very dangerous place, but our understanding of the positive emotions is improving. The evolution of science over the very recent past has brought us closer to spirituality, not further away. Most of the scientific studies cited in this book in support of the positive emotions are less than ten years old. Over the last decade American medical schools and the life sciences in general have made an increasing effort to rescue the baby of spirituality from being thrown out with the religious bathwater.[33] A course on positive emotion is currently the most popular course at Harvard College.[34]

For millennia, theologians, largely male, have suggested that spirituality was about basic intellectual questions like "Who am I? Why am I here? What happens to me when I die? How can I please my God?" These dry, cognitive questions are about patriarchal gods and "me." In the last century, however, cultural anthropologists (such as Margaret Mead), ethologists (such as Jane Goodall), and neuroscientists (such as Andrew Newberg) have been more likely to suggest that spirituality reflects limbic questions about love, community, positive emotions, and the feeling of "being one with the universe."

Even since the Enlightenment, underneath our rational, postmodern, sophisticated radar screen, human spirituality has continued to evolve culturally. Alfred Nobel grew rich selling the world explosives; his descendants are today as invisible as the ruins of the first Troy. Only Nobel's spiritual legacy of prizes for beauty, truth, and peace live on. You do not have to go back very far in time to find an era when the plague of intertribal wars that afflict Africa today afflicted the entire globe. Over the past two thousand years, larger and larger groups of ethnically diverse people have learned to live together cooperatively. From the unification of China after the chaos, of "the Warring States" two millennia ago to the European Union in the twenty-first century, humanity is moving toward the mystical "oneness" that we associate with spiritual ecstasy. Hope, forgiveness, and compassion have all played critical roles.

The twenty-first-century United Nations, for all its difficulties in herding cats, works hard to bring about empathic cooperation between nations—a very new phenomenon. Like Samuel Johnson's famous dog walking on its hind legs, it is not that the United Nations walks haltingly that we should criticize. It is that the United Nations walks at all that should provoke our heartfelt applause. A century ago a functioning World Health Organization would have been as unimaginable as a jet plane.

Another clear example of the survival value of spirituality is revealed by the recent history of Cambodia. In 1975 the Khmer Rouge gained absolute control of the country, then systematically, and for mostly idealistic, cognitive, "Marxist" reasons, tried to abolish Buddhism and familial love. Pol Pot believed that sentimental attachment to family members and to economically wasteful Buddhist temples impeded rational, rapid social progress. He made such inefficient attachments punishable by death. (It is not just "religious" Muslims and Christians who have made heresy a capital offense. Atheists have been equally enterprising.) Pol Pot's idealistic regime hoped to instill in young children, separated from their families, an attachment to agrarian simplicity and to create a society without memory of urban decadence, monastic indolence, or that root of all evil, money. Thoreau, Jefferson, and Mohandas Gandhi all might possibly have admired some of Pol Pot's ends—just not his means.

Four years later, when the Khmer Rouge regime fell, the Cambodian children, now orphans, remained passionately attached to what remained of their extended families, and Buddhism rapidly reasserted itself as a high point of village life. The recovery of Cambodian villages from left-brain disaster was not a result of do-gooder central planning; rather, the human brain is hardwired for loving, spiritual resilience. Yes, *The Lord of the Flies* holds some truth, and child murderers exist, but not in the same numbers as

Cambodian children who valued love and spirituality over a rationally, but heartlessly, planned society. Ever since the Enlightenment, underneath our rational worldview, human spirituality has continued to evolve culturally.

Is this miracle of human evolution, as Teilhard de Chardin hinted, due to a lonely, loving God patiently waiting until an evolving universe can achieve the "divinization of humanity"?[35] Are we destined to become gods? I personally rather doubt it. In time, science may reveal such touching faith to be no more than metaphor, but a metaphor underscoring a powerful truth. Just as sometimes through the rational exercise of left-brain free will we can substitute wonderfully tasty Twinkies and ice-cold Coca-Cola and martinis for our biologic need for fiber, boring broccoli, and the four basic food groups, just so for a while we can substitute dispassionate science, lukewarm humanism, and exciting negative emotions for the passionate positive emotions of the mammalian human heart. Over the long haul, however, our survival depends not just on "good ideas," clever marketing, and drugs, sex, and rock and roll but also on following the laws of biological and spiritual nutrition. Science and dogmatic religions, too, can help us to survive, but not for long if, like the Khmer Rouge, they lack compassion and humility.

۞

Besides genetic and cultural evolution, there is yet a third form of evolution at work in the maturation of human spirituality—adult development. Our mastery of the positive emotions grows as we mature. Having sketched the development (phylogeny) of positive emotions for the species over the millennia, let me sketch the individual embryology (ontogeny) of positive emotions over a lifetime.

The maturation of our organs is largely completed by puberty. Indeed, after age twenty, nearly every organ in our body begins inexorably to decline. Only the human brain—and thus our capacity for integrating the prose and passion—continues to develop biologically until at least age sixty.[36]

The life of John Newton provides an illustration of increasing morality during adulthood.[37] During his early adulthood, Newton, the author of the hymn "Amazing Grace," evolved from being an adolescent seaman who reveled in anti-Christian blasphemy and profane verse to a ship captain who flogged his seamen for blaspheming. As a young man, John Newton himself had suffered the humiliation and iron shackles of slavery, yet once "over thirty" he perceived no conflict in becoming a captain who transported to the colonies, and then marketed, shackled slaves.

Hymn writing replaced his once scurrilous adolescent verse. Like the Christian authors of the Declaration of Independence, John Newton penned his hymn of gratitude to the "God who saved a wretch like me" without empathy for the wretches it excluded. To middle-aged John Newton, as to middle-aged Thomas Jefferson, life, liberty, and the pursuit of happiness did not apply if you were the wrong color or valuable merchandise.

Human brains, like human culture, take time to mature. Thus, it took both the cultural unfolding of England's Enlightenment and the maturation of his own central nervous system for the obediently Christian ex-slave captain, now Reverend John Newton, to become in late adulthood a passionate and dedicated abolitionist. For him the development process took forty years! Maturation and spirituality unfold together, but not very fast.

In a masterful study, Boston psychoanalyst Ana Maria Rizzuto studied how children develop their private image of God. In so doing, she charted the development of preverbal spiritual ideation. "Around the age of three the child matures cognitively to the point of being concerned with animistic notions of causality. . . . Through questioning he tries to arrive at a final answer and is not satisfied with scientific explanations. The child wants to know who moves the clouds and why. If told the wind, he wants to know who moves the wind, and so on. . . . This ceaseless chaining of causes inevitably ends in a 'superior being.' "[38]

In the modern three-year-old, Neolithic animism is still alive and well. At age three, my brother, now a most rational physician and grandfather, spent his New York City nights in an exciting world populated by "rokers" and "dophies." At night, when scared, he needed to take a roker (the spire on the Chrysler Building) to pin dophies (the scary monsters that flew around his bedroom at night) to the ceiling.

Then, Rizzuto goes on to caution, "the fictive creations of our minds—those of creative artists for example—have as much regulatory potential in our psychic function as people around us in the flesh. . . . Human life is impoverished when these innumerable experiences vanish under the repression of a psychic realism that does violence to the ceaseless creativity of the human mind."[39] As we mature, we forget that we once held in our mind's eye the vivid image of the God of our understanding. With gentle urging, Rizzuto was able to get adults to draw what most children and many preliterate people can draw without urging—their image of God. Of course, none of them looked quite the same, and a lot of the drawings resembled family members.

Literacy exerts the same effect on children's faith development as the invention of the alphabet and printing exerted on the development of mankind. By kindergarten, children are already being schooled to abandon animism as well as tears and noisy joy. No longer is the child's mind filled with the "right-brain," elemental, supernatural, uncanny, and sacred imagery that fills the minds of both illiterate hunter-gatherers and postmodern three- to four-year-olds with omen, portent, and awestruck wonder. During grammar school the once marvelous reality of Santa Claus vanishes as progressively and as inexorably as the Cheshire cat in *Alice in Wonderland*. Depending on the culture, the poet, the dreamer, the shaman, or the religious mystic sometimes retains the capacity to regress to the mind of the three-year-old and thus retrieve early nonverbal creative powers from domination by the left-brain rational prose. These literally visionary individuals help us to understand more fully our tenuous place in the universe.

The incorporation of rituals is part and parcel of adult development, but they have a downside. One of the drawbacks of human emotional development is that sometimes what was once vibrant in our hearts becomes ever more petrified to fit into the rigidly formatted software of our culture. Remember how the Victorians ritually immobilized their bodies into tightly laced corsets and draped the legs of pianos lest they arouse sexual desire.

Obviously, there is also an upside to adult development. With maturity, our positive emotions become increasingly linked to community welfare rather than to looking after number one. In one 1930s study of the "wishes" of adults, among the twenty-five-year-olds, 92 percent of all wishes were directed toward the individual himself, but among the sixty-year-olds only 29 percent of wishes were directed toward the self; 32 percent of wishes were directed toward the family and 21 percent toward mankind in general.[40] The self-absorbed Depression-era twenty-five-year-olds, of course, matured to become the parents who were so horrified by the self-indulgence of their 1960s "flower children." Like adolescents from the beginning of time, the 1960s "flower children" talked a more altruistic game than they played. Since the beginning of history, fifty-year-olds have regarded twenty-year-olds as selfish. Fifty-year-olds forget that being selfish is part of a young adult's developmental task. As developmentalist Carol Gilligan points out, we have no self to give "selflessly" away if at first we are not "selfish."[41]

The study of wishes was conducted by an influential Berkeley professor, Else Frenkel-Brunswik, who helped to educate her more famous Berkeley colleague Erik Erikson. Erikson titled the midlife transition of youth into middle age "generativity," and he saw the virtue of midlife as a shift toward care of the next generation. Put differently, as we abandon our own wishes for Barbie dolls and the beat of reindeers' hooves upon our own roofs, we replace these dreams with the heartwarming task of filling the Christmas stockings of our children. Our sexual prowess declines steadily after sixteen; our muscular power declines steadily after twenty-five. The capacity of our brains to care for people outside of our kinship pattern develops all of our lives. That is how the developing brains of human adults are genetically programmed, but such individual psychosocial progression must be catalyzed by cultural evolution.

With maturity comes an increasing ability not only to modulate but also to differentiate our negative emotions. For example, when are our tears from anger, indicating that we should push people away, and when are our tears from grief, indicating that we should hold people close? This is a distinction that most grandparents can make and many twenty-year-olds cannot.

Jean Piaget, the great Swiss child developmentalist, pointed out that children's morality—quite independently of religious instruction—matured from primitive selfish belief into, first, rule-bound piety, and then, into adult altruism.[42] This individual maturational process is strikingly similar to the evolutionary maturation of tribal into urban faith traditions. Piaget used a child's rules for playing marbles to illustrate how children's rules of morality evolved beyond the three-year-old's self-centered amorality (for example, might makes right, God is on the side of the big battalions, and almighty Zeus can sleep with anyone he chooses). Between ages six and ten, rules for marbles, like the Ten Commandments, become engraved in metaphorical stone. Without intending a pun, Piaget called this developmental stage of thinking "concrete operations." There is only one way to play marbles, and all other ways are wrong. The concrete retaliatory rights of others become paramount. The black-and-white Old Testament Talion laws (an eye for an eye and a tooth for a tooth) of early tribal development take over. Justice trumps care. Vietnam villages, like Torquemada's heretics, have to be destroyed in order to "save" them.

In adolescence both limbic passion and neocortical intellectual intolerance become tamed by the facet of cognitive development that Jean Piaget termed "formal operations." Adolescents discover that there are many ways to play marbles and that losers, too, deserve mercy and applause. Motivation and cause become important. Breaking one cup on purpose deserves more severe punishment than breaking ten cups by mistake. What is more, Piaget noted, such moral maturation takes place as a result of nonverbal schoolyard and biological development and not from lexical "Sunday school" instruction. Only mature adults can conceptualize the folly of zero-sum games.

Just as Galileo's telescope and Francis Bacon's experimental method forced devout Christians to abandon some beliefs and gave birth to the Enlightenment, just so Piaget observed that by the time children are in their teens they develop the capacity to place general principles over concrete thinking. This may mean accepting that our earth is not the center of the solar system. This may mean understanding that God, Allah, Yahweh, and the awe induced by experiencing unselfish love may mean the same thing.

Formal operations permit us to shift from the specific to the abstract. The Golden Rule provides one such example. Like the Golden Rule, the capacity for formal operations occurred late in the phylogeny of our species, just as it occurs late in the evolution of the individual. Formal operations allow us to class both members of Hamas and members of the Boston Tea Party gang as freedom fighters *and* as terrorists. The gallant B-17 and B-29 crews that gave their lives destroying Hamburg and Tokyo were both patriotic heroes and terrorists, sometimes suicidal murderers of tens of thousands of innocent women and children. But remember, I write these words as a seventy-two-year-old grandfather. At twenty, such heretical thoughts would not have crossed my patriotic mind. At thirty-five, I was still surprised to discover that when my post-1960s children played cowboys and Indians, they sided with the Native Americans.

Our capacity to plan and act maturely is powerfully affected by our frontal lobes. Although our frontal lobes are often identified as the most recently evolved part of the human neocortex, recent studies of both neural brain structure and function suggest, paradoxically, that the frontal brain gyri most relevant to emotion, especially the ventromedial gyri, are actually as much part of the archaic limbic system as they are part of the most recently expanded neocortex.[43]

As we mature, our frontal lobes become ever more securely wired to the rest of our limbic system. In more scientific language, the embryological myelinization (insulation) of the connecting neural tracts increases, at least until we are sixty.[44] Myelinization of nerve fibers speeds their conduction and allows the neocortex both to modulate and to be modulated by the more primitive emotional centers in a more nuanced and experience-based fashion. Thus, with adult maturation, planning becomes ever more smoothly linked with passion; we become more like "grown-ups" and less like adolescents. At age eighteen, elopement is romantic and exciting, but if the marriage is going to last for more than a few weeks, relatives with lingering gratitude for a lovely reception are so much more fun than relatives with lingering resentments. And wedding presents sure do facilitate setting up a home. We can plan for the present or for the future; it is all in our frontal lobes.

Maturation, however, does not take place overnight. Adolescents, like religions, strive for identity and unity. Teenagers need dogma. If you do not believe your identity is your only identity, you have no identity. Religious communities, like adolescent cliques, are deliberately homogeneous. Such communities tend to exclude or even attack other communities. Thus, the very Darwinian British humanist Richard Dawkins was not entirely wrong in asserting that the cultural memes of intolerant religions, like the warring adolescent patriots of all ages, are analogous to a dangerous virus.[45] Nevertheless, the identity formation of adolescence also reflects a developmental necessity.

Jane Loevinger, a developmental psychologist at Washington University in St. Louis, and James Fowler, a developmental psychologist and theologian at Emory University, both devoted their lives to carrying Piaget's ideas further into adult development.[46] In Loevinger's model, belief evolves into trust, and piety evolves into tolerance. Loevinger asks us to focus on three sequential adult stages: the conformist, the conscientious, and the autonomous. In Loevinger's conformist stages, morality is evaluated in terms of concrete externals rather than in terms of emotions. You love a woman if you give her an engagement ring. You can be trusted to have a child when you have a valid marriage license. You were admirable if you enlisted in the United States Marines in January 1942. Russia is "the Evil Empire," and the American flag is emblazoned with colors that don't run. Most laws and most religious dogma work at this level. So do the minds of a lot of devout patriots in all of the world's nations. If you are not with us, you are against us.

As individuals mature, they reach Loevinger's conscientious stage. Love means you put your mate's needs above your own lust. You can be trusted to have children when you are able to care for them properly. You learn to entertain the possibility that a man might still have been admirable if in 1942 he preferred jail as a conscientious objector to killing other human beings. You value ecumenical religious services, and sometimes you support the United Nations over your own country's interests. You learn to differentiate your emotions and master Piagetian formal operations.

Loevinger believes, and I agree, that some, but not most, adults evolve further into what she calls the autonomous stage. By autonomous she means trusting others to be autonomous. Rather than giving the hungry a fish, you teach them how to catch fish themselves. Defining love becomes more difficult than just the Golden Rule and involves the paradox of two people with different needs having to achieve solutions that satisfy both even if that means separation. As a conscientious objector in World War II, you can respect your granddaughter who, with patriotic conviction, volunteers for combat duty in the "liberation" of Iraq. In other words, the autonomous stage involves a profound and empathic level of moral reasoning. Prose and passion, obedience and desire are seamlessly integrated. The number of emotions that one can pull up into consciousness become more nuanced and more numerous.

In late adulthood, cognitive development may continue beyond Piaget's formal operations into what Harvard psychologist Michael Commons has termed "post-formal operations."[47] Post-formal operations involve appreciation of irony and of paradox. By paradox I mean learning to trust a universe in which the uncertainty principle is a basic axiom of quantum physics, in which good and evil exist side by side, in which innocent children die from bubonic plague, and in which to keep something you have to give it away. As in quantum mechanics, certainty is an impossibility. Only faith and trust remain. The frontal cortex, the seat of our social morality, can be both limbic and neocortical at the same time. It took the Catholic Church two millennia of cultural evolution and John Paul II eighty years of personal maturation for a Vatican pope to master paradox and finally refer to Jews and Muslims as "brothers." If the bad news is that maturation takes a long time, the good news is that once you learn to ride a bicycle or fully understand that all women and all men are created equal, it is hard to forget.

A Study of Adult Development questionnaire asked a seventy-five-year-old Presbyterian minister the provocative question: "Taboos on obscenity, nudity, premarital sex, homosexuality, and pornography seem to be dead or dying. Do you believe this is good or bad?" He wrote: "NEITHER. What human beings need are limits to their behavior *and* freedom to realize their true selves—we really need a societal consensus on limits balanced with freedoms. I think these limits and freedoms and the balance between them change with the culture." In his wise and moral answer, paradox followed paradox.

With maturity, this minister had developed the skill to imagine the world from eyes other than his own. He appreciated that emotionally laden issues could not be solved by dogmatic recourse to personal beliefs of right and wrong, of Red State versus Blue State. The minister had replaced a child's belief in a just God with trust in the value of a group conscience, and he understood that not all groups would share the same group conscience. Like Albert Einstein, as we mature, we understand that time is an important dimension that determines the shape of reality. But remember, the minister wrote his reply when he was seventy-five years old. Deepening understanding of the relativity and complexity of life transforms immature belief into mature trust and transforms rigid religious belief into spiritual empathy. Or to translate the idea into the rhetoric of Saint Paul and into the poetry of the King James Bible: "When I was a child, I spoke as a child, I understood as a child, I thought as a child; but when I became a man, I put away childish things. For now we see through a glass darkly; but then face to face" (1 Corinthians 13:11–12).

In closing this chapter, a note of caution is needed. I suggest that a faith emphasizing trust and positive emotion is more mature than a faith made up of words, prohibitions, and rigid beliefs. Am I not asserting that one is better than the other? In so doing, I risk inventing a circle that draws me in and excludes others. Butterflies, however, are not better than caterpillars, nor are grandparents better than the grandchildren they adore. Butterflies are only caterpillars at a different level of maturation. Feelings and passion are not better than prose and belief; they simply arise in different parts of the brain. Only connect the prose and the passion! That is what human evolution is all about.

Over time, just as evolving humanity is better shielded by science from capricious famine and infant deaths, just so its faith traditions—once dependent on the protective but negative emotions of abject fear and righteous anger—can give way to the positive emotions of faith, love, hope, joy, forgiveness, compassion, and awe—the positive emotions whose biologic underpinnings will serve as foci for the next seven chapters.

4

Faith

৩৬

*Since Paleolithic times, by far the overwhelming
majority of human beings on this planet have been
men and women of faith.*

—WILFORD CANTWELL SMITH, *Faith and Belief* (1979), p. 6

ঞ্চ

To me, your faith may be an object of curiosity or contempt. To you, my
faith may merely consist of a set of implausible beliefs. Yet, to me, my faith
reflects my trust in the universe, and I presume the same is true for you. Trust
is my master, and trust permits me to master. I will never be the same person as I was before I gained or regained my trust in the universe. But note
that, to define faith, I refer to the emotion trust, not the cognition belief.

Let's listen to Maria, the heroine of the film *The Sound of Music*. She
has left the abbey and is walking up the path to the formidable Captain
von Trapp's mansion. We take her seriously, not just because of what she
says, but also because of her unshakable faith. She has confidence in the
sunshine, she sings. She has confidence in the rain. (Richard Rodgers and
Oscar Hammerstein, "I Have Confidence," *The Sound of Music*, 1965.)

Faith, of course, has many meanings. We can conceptualize faith as belief and fight over our different cognitive realities for the rest of the afternoon. Or we can agree with Maria, who describes faith as trust and confidence, and becomes a pleasant companion for the rest of the movie. Gandhi once remarked to an English friend, "I don't think much of your Christianity, but I like your Christ."[1] In other words, Christian *beliefs* annoyed Gandhi, but he trusted Christ's *behavior*. This exemplifies the two different types of faith: belief in religious dogma that led to the Spanish Inquisition, and faith in a man who spoke of what was in his heart and lived his message, as Maria was about to live hers.

Trust will be the sense in which I discuss faith in this chapter. The distinguished Harvard psychiatrist Gregory Fricchione explains, "Trust is a distinguishing feature of human relationships. . . . Trusting approach activity . . . is a sine qua non for altruism and true love."[2] Most religious traditions have developed mystical and meditative rituals of silence, prayer, dance, sacred drug ingestion, or fasting to heighten the emotional experience of trust. In a well-controlled study designed to test the trust of "investors" in each other, investors given intranasal oxytocin, sometimes referred to as the "cuddle hormone," were more likely to trust their partners than investors given a placebo.[3] Oxytocin works on mammalian limbic structures, not on the *Homo sapiens* neocortex.

When we speak of people's faith, we usually refer to their faith tradition—an amalgam of their religious beliefs, their cultural traditions, *and* their emotional trust in the universe. "Faith tradition" is a broader definition than the one I shall be discussing. Our faith tradition is the personalized version of the religion that we have been taught, superimposed upon our own neurobiology.

Faith, as I shall use the term, involves basic trust that the world has meaning and that loving-kindness exists. Such faith should be our human birthright. An atheist may have faith. The absence of faith is nihilism, not atheism, not disbelief in a lexical God. The Buddha in spirit, if not in the letter, dethroned the Hindu gods, and yet no one would suggest that Buddhists lack faith. A nihilist loves no one and is loved by no one, does not care for truth or appreciate beauty, has lost hope and knows no joy. Worst of all, nihilists find no meaning in life. As Erik Erikson noted, it is a terrible thing to be without basic trust in the universe. Christ wanted us to feel, not think, that we were loved. For the godless Buddhists, because the Dharma exists, because morality is a fact of nature, life has meaning. The Buddha taught, "As with her life a mother cares for her own, her only child, so in your hearts and minds let there be boundless love for all creatures great and small."[4] That was the faith that the Buddha spent forty-five years of his life trekking the length and breadth of India to share with all he met.

In Hebrew and in Latin, faith is not a singular state but an active verb. We *do* faith; we do not *have* faith. When I suggested to a friend that Sunday school was a place where one learned religious dogma, she flatly contradicted me. "No, George, for me Sunday school was a loving experience." She did not have faith. She did faith. Basic trust, like God, is not a noun: it is an experience.

Faith can become manifest in three rather different ways. First, faith can be expressed through the culturally determined symbols, beliefs, rituals, and common prayers that undergird a specific faith tradition. As such, faith, like language and culture, is one among many. Second, faith can be expressed through a trusting commitment to compassionate behavior and community building. This is the context within which passionate missionaries, Christ, and the Buddha did faith. Finally, faith can be experienced through positive emotion, through a personal sense of inner illumination, awe, and a longing for the sacred; this was Saint Paul's experience on the road to Damascus.

Our faith tradition usually combines the beliefs given us by our religion with the emotional depth and faith in the universe given us by our spirituality and by those who have loved us. The terms "religion" and "belief" are straightforward. However, the words for "faith" and "spirituality," like the words for all emotions, resist lexical definition. The best definition of faith as a positive emotion that I know of comes from Albert Camus's great novel *The Plague*.[5] A child has just died in agony from bubonic plague. Father Paneloux and Dr. Rieux are arguing over the meaning or meaninglessness of the tragedy:

"I understand," [Father] Paneloux said in a low voice. "That sort of thing is revolting because it passes our human understanding. But perhaps we should love what we cannot understand."

[Dr.] Rieux straightened up slowly. He gazed at Paneloux, summoning to his gaze all the strength and fervor he could muster against his weariness. Then he shook his head.

"No, Father, I've a very different idea of love. And until my dying day I shall refuse to love a scheme of things in which children are put to torture."

A shade of disquietude crossed the priest's face. "Ah, doctor," he said sadly, "I've just realized what is meant by 'grace.'"

The priest's parochial term "grace" may be translated to a general audience as trust. And so at this point there is nothing more either of them can do except to choose: to lose or to retain Maria's confidence in the universe. When children die and we are helpless, whose path will be more healing, the priest's faith or the doctor's outrage? I guess it all depends. I only offer the vignette to illustrate that faith is the foundation of trust in the universe.

Faith also underscores our trust in the power of positive emotions over negative emotions. Consider again Antoine de Saint-Exupéry's fable about a little prince, a fox, and an aviator. Toward the end of his book *The Little Prince*, Saint-Exupéry relates the following exchange:

So the little prince tamed the fox. And when the hour of the prince's departure [death] drew near—

"Ah," said the fox, "I shall cry."

"It's your own fault," said the little prince. "I never wished you any sort of harm; but you wanted me to tame you." . . . [i.e., you wanted me to teach you to love me and to have faith in me, or, in Saint-Exupéry's words, "to establish ties"]

"Yes, that is so," said the fox.

"Then it has done you no good at all!"

"It has done me good," said the fox, "because of the color of the wheat fields."[6]

A little while before, the fox had told the little prince: "I do not eat bread. Wheat is of no use to me. . . . And that is sad. But you have hair that is the color of gold. . . . The grain, which is also golden, will bring me back the thought of you. And I shall love to listen to the wind in the wheat."[7] Through loving the little prince, the fox has learned to hold the little prince in his heart—and so the still weeping fox has faith that the prince will live on. And that is the difference that faith makes—to go on loving the evidence of things not seen, the substance of things hoped for.

※

Instead of groping further for a lexical definition of faith, with which you are likely to disagree, let me offer an illustrative example. Studied for sixty years, Bill Graham (a pseudonym) was a member of the Study of Adult Development. He grew up without ever having been given a chance. At age sixty-eight, when asked about his childhood, Bill Graham told his interviewer, "I don't have any pleasant memories of childhood," and explained that his early years were full of "abuse, starvation, lack of love, and aloneness." Review of his research record compiled fifty years earlier revealed that he was not exaggerating.

When he was three and a half years old, Bill Graham's mother gave him up to foster care. By age twelve, he could not even recall what his mother had looked like. None of his unempathic foster caretakers had thought to give him her picture. Indeed, Graham did not even know where he had lived before age six—his age when his father was committed to a state hospital for syphilitic psychosis. From age six to eleven, he lived with a foster family in South Boston who regularly beat him. These foster parents, he believed, were more interested in the state aid support money than in Graham. "I always knew someone was coming to visit because I got fed and cleaned."

"I was young enough to mess my pants and to be thrown down the stairs because of it," Graham recalled. "I remember being beaten and not having food." But he explained that by far "the most abusive thing was nobody caring. . . . Having no one to care for me, no one responsible." Asked how these experiences of abuse affected him as an adult, at age sixty-eight he could reply, "I learned to be more compassionate. . . . Shit happens and you get over it." He made resilience sound so easy. But how? It had only taken fifty years.

When Graham was forty-seven, his interviewer had written, "He has had the worst childhood of the men that I have seen. Yet," the interviewer continued, "I was struck that with a background of such deprivation he has gone on to mold a rich and full life for himself. I have seen few other subjects who seemed as enthusiastic about their activities as Graham." But why? Because by the time Bill Graham was forty-seven, he had been strengthened by almost two decades of loving marriage.

Although he had been a boy from a no-hope background, with all of the risk factors that resilience researchers believe damn such children to poor adult outcomes, Graham married well. Through the alchemy of strong attachment—in Graham's case, to a woman ten years older than himself who spoiled him—Graham eventually attained emotional safety. It was obvious to the interviewer that the newly married twenty-five-year-old Graham was very proud of his wife, and she, in turn, informed the investigator that she thought Graham was wonderful—and that her parents thought so too. For the first time Graham felt that he had a real home.

It was noteworthy that at age twenty-five Graham was not at all religious. He attended services only occasionally. By age forty-five, he had stopped altogether. Instead, he had found his higher power within a secure and loving family matrix. At age forty-five, Bill Graham described his wife as "devoted to me and the family." She was "unselfish, kind, loving, and generous." He was deeply touched by her understanding and reassured by the fact that she was dependable, considerate, and an immaculate homemaker—so different from the squalor in which he had been raised.

By age forty-seven, his loving actions spoke louder than any words.

Even though his psychotic father had never cared for him, Bill Graham, once adult, took his father out of "the inhumane conditions of state hospital" so that his father could live with him. In the last years of his mother's life, when she was lonely and isolated, Graham also regularly visited the woman who decades before had given him up to foster care. Love and forgiveness denied to Graham as a child were not learned in childhood or in Sunday school but, I believe, from the internalization of his wife's unselfish love. You cannot be taught love; you can only breathe it in and absorb it. Love, you see, is limbic, not intellectual. In any case, as an adult, Graham cared for two parents who had not cared for him.

Then, when Bill Graham was fifty-three, his wife of thirty-three years died tragically from cancer. For the next seven years, his life was in disarray. Shortly after his wife's death, he explained to an interviewer:

I lost my wife, okay? It's very simple to say, "I lost my wife," but that's not true. That's not true of anyone. In no significant sequence, in no particular order of importance, I say I lost a friend, I lost a lover, I lost a mother, I lost a sister, I lost a doctor, a nurse, a teacher, a finance expert, a fighter. I lost many, many people when I lost this one person. That's a lot. A lot of people think it's just . . . a wife, just a person, just one person. But unless you've walked that path, it's hard to imagine all the things you have to do for yourself all of a sudden.

Graham for years found his life without meaning. At fifty-eight, five years after his wife's death, Bill Graham was hospitalized, like Tom Merton, for major depression; he had lost love and was without hope or faith. After his discharge from the hospital, he became physically disabled by a bad back. He was mentally, physically, and spiritually ill. He was consumed by negative emotions: anger, fear, despair, pain, and even hunger.

Ten more years passed, and at age sixty-eight, Bill Graham was a much happier and very spiritually committed man. What had happened? Although raised a Catholic, Graham told the interviewer, "I had found that it didn't serve me." At age sixty, at the same time that a successful remarriage relieved

Graham's heartache, a Catholic priest who called himself a spiritual healer had relieved Graham's backache, which had been at the root of his physical disability.

All forms of spiritual healing have in common empathy, healing within a circle of caring persons, permission to feel and express emotion, shared responsibility for pain, and reverence for life rather than for self. Such "blessings" lower blood pressure, ease pain, relax muscles, and postpone death.[8]

Wanting to learn more about such healing, Graham began his own spiritual healing mission. After starting to work as a healer, Graham found further purpose in life. Since then, he has entered into the "happiest years of my life," for the process of "passing it on" often heals the giver more than the receiver. Bill Graham describes his work as a "ministry of hope"—the hope that for a decade he had been so desperately without.

The laying on of hands, Graham explained, awakens a natural healing process in the body. He is convinced that such healing is effective, but he acknowledged that he did not understand how faith healing works. He did not try to put his healing love into words. That was unnecessary. Although Graham gained comfort from helping people, he did not wish to take credit for the healing process. Rather, "it is important that people know I don't do it. I say to them, 'Don't thank me . . . go and praise God.' " He could have just as accurately said, "Don't thank me . . . go and praise unselfish love."

The story of Bill Graham, like the story of the woman who rescued her son's murderer and the lives of Mandela, King, and Gandhi, illustrates the survival value of positive over negative emotion. What is different about the story of Bill Graham is that he chose to identify such positive emotion as spiritual.

ॐ

Faith is literally inspiration. *Spiro:* I breathe in. I depend upon that which I cannot see. Faith always involves taking in. But faith is more visceral than cognitive. Trust is rooted in the emotional experience of love, attachment, and gratitude. Neurobiologically, faith begins with our trust in the mammalian separation cry. I have faith that if I fall and cry out, someone will pick me up—"that I once was lost but now am found, was blind but now I see."

For some, faith is merely belief; for others, faith is trust; but there are important differences between belief and trust. The price of depending upon language to promote cultural evolution is that experiences become reified and the ineffable becomes concrete. For example, just as originally the word "manufacture" meant "made by hand," originally belief meant "to cherish, to hold dear," and was first cousin to love (*lieben*) and libido.[9] Today the words have lost their earthiness. Today the inflexible belief in the concrete Creed or Credo of the Christian faith inadvertently, or sometimes deliberately, annoys people with other beliefs. The concreteness of the modern usage of belief reminds me of an old chestnut. The applicant for membership in a conservative Protestant church is asked if he believes in baptism. "Believe in baptism?" the applicant exclaims. "Heck, I've seen it!" Always the limbic spirit of faith is more compelling than the letter.

Good lawyers and charismatic cult leaders with their clever arguments make us believe; good mothers, saints, and positive emotion help us to trust. Belief is so exact that we think we can add up the bill. Trust always involves casting bread upon the waters with its return being only a matter of faith, not contract. "Believe what I say" stands in stark contrast to "Don't trust what I say; trust what I do."

The ambiguity of whether faith is to be defined as a positive emotion or concrete belief is illustrated by an example from the early Christian church.[10] The story is told about one of the early desert fathers, Abba Poemen. Some church elders came to Father Abba and rather sententiously asked, "When we see brothers who are dozing during the liturgy, shall we rouse them so that they will be watchful?" Father Abba replied, "For my part, when I see a brother who is dozing, I put his head on my knees and let him rest."

Cognitive science, another new discipline of the late twentieth century, has suggested that much of the order that physics perceives in the world is no more than dogmatic belief "imposed by the prisms of our nervous system, a mere artifact of the way evolution has wired the brain."[11]

During adult maturation, cognitive religious *belief* tends to evolve toward emotional spiritual *trust*. But the issue is not simply cognitive versus emotional, but immature versus mature. Immature faith draws a circle that pencils some people out. Mature faith draws a circle that pencils all people in. It was the certainty of belief that allowed Cotton Mather to crush imaginary witches at Salem, Torquemada to burn imaginary heretics in Spain, and a recent attorney general to trumpet that "the United States has only one King and his name is Jesus." It is almost always immature and illusory to maintain, "It is my way or the highway."

In a careful study of twins, a University of Virginia psychiatrist, Kenneth Kendler, observed that high levels of "personal devotion" (frequent church attendance, prayer, and seeking spiritual comfort) were strongly and positively correlated with increasing age.[12] In the same study, however, as adults became older, their religious "conservatism" (their literal belief in the Bible and in a belief that God rewards and punishes) weakened and they became more spiritually inclusive. In other words, with maturity, the patriarchal model of pleasing God *only* if you meet *His* expectations gave way to a more maternal spirituality of forgiveness and unconditional love.

Faith, like humor (a positive but not a spiritual emotion), allows us to contemplate suffering without despair. I am reminded of a recently widowed English friend who sought comfort from her Anglican priest. She told him that in her bereavement she was surprised to find herself experiencing increasing empathy for the suffering of AIDS patients and for the pain they had experienced owing to widespread intolerance for their homosexuality. No, she was wrong, insisted her priest; he knew that homosexuality was a sin against God, and the Bible's condemnation proved it. In her grief, she was stung by his criticism. She tried to argue for her faith in the commonality of human suffering. Finally, the priest could bear her openness no longer. "Clearly, you are too liberal to be a Christian!" he exploded. The rigid certainty of her minister's belief repudiated the loving trust in which my widowed friend was trying to find comfort. Like good science, mature faith can usually distinguish the forest from the trees. Jesus Christ, after all, was probably too liberal to be a "Christian" in that priest's estimation.

෪

Our faith arises from three sources—one source is conscious (neocortical), and two are unconscious (limbic). These three sources are our cognitive need for certainty, our social need for community, and our emotional need for trust. The first source of faith comes from the conscious human wish to provide plausible, if often confabulated or dogmatic, certainty in the face of ambiguous and mysterious reality. Ambiguity makes us anxious; certainty calms us; and usually, at least initially, we do not care if such anxiety-relieving certainty is true. This first source we call *belief*. The cave dwellers did it; Karl Marx did it; Sigmund Freud did it. All the great religious leaders did it. They all provided frightened humanity with a scientifically unjustified certainty about the world.

When people whom we love die, we need to believe that we will meet them again. The danger is that the line between self-soothing trust and self-soothing delusion is unclear. Insanity, brain toxins, brainwashing, deafness, and terror can all lead to mental confusion that in turn can lead the individual brain to reorganize faulty perception into anxiety-relieving delusional and/or paranoid certainty. To relieve uncertainty about a romantic partner, we may visit a fortune-teller in a foreign city or pull petals from a daisy ("she loves me, she loves me not").

To turn to a more negative facet of faith, delusions, especially persecutory delusions, are often contagious, and thus we sometimes have blind faith in irrational leaders and dangerous systems of "religious belief." But the way to distinguish such unshakable beliefs is to ask whether they are empathic or paranoid. In contrast to Hitler's projection that all Germany's ills were caused by Jews, consider the famous waking dream and more trusting faith of Martin Luther King Jr.: "I have a dream that my four little children one day will live in a nation where they will not be judged by the color of their skin. . . . This is the faith that I go back to the South with . . . knowing that we will be free some day." In short, deep spiritual faith rests in the heart as well as the intellect and is free of projection and delusion.

Apocalyptic cognitive visions of the incipient end of the world in which only the elect are saved, such as can be found in the Bible's Book of the Revelation to John, have spawned many religious sects and have little to do with positive emotions and spiritual faith. Undoubtedly, the hopeful faith of Martin Luther King Jr. saved countless lives; the possibly delusional faith of the Mormons' Joseph Smith has cost more than a few.[13] But then, so have all of the world's major religions.

> We are the Lord's elected few.
> Let all the rest be damned.
> There's room enough in Hell for you.
> We don't want Heaven crammed.
>
> —NINETEENTH-CENTURY PARTICULAR BAPTIST HYMN

The Particular Baptists are not a sect that has thrived. In contrast, Reverend King was awarded the Nobel Peace Prize. The Mormon elders were sane enough to learn from experience. Thus, instead of going to war with the United States over Joseph Smith's and Brigham Young's unempathic belief in polygamy, they accepted the will of the majority and abandoned polygamy, and for a while Mormon religious community spirit, not their cognitive beliefs, made Utah the most law-abiding state in the Union. Utah, still by a wide margin, has the lowest rate of alcohol-related automobile fatalities in the nation. By their fruits shall ye know them.

A second, less conscious source of faith and trust is our need for loving community. Admittedly, love originally arose from the mammalian intimate connection we needed to care for often annoying children and from our need to temper our own valuable, but often disruptive, negative emotions. However, much of the social power of love comes from culturally mediated institutions based on trust, like marriage, child care, and hospitals. Within these bonds we create fables and maxims for empathy and altruism that trump the more selfish pull of self-preservation. Our consciously motivated rules for familial attachment and for communal gatherings like Thanksgiving, so necessary for our survival as a species, are how we semiconsciously use faith to maintain community. The danger is that such loving traditions will petrify into religious intolerance.

Our limbic brain provides the third source of faith and trust. This third source of faith is sometimes called inner illumination, and it involves involuntary emotion, ecstasy, and mystical experiences. Inner illumination can be produced both by neurological stimulus from within (for example, a near-death experience) and by neurological stimulus from without (for example, through consciously willed meditation).

To be useful, inner illumination, like intuition, can never be "all about me." Empathy—intuition linked to the other—is almost always valuable. Projection—intuition linked to the self—is almost always unhealthy. Nevertheless, while cognitive belief can usually be modified by argument, cognitive belief, crystallized by either inner illumination or paranoia, can become impervious to argument. This is what can make religion so dangerous. Like the delusions of a madman, faith fueled by limbic illumination can become the very antithesis of reason. As English psychiatrist Anthony Storr notes, "We tend to treat infatuated lovers with the same tact that we extend to believers whose faith we do not share and to mad men whose delusions we perceive as absurd."[14] It is sometimes hard to distinguish the romantic infatuation of an adolescent from the improbable convictions of a religious zealot.

Mystical limbic experiences of faith—whether from within or without, whether from epilepsy and/or divine visitation or from disciplined meditation, breathing, fasting, and prayer—are unique. They are as alerting, as "never to be forgotten," and as real as any other profound emotional experience. These limbic experiences produce the same deep sense of trusting inner calm that I shall discuss in the chapters on joy, love, and awe. Trust and confidence, like the other positive emotions, stimulate our parasympathetic, not our sympathetic, nervous system. The sympathetic nervous system is *catabolic*: fight-or-flight uses up the body's resources. The parasympathetic nervous system is *anabolic*: faith, hope, and cuddling build up the body's resources.

But how do we know if the mystical limbic message is from God or the

Devil? How do we know if the divine message that may shape our faith and belief for decades is in the service of good or in the service of evil, in the service of loving trust or reptilian greed? In more scientific terms, how do we reliably distinguish between empathy and projection, between a loving mystical experience and psychosis? Too often we do not have a clue. After all, both empathy and projection maintain, "I know what you are feeling and what is good for you." Great junior high school teachers and self-indulgent pedophiles both believe that their love is serving the young. Thus, how to distinguish spiritual inspiration from frank delusion has long worried spiritual directors—especially within the Catholic religious orders—just as much as religious convictions have worried geneticist Richard Dawkins and philosophers Daniel Dennett and Sam Harris.

The fact that faith is occasionally based solely upon inner illumination can make it extremely dangerous, for in such cases there are no checks and balances against autism and delusion. The dangerous fixed beliefs of faith and the tendency of faith to impose certainty without evidence has caused some intelligent critics of religion to throw the baby out with the bathwater. Sam Harris can exclaim, "Our enemy is nothing other than faith itself." Then, in case there is something about "enemy" that his audience might miss, Harris drives his point home with italics. "The only demons we most fear are those that lurk inside every human mind: ignorance, hatred, greed, and *faith* which is surely the devil's masterpiece."[15]

Recent studies by Jeffrey Saver and John Rabin have clarified the criteria for distinguishing mystical experiences from insanity.[16] In mystical experiences, visions are usually visual and last for minutes or hours. In paranoid schizophrenia, hallucinations are usually auditory and can last for years. In schizophrenia, the dominant affect is most often terror, and schizophrenic religious delusions are more often associated with omnipotence. In mystical experience, the affect is more often joy and ecstasy, and the individual religious illusions are not of omnipotence but of being a humble servant to a higher power. The language of mystical experience is easily communicated and is socially empathic. The language of schizophrenia is bizarre, eccentric, difficult to understand, and often socially inappropriate. Paul's Second Letter to the Corinthians is pretty straightforward, benign, and easy to understand. The Revelation to John is bizarre, terrifying, and to many incomprehensible.

A thoughtful student once asked me, "But why do groups of individuals seeking spiritual connection so often create brutalizing institutions?" The question must be addressed by every faith tradition, but the answer is the same. Brutality occurs when projection replaces empathy. Sometimes in a quest for unity rather than community, religions forget to love their neighbors as themselves. Totalitarianism and selfish desire for dominance take the place of unselfish love. The Spanish Inquisition was not so much an effort to reform and reinvigorate the Catholic faith as it was an effort to unify Spain and then Mexico under the power of the crown. The ongoing bloody conflict between the Sunni Muslims and the Shiite Muslims over control of Iraq cannot be blamed on the unifying spiritual vision of the Qur'an. When faith is about selfish politics, or when projection replaces empathy, it becomes destructive. As with paranoia, selfishness is not susceptible to another's point of view. Faith, then, is not the danger; the danger is the lack of empathy and the false beliefs of those who profess faith. Inner illumination, to be safe, must perceive others accurately.

Mental health and maturity share two important characteristics. They take both reality and the other person into account. Mental illness, like immaturity, ignores not only inanimate reality but also the reality of the feelings of others. Like the adaptive functions of psychosis, the false beliefs of religious faith can diminish the pain of grief and social isolation by providing either imaginary friends or obedient disciples. Delusions, whether psychotic or religious, preserve self-esteem by blaming others. In sum, whenever the quest for loving inner illumination becomes a fanatical "all about me" belief system, the result is catastrophe. The intolerant faith of the "moral majority" in the contemporary United States, of the Taliban in Afghanistan, of the murderous Jewish Law in the Book of Deuteronomy, and of the Catholic Inquisition is more typical of a selfish quest for power than of the billions of ordinary people who "do" religious faith and trust a loving universe.

The answer to how we can distinguish loving trust from dogmatic belief, and thereby distinguish projection from empathy, can be found only through dispassionate, scientific follow-up. Loving inspiration inspires trust for centuries; fanatical belief is usually short-lived, and often while it lasts, fanatical belief must be enforced by violence. Jim Jones of Jonestown notoriety, David Koresh of Waco, Texas, and Bhagwan Shree Rajneish of Poona, India (and then of Antelope, Oregon) are but three of several examples of lonely, paranoid gurus who needed armed guards to keep their "devoted" disciples from fleeing.[17] Trust, like my friend's experience in Sunday school, is spiritual and enduring; beliefs, gurus, and religions, like adolescent loves—and even science—may prove false.

In short, I believe that the same limbic wiring that prepares us to receive and retain love also provides us trust and comfort when no visible loved one is present. The scurrilous schoolboy jingle "I don't care if it rains or freezes, I am safe in the arms of Jesus" contains more truth than young urchins appreciate. After all, a grown man three thousand years ago noted, "The eternal God is thy refuge, and underneath are the everlasting arms." Deep faith helps us to believe in love even when it is not before our eyes. Even the acerbic and bestselling atheist Sam Harris, perhaps reluctantly, was moved to acknowledge, "Faith enables many of us to endure life's difficulties with an equanimity that would be scarcely conceivable in a world lit only by reason."[18]

Moreover, the personal resources gained during the positive emotional states of faith and inner illumination can be enduring.[19] A broader, more compassionate view toward the world lasts after the intense mystical experience of "divine" love or joy has passed. Our faith, then, becomes a lasting reservoir of positive emotion that can be drawn upon in future moments of crisis. When kneeling at a communion rail, or prostrating oneself in a mosque, or meditating in the lotus position, past positive emotions and early memories of parental love return. Prayer often brings back reminiscences of our own private Camelots where "the rain may never fall till after sundown. By eight the morning fog must disappear."

The distinguished German theologian Rudolf Otto (1869–1937) captured the faith experience well when he coined the polysyllabic label "mysterium tremendum et fascinans" to describe the eerie, ineffable, sublime feelings of wonder and connection that deep faith brings.[20] William James observed that the effort of science to capture the energy and reality of faith is analogous to trying to appreciate through photography a freight train going fifty miles an hour. Similarly, our still very limited human brains reduce the unimaginable intensity of atomic fusion within the sun into the tidy inspirational experience of a sunset.

> *Great Father of glory, pure Father of light,*
> *Thine angels adore thee, all veiling their sight;*
> *All laud we would render: O help us to see*
> *'Tis only the splendor of light hideth thee.*
>
> *Immortal, invisible, God only wise,*
> *In light inaccessible hid from our eyes,*
> *Most blessed, most glorious, the Ancient of Days,*
> *Almighty, victorious, thy great Name we praise.*
>
> —WALTER CHALMERS SMITH (1867)

5

Love

⁂

At every important stage in our life it is human
affection that nurtures us, sustains us and comforts
us. . . . To me the image of a mother's breast feed-
ing her baby is the most potent symbol of human
love.

—DALAI LAMA, *Visions of Compassion* (2002), pp. 70–71

ৡৡ

Modern ethology and neuroscience make clear that all mammals are hard-wired for love. Of all the fauna on earth, however, *Homo sapiens* is the most radically dependent on love. Thus, ethologist Konrad Lorenz called love "the most wonderful product of ten million years of evolution"; psychoanalyst Erich Fromm wrote, "Without love humanity could not exist even for a day"; and Saint Paul concluded, "And now abideth faith, hope, love, these three; but the greatest of these is love."[1]

Mammalian love involves attachment that is selective, enduring, and often remarkably unselfish. If the loved one leaves, the grief that ensues is also selective and enduring. Not all mammals manifest such attachment, but many do. The Greek philosophers did not understand this. Their *agape* (universal unselfish love) is not selective, and the Greeks' *eros* (instinctual desire and lust) is not enduring. Once he satisfies his lust, the romantic troubadour loses interest. Howard Hughes was a man remarkably incapable of lasting love or attachment. Yet he had passionate "not-love" affairs lasting weeks to years with many of the most beautiful movie stars of his day. It was just that after having sex with them, Hughes had no wish to share their bed.[2] In contrast, a mother bear spends most of her day with her cub, and just try borrowing her bear cub for even five minutes.

Before I discuss the importance of love further, I shall offer a case history to illustrate both what I mean by attachment and spiritual evolution. Tom Merton suffered a bleak childhood and a depressed adulthood. As a young adult, Merton (a pseudonym) was one of only eight—out of the 268 college men from the Study of Adult Development—who ranked at the very bottom of the scale measuring personality stability. And Merton's childhood had been ranked as even bleaker than the childhoods of the other seven. As adults, all the other seven men from barren childhoods continued to fail at life. All but two were dead by seventy-five, and those two were physically disabled. In sharp contrast, at age eighty, Tom Merton was not only alive and vibrantly happy but also still playing competitive squash. Why? What had saved him? Or perhaps, who had saved him?

By hiding his lovelessness behind a facade of fragile cheerfulness, Merton had been admitted to a study of normal college boys. In college, however, he soon revealed an intractable hypochondriasis that prompted the usually sympathetic college internist to grumble, "This boy is turning into a regular psychoneurotic." A staff psychiatrist called Merton "distant, suspicious, floundering, and stubborn." As Tom Merton had explained to his study interviewer: "Dad and I have never gotten on very well. . . . He has done nothing that I consider a father should do for his children. . . . Mother hasn't exactly made up to us for Dad's shortcomings." The study's social investigator agreed. She described Mrs. Merton as "one of the most nervous people I have ever met. She is a past-mistress in self-deception."

Tom Merton had been cared for in all the wrong ways. Throughout his childhood a succession of chauffeurs had driven him to school, and he had often been kept from playing with neighborhood children. But his parents' overprotectiveness did not extend to caring for him themselves. Until Merton was six, he ate his meals, alone, in his playroom. At age forty-six, Tom Merton sadly affirmed his earlier statements about his family and wrote laconically, "I neither liked nor respected my parents." On graduation from medical school, Tom Merton had tried to join the short-lived ranks of the other seven unloved study men. He made a suicide attempt. Afterwards, as a timid bachelor, he spent the next seven years sabotaging his halting efforts to become an independent physician and husband.

Then, at age thirty-three, a change began. Following a broken engagement, Tom Merton was hospitalized for fourteen months with pulmonary tuberculosis. For whatever reason, at thirty-four Tom Merton arose from his sickbed to become an independent physician, to get married, and to grow into a responsible father and clinic leader. Many years later I met Dr. Merton for the first time. Uneasily, I asked how he had coped with that hospitalization. For most young men, such a prolonged incapacity in their thirties might have been devastating, but not for Tom Merton. Referring to his hospitalization as "that year in the sack," he explained, "It was neat, I could go to bed for a year, do what I wanted, and get away with it." Later he confessed, "I was glad to be sick. My poorly met dependency needs had found an acceptable harbor."

Perhaps more important for Merton, his illness had opened the door to rebirth. In his sickbed he experienced a vision of Christ coming into his room. "Someone with a capital 'S' cared about me," he wrote. "It made me feel that I was nutty for awhile, but in the Catholic Church it's known as Grace." The playwright Eugene O'Neill, from an equally dysfunctional family, had felt the same way about *his* hospitalization for tuberculosis. With the right caretakers, invalidism can allow some people to feel loved.

"That year in the sack" began the process of putting Merton in touch with the people who had loved him. The first step was not religion, but psychotherapy. At age fifty, Merton wrote to the study, "I don't go to church at all. I hate organized religions." Despite his religious experience in the hospital, from age forty to sixty psychoanalysis replaced the Episcopal Church as the source of Merton's faith. "Psychoanalysis is my home and my church." Psychoanalysis, however, is very different from major religions. Psychoanalysts are suspicious of positive emotion, avoid eye contact, and encourage the patient to make psychoanalysis "all about me." On the more positive side, unlike many other therapies, psychoanalysis allows a person to feel empathically and emotionally "seen." Suffering is respected, not swept under the rug.

Dr. Merton's analysis helped him recall that up to age five he had had a close relationship with his nurse. At the age of sixty-six, he explained:

> She was a person in my infancy that I rediscovered in my more Klein- ian hours [his psychoanalysis in 1981 and 1982]. I have reason to be- lieve she was a warm woman. My mother spoke of her as "Pearl, the dirty girl." I found [my memory of] her by following the trail of associ- ations to abalone and mother-of-pearl, which were very affect-laden for me. Whatever her role, and that of her successors in trust, I know also that I absolutely loved my teachers. Some of them cared about me too . . . sent to school to be properly educated, I learned about proper loving.

More years passed, and Merton again wrote to me of his rediscovery of his early nurturing:

> Is it the re-finding of the love that matters? Or is it the chance to re- celebrate and to re-celebrate again and again the bond that holds? An image comes to mind—the empty wine bottle used as a candlestick. The wine may have been the initial warmth in life, but once it is gone only the cold and empty glass bottle remains—until in memory we re- light the candle of conviviality, and as it drips, it transforms the sym- bol of the warmth that was spent into a differently shaped, differently colored object—alive with new warmth. Early loves may be "lost" be- cause they were taken for granted and never reinforced by review. Rec- ollection and retelling have a way of making them increasingly visual and real.

Earlier, after a painful divorce, Merton had become severely depressed. He had lost not only his wife but also his savings, his job, and his network of professional colleagues. "It was as if blue-black ink had been spilled on my mind." Merton again required hospitalization—this time in a psychiatric, not medical, facility. It was at this point in his life that, for the first time since college, Dr. Merton returned to the Episcopal Church. At age sixty, he described his process of re-involvement with church: "It was like sleepwalking at first, but bit-by-bit I've gotten involved. . . . Something got put into me that was never really there before." For the next twenty years, Merton became one of the most beloved members of his congregation. His reinvolvement with the Episcopal Church facilitated his capacity to make his life all about the other.

Perhaps the most significant further clue to Merton's slow transformation from crippled young man to resilient, spiritual octogenarian came from his answer to my question "What have you learned from your children?" Tears in his eyes, Merton blurted out, "You know what I learned from my children? I learned love!" And I believed him. The same year Tom Merton had written to a college friend, "Before there were dysfunctional families, I came from one. As *The Velveteen Rabbit* [a children's book describing how a stuffed rabbit came to life through a child's love] recounts tenderly, only love can make us real. Denied this in boyhood for reasons I now understand, it took me years to tap substitute sources." In more neurobiological terms, it is our affect-laden hippocampal memory of past attachments that helps to make us feel real.

Still another decade passed. At age seventy-seven, Tom Merton granted me another interview. He was actively involved in community life. He was also in love and nurturing a beautiful garden. Beside his chair were recent pictures of the children who had taught him to love—a picture of his daughter and her husband and a picture of Merton and his son on their recent climbing expedition in the Tetons. He was very active at his church, working to make it a center for community life. He helped with pastoral care and served as a lay eucharistic minister, which meant visiting shut-ins to provide communion. He was still playing competitive squash, but his opponents were now all much younger than he was. On the squash court no one near to his age could keep up with him. I came away from the interview confident that he had evolved into one of the best-adjusted men in the study.

Thus, at age seventy-seven, the once desperately unhappy Tom Merton now viewed the past five years as the happiest in his life. And that is the difference that love makes. Loving, selective, enduring attachment allows the severely deprived to heal. Yet scientists find such love difficult to talk about.

We are a clever species. We can sail, even fly, around the entire globe—alone. But we are unable to tickle ourselves or give ourselves a relaxing back rub—alone. Howard Hughes, industrialist, movie mogul, scratch golfer, and brilliant aviator, with all his millions and the ability to inspire love from others, died alone after twenty years of joyless self-absorption. Why? Because Howard Hughes could not permit himself to love or to feel loved.[3] For it is not enough to be loved; we need to be able to take love in, and we need to be able to give love back. Hughes could do neither. Tom Merton could. A miracle? No, it is how most brains are wired.

To understand love, the usually helpful resources—the ancient Greeks, the poets, and the psychologists—all fail us. They become preoccupied with lust, which even reptiles are capable of manifesting.

The Greeks and the poets rarely understand mammalian love. In order to understand unselfish love, we must rely upon neurobiology and ethology. The ethologists studying chimpanzees and the evolutionary anthropologists studying hunter-gatherers show us rather than tell us what real love is about. Certainly, love is not about words. Love is about attachment, music, odors, and the spiritual ecstasy that, depending on the speaker's choice of words, we can call many things, including God. "God is love and those who abide in love, abide in God and God abides in them" (1 John 4:16).

The spirit behind the New Testament words "God is love" can be found in the Qur'an and the Bhagavad Gita. It can be found in the writings of

Judaism, Buddhism, and Taoism. Even the self-consciously atheistic *Great Soviet Encyclopedia* explains to us, "Love is the point at which the opposing elements of the biological and the spiritual, the personal and the social, and the intimate and the universal intersect."[4]

A pilgrim described his ecstatic visit to Mecca as follows: "As you circumambulate and move closer to the Ka'ba . . . you are a new part of the people. . . . The Ka'ba is the world's sun whose face attracts you into its orbit. . . . You have been transformed into a particle that is gradually melting and disappearing. This is absolute love at its peak."[5]

Eros, the instinctual and lustful love, springing from the instincts of our hypothalamus, is all about self and all about preservation of "selfish" genes. Eros often evokes the negative emotions of jealousy and envy. In contrast, deep attachment evokes the positive emotions of gratitude and forgiveness. Unselfish mammalian limbic love is all about the other. "Love is the amazing realization that another person actually means as much or more to me than myself."[6] Mothers have understood this for millennia.

Mammalian love is more evolved in primates than in bears. Primates can engage in hours of parenting behavior a day—even if the child is a grandchild. Primates can satisfy their mutual lust and then spend the following hour affectionately grooming each other. Human unconditional love is a further evolution of mammalian love. As the human cortex learns to connect the prose and the passion, mature cognition allows us to generalize from unselfish mammalian maternal love to people more and more different from us. Of course, bred to be loving, golden retrievers seem to have mastered unconditional love since puppyhood.

Co-investigators Helen Fisher and Arthur Aron have used neuroimaging at Stony Brook University to study love in college students.[7] They found that in the early months of falling in love, viewing one's lover's photograph lit up only the more primitive regions of the brain reward circuitry, but after two years of loving attachment, it was the anterior cingulate and insular cortices, with their mirror and spindle cells, that showed the greatest activity. With time, "all about me" eros can evolve into empathic attachment.

Love is different from compassion in that compassion is neither specific nor enduring. As we shall see in chapter 7, compassion is the desire to separate others from their suffering. And what is the difference between specific, enduring human love and true agape? Imagine a stone dropped into a pond. The first circle reflects a child's fierce, unreflective attachment to her mother. The farthest ripple reflects the unselfish devotion to all living creatures (agape) that, in our imagination at least, we attribute to Christ, Schweitzer, and the Buddha. Most mature adults live somewhere in the middle of these expanding ripples.

In writing about love, poets have as much trouble as the ancient Greeks. Poets, caught up in their own subjective palpitations, often confuse love with desire. In *As You Like It*, Shakespeare's description of youthful love, "Sighing like a furnace, with a woeful ballad made to his mistress' eyebrow," is not what real love is about. The vividness of the poets' intense subjective experience obscures their perception. For example, where is the dividing line between the beliefs of a deeply in-love teenager and the delusions of a madman? How many, I wonder, of the "forever" loves described in the world's great poetry lasted even a decade? As Shakespeare, a great ethologist as well as a great poet, warns us, "Love is blind and lovers cannot see the pretty follies that they themselves commit" (*Merchant of Venice*, 2.6.36). Real love involves behavior visible and plausible to lover and beloved alike.

If poets are blind to love, psychologists are struck dumb. For decades, psychologists tried not even to mention love. They deliberately ignored it. In his 1958 presidential address to the American Psychological Association, ethologist Harry Harlow was driven to exclaim, "Psychologists, at least psychologists who write textbooks, not only show no interest in the origin and development of love or affection, but they seem to be unaware of its very existence."[8]

Academic psychology has always had difficulty dealing with the passionate reality of a child's inarticulate longing for his parents, of any mother's unshakable devotion to her child, and of the immutable bond that ties spouses together for half a century.[9] Until very recently, psychologists described the capacity for love as acquired and not as an innate biological potential. Love was deemed a learned response and a "culturally created emotion not a natural need."[10] For love to occur, other people were merely "secondary reinforcers."[11] In this view, the medieval troubadours seem to have brought love to Europe. Nothing could be further from the truth.

Even when the social scientists finally got around to acknowledging love, they made it sound awful. Behaviorist John Watson thought of love as nothing more than "an innate emotion elicited by cutaneous stimulation of the erogenous zones."[12] In their efforts to be dispassionate, the psychoanalysts proved equally obtuse. Although Sigmund Freud was able to focus upon many emotions that others found unbearable, especially grief and lust, he blinded himself to human attachment. Freud once reduced love dismissively to "aim-inhibited sex." In defense of Freud, he may have been unconsciously trying to avoid the countertransference—God forbid that I say "love"—involved in the intense attachment between psychoanalysts and their patients. For a while, John Bowlby, a psychoanalyst *and* an ethologist who did stress the importance of attachment, was not only unread, uncited, and unseen but also became a nonperson of psychoanalysis.[13] Even today most modern psychoanalysts render deep attachment insipid and inanimate by relabeling love "object relations." New mothers do not get up in the middle of the night for objects; widows don't weep at gravesides for objects.

Like poets, the early psychoanalysts confused reptilian instincts like lust and hunger with mammalian positive emotion. The fact that human attachment is more important to children than hunger for the breast was not easy for the psychoanalytic establishment to grasp. Anna Freud described infant love as follows, "He [sic] forms an attachment to food— milk—and developing further from this point to the person who feeds him and the love of food becomes the basis of love for the mother."[14] Sigmund Freud, like his daughter, erroneously believed that an infant's connection to its mother was through its mouth and stomach, not through its eyes, ears, and skin. The neuroscience of Freud's day was still too young for him to appreciate that an infant's brain is more highly connected to its skin than to any other organ.

It took Harry Harlow's work with rhesus monkeys to bring love to psychology. In conjunction with John Bowlby's observational studies of real, not theoretical, infants, Harlow's studies, based on the discipline of ethology, not psychoanalysis, proved the Freudian view of attachment categorically wrong. (And I write this as a member of a Freudian psychoanalytic society.) As Harry Harlow noted, baby monkeys separated from their real mothers become more attached to a cuddly terry cloth "mother" without milk than to a wire "mother" surrogate with milk. Love is about eye contact and cuddling, not hunger and sex.

Perhaps I should look in the mirror before I mock the poets and psychologists. For most of us, love, like joy, is sometimes difficult to bear. Love makes us all feel so vulnerable that sometimes we are afraid to take love in.

Dr. Adam Carson (a pseudonym), a member of the Study of Adult Development, was a very loving man. He had no difficulty telling me about his sex life, but he demonstrated difficulty in "knowing" how he felt about love. Years before my last interview with Dr. Carson, his wife had written to me:

> To me Adam is the most remarkable, patient, and considerate man I have ever met. He is very intuitive. I feel you are the one person that knows how lucky I really am. He gives so much to all his patients, friends, and family.

A few years later my last interview with this seventy-eight-year-old physician had progressed until the sun began to set upon his lovely garden terrace in Dover, Massachusetts, and the air grew chilly. Dr. Carson suddenly interrupted himself and said, "I am going to bring out a sweater for you, George, so you won't have to sit there wondering if you can have a sweater." As when I had interviewed him in 1967, now, thirty years later, warm in his cashmere pullover, I was again flooded with understanding of why this empathic man's patients and wife loved him.

Then he confirmed two of my intuitions. First, that his patients really did love him, and second, that he had trouble holding their gift of love in consciousness. Dr. Carson suddenly blurted out, "Let me get some exhibits." He then proceeded, rather sheepishly, to bring out a beautifully bound, silk-covered presentation box. In the box were at least one hundred letters from grateful patients. For his seventieth birthday, he told me, his wife had secretly obtained his patient address list. She had asked his longtime patients to send to her personal letters to commemorate their long relationship with their beloved physician. The letters that came back were deeply caring, often with photographs pasted to the bottom.

Dr. Carson showed me the collection of letters. Then he turned to me and said, "I don't know what you will make of this, George, but I have never read them." His eyes were filled with tears, and he blurted out, "I can't bear to talk about this." The depth of his feeling, his obvious attachment to his patients, was deeply moving. Yet I was stunned by his inability to let himself fully savor the fact that his patients had loved him back. We all need to help each other not only to bear grief but also to bear love!

❧

Attachment does not live in the stomach, where the early psychoanalysts tried to put it; nor does love live in the lexical, rational, neocortical brain, where the philosophers and theologians try to put it. Remove a mother hamster's entire neocortex, and she will seem feeble-minded in a psychologist's maze. But she can still love and raise her pup. Damage her limbic system only slightly, and she can be a wizard at mazes but an utterly incompetent mom.

Nor does love live in the hypothalamus (the sublimbic brain) that gives impetus to Freud's "id" and to the eros praised by red-blooded, passionate poets. Love lives within that part of the brain where smells, caretaking, and memory all come together—especially in the limbic anterior cingulate gyrus. Thanks to our limbic system and its surrounding temporal lobes, instead of intellectual neutrality there is commitment. Instead of analysis there is encounter. Instead of lust there is mystical union.

In short, love, like spirituality and grief, exists in the same "olfactory" brain that encourages mother rats to sniff to find their babies in the dark. Evolution has given mammals emotional attunement and eye contact, and they use them to tinker with one another's physiology, to adjust and fortify another's fragile neural rhythms in a collaborative dance of love.[15] A stressor that raises an isolated animal's plasma cortisol levels (a measure of stress) by 50 percent does not increase cortisol levels at all when the animal is surrounded by familiar companions.[16]

> *If music be the food of love, play on . . .*
> *O! it came o'er my ear like the sweet sound*
> *That breathes upon a bank of violets,*
> *Stealing and giving odor!*
>   —SHAKESPEARE, *Twelfth Night*, 1.1.I, 5–7

In humans the olfactory/memory brain of primitive nocturnal mammals has evolved into the more visual-auditory/memory brain that causes sad movies and sad songs to evoke lost loves and make us cry. Of course, the perfume or scent of an unwashed pillow slip of an absent lover can evoke the same response. The mammalian separation cry, one of the hallmarks of the mammalian limbic system, is tightly bound to empathy, compassion, and companionship. And the tragedy of individuals with Asperger's syndrome (a form of autism) is that they are capable of every human mental activity except empathy and attachment. In contrast, children with Down's syndrome, who seem to us so crippled by intellectual challenge, can radiate deep and meaningful attachment.

We remember our telephone numbers and the multiplication tables by rote; the process is cognitive and without feeling. We can retrieve such memories quickly and voluntarily. They live in what cognitive psychologists call explicit memory. We can recite such memories word perfect—until we grow old and forget. In contrast, we remember people, smells, melodies, and moments of personal crisis by implicit memory, analogous to the way dogs remember their masters by their unique smell. The sudden memory of a lost love during a movie may startle us as we weep inexplicably. Like the rules of grammar and riding a bicycle, love provides memories that still remain when we are otherwise crippled by dementia.

Our awareness of smells begins gradually and lingers even when we push the source away. Similarly, memories of sustaining (or destructive) relationships can occur involuntarily. Slowly and inexorably, they alter our state of mind. Such memories are evoked by odor, music, and symbol, but not by command. Unfortunately, even if we are poets, our capacity to give words to our memories of loved ones often fails us. Nevertheless, the memory of our lovers' perfume may linger long after their more easily verbalized telephone numbers have faded forever. Babies with little explicit memory (verbal memory of "facts") can distinguish the aroma of their own mother's milk from the milk of all other mothers with perfect accuracy. I recall a woman incapacitated by Alzheimer's who, upon hearing a certain man's name—dead for fifty years—exclaimed, "Oh, John, I was once very much in love with him!"

Once again, when words fail, song comes to our rescue. As Oscar Hammerstein's lyrics from *South Pacific* remind us, "You touch my hand and my arm grows strong." Music goes straight to the heart and soul; words often get ensnared by the mind. Thus, hymns and psalms are usually more comforting than sermons. Put in simple terms, we assimilate the people we love by suffusing them with positive emotion so we can take them inside and, as it were, metabolize them. Then, once we take them inside, like Tom Merton, we are changed forever.

༆

So why did natural selection create unselfish love? The nature of human unselfish love becomes clearer if we reflect upon life in the African savannas one or two million years ago. On those sparsely wooded plains evolved our hairless ancestors who took several years to reach maturity. Although they lived in a land richly endowed with carnivores, our ancestors could not run like the gazelle, burrow like the rabbit, climb trees like the gibbon, fly away like the flamingo, or fight back like the elephant. If humans did not band together, they perished. Humans do not even have fur like the ape for the young to cling to; instead, the human mother must cling to her young. In order to survive, humans had sometimes to subordinate both hunger and sex per se to the development of an inborn altruistic social organization. From such social bonding came lasting attachment and the survival of their young. On the savanna a young gazelle can survive with "selfish" genes. As soon as it is born, it can walk. In contrast, if not born into an unselfish human community, the *Homo sapiens* child is destined to become some predator's lunch.

The increased brain size and prolonged dependency of evolving humans have each catalyzed the other. Unconditional and forgiving love became essential to human survival, but such attachment is not rigid and reflexive, as is the gosling's imprinting on the mother goose or a mother bluebird's stereotyped care of her young. Rather, love in primates depends on emotionally motivated decision making and on flexible, if not quite "free," choice. Thus, unlike geese and bluebirds, humans have developed religious memes to reinforce their caretaking behaviors. But all this has required an increasingly complex and, thus, larger brain.

In short, humans have survived by sophisticated social bonding—characterized by unconditional attachment, forgiveness, gratitude, and affectionate eye contact. True, the negative, but self-consuming, emotions of disgust, anger, fear, and envy have often allowed individual humans to push other humans away or to selfishly exploit them. The positive emotions, however, of love, joy, hope, forgiveness, compassion, and trust have allowed humans to draw close to one another and to survive more successfully. Yes, fear draws people together too—but without the sharing.

The evolution of the limbic system molds lust into lasting and specific attachment. The two species of chimpanzee and *Homo sapiens* are the only three mammalian species to make eye contact while nursing, and bonobo chimps and *Homo sapiens* are the only two species to make eye contact during sexual intercourse.[17] *Homo sapiens* is arguably the only species to have clear female orgasm, and one of the few female mammals to remain sexually receptive year-round.

Evolution has liberated human love from the reflexive neuroendocrine dominance by the hypothalamus and instead has led to mate choice and bonding based on relatively flexible motivation. The "moral," mature, and cause-and-effect mentalization within the frontal lobes takes over from adolescent hypothalamic impulse. With maturity, empathic attachment replaces sexual greed.

꿃

Love, like the sacred and our image of God, has a timeless quality. The novelist Laurence Durrell reminds us that "the richest love is that which submits to the arbitration of time." Saint Paul reminded us that "love suffereth long, and is kind; love beareth all things, believeth all things, hopeth all things, endureth all things" (1 Corinthians 13:4, 7). In contrast, lust marches to a marvelous but much more urgent drummer. The object of a passionate one-night stand may seem boring and ugly the next morning. But what a wonderful evening!

If we read, one at a time, the love letters and poems of a man with four marriages and five mistresses, they may each seem convincing until we look at his life course. In contrast, a couple discussing love at their fiftieth wedding anniversary may sound trite and boring until we add the dimension of time to the equation. A wise editor once reminded me, "George, it is not that divorce is bad; it is that loving people for long periods of time is good." An octogenarian judge told me that he had fallen in love with his wife in eleventh grade. At age sixty-five, he observed that his love for his wife Susie was now "much deeper than at the beginning." Twelve years later, at age seventy-seven, he confided to the study, "As life gets shorter, I love Susie even more."

However, the growth of love is like the passage of the hour hand. Love may evolve so slowly that the process is almost invisible. Glaciers progress, flowers bloom, and we fall deeply in love, but we may never actually see the forward motion. Who can deny that many children love their grandmothers for a lifetime, but such love is never love at first sight. In contrast, love at first sight can happen in milliseconds, and I suspect that half of all marriages that do not last a year began quickly. Love at first sight is often lust, illusion, transference, or narcissism. It is about breasts and lips and seeing one's self in the other person. In Andrew Marvell's "To His Coy Mistress," the poet urges, "Had we world enough and time, this coyness, lady, were no crime. . . . But at my back I always hear time's winged chariot hurrying near." But that is lust, not love. Admittedly, lust is delightful, but it is all about me.

In contrast, the timelessness of meaningful love is reflected in the poem Walt Whitman wrote after Abraham Lincoln's death. "When lilacs last in the dooryard bloomed, and the great star early droop'd in the western sky in the night, I mourned, and yet shall mourn with ever-returning spring." I suspect very few people learned to love Abe Lincoln overnight. He was ugly and morose. Real love takes time.

Thus, contrary to current Western fashion, not only have arranged marriages been far more common in human history than "marrying for love," but follow-up of such arranged marriages reveals them to be as enduring. The elderly widow from a Hindu arranged marriage grieves as deeply at her husband's funeral pyre as does any modern married-for-love Scarsdale widow at a suburban funeral home. Human attachment takes time.

ॐ

So how do we learn love? How do we become agents of love? Not through Sunday school, not through the Internet, not ever by words alone. We learn to love through neurochemistry, genes, and identification.

In part, enduring selective love is catalyzed by genes. The crippling social limitation of infantile autism is almost wholly genetic. For unknown, but highly heritable, reasons, autistic individuals are unable to take love in and thus unable to give love back. On the other hand, enduring love in humans is different from that in insects. Insects have genetic communication systems for "altruistic" behaviors that are sometimes impressively sophisticated, but they neither invent them nor teach them to others. The waggle dance of the honeybee and the odor trail of ants contain symbolic elements, but their altruistic performance and meaning are genetically inborn and cannot be altered by learning. Unlike human compassion, the genetically mediated "altruism" of insects is not culturally contagious.

In part, enduring selective love is catalyzed by chemistry. Neurochemistry provides ingenious models of nonverbal communication and catalyzes the involuntary mechanisms of positive emotion. The brain hormone oxytocin is released when all mammals give birth. Oxytocin seems to permit mammals to overcome their natural aversion to extreme proximity, and thus oxytocin has been rechristened the "cuddle hormone." As previously stated, if they are genetically deprived of oxytocin, monogamous, maternal, loving *prairie* voles (a species of rodent) turn into another subspecies—the heartless, promiscuous, pup-abusing *montane* voles. Without oxytocin, parental cooperation and responsibility vanish.[18] In human newborns there is a short-lived overproduction of oxytocin receptors.[19] Oxytocin goes up in human puberty in parallel with adolescent crushes. Put a newborn baby in a mother's arms or bless a couple's sexual union with mutual orgasm and brain oxytocin levels rise.

The oxytocin-rich dopaminergic brain centers are an intimate part of the human limbic system. The nucleus accumbens (in voles), the ventral tegmentum (in rats), and the anterior cingulate gyrus (in humans) have all been shown to be closely involved in lasting mammalian attachment. All are heavily dependent on the neurotransmitter dopamine, and interestingly, these same three brain centers also contain opiate receptors and are linked to heroin addiction—an ersatz and often lethal "love" that is also selective and enduring. Opiates are the only chemicals that can comfort a baby animal separated from its mother. Or as one chronic addict described it, "You don't really get lonely on smack [heroin]. It's like having a lover."[20]

In part, enduring selective love is catalyzed by identification. Unlike honeybees, humans do not come into the world knowing how to dance. If all human love is a dance, it still takes two to tango—and usually at the beginning an experienced tango teacher. Thus, chemistry, genes, and survival of the fittest are only part of the story. True, the evolutionary march from fish to cold-blooded reptiles to Harry Harlow's loving monkeys reflects the power of genes to lay the groundwork for love. For enduring mammalian attachment to occur, however, loving environments and identification with others are as critical as chemistry to sculpt the brain.

If, as Lieutenant Joe Cable sings in *South Pacific*, "you've got to be taught to hate and fear," you also have to be shown how to love. Thus, the behavioral self-regulation that we associate with love does not come from a solitary brain, but from one brain's evolving and becoming shaped through attachment to a beloved other. Monkeys raised in isolation go on eating binges and cower in corners. Instead of playful roughhousing, they fight with their peers unto death, and they never really get the hang of copulation. All their lives such isolated monkeys remain inept "at doing what comes naturally." In contrast, isolated monkeys who are subsequently raised by mothers or with siblings for even one year can learn to roughhouse—gracefully stopping once social dominance is achieved—and skillfully negotiating the dance steps to successful impregnation. Remarkably, as the life of Tom Merton illustrates, sustained loving environments in adulthood can help undo the damage of childhood isolation. Without recovering the memory of his loving childhood nanny and without his own children's later attunement with him, Dr. Tom Merton might never have learned how to give and receive love. The multiply orphaned Leo Tolstoy was an impulsive, unempathic narcissist until his wife, Sonya, entered his life.

As the parables, hymns, and uplifting narratives of the world's great religions suggest, the biology of love is catalyzed by social example. This was demonstrated in a series of ingenious experiments by University of Virginia psychologist Jonathan Haidt and his students. By showing new mothers video clips reflecting love and gratitude, they increased the leakage of milk and/or nursing behavior (both evidence of oxytocin release). These effects were much less evident if the mothers were shown humorous or neutral videos. Again, when they showed college students documentaries of heroic altruists and uplifting segments from The Oprah Winfrey Show documenting displays of gratitude and unselfish love, Haidt and his colleagues evoked in the students a sense of calm, a warm feeling in the chest, and an impulse to help others, which was not in evidence after the same students viewed neutral video clips.[21]

Love, especially unconditional love, also cures people—both those who give it and those who receive it. To receive love is transformational. Kissed by a loving princess, the ungainly frog becomes a prince. Made ugly by myriad tubes in all his orifices, the dying centenarian is made beautiful once again by the caring hospice nurse who holds his hand. Love, like the other positive emotions, is religion without the side effects.

Healing love, of course, always involves appropriate boundaries. Eye contact and touch, as in mother-child interaction, must always be kept separate from lust and selfish eros, or the other person will feel violated. The good hospice nurse, the committed parish priest, the dedicated caseworker, even a best friend, needs to remember that a favorite grandmother, not a charismatic lifeguard, is the proper model for the connectedness, the passion, the commitment, and the wise limits that create therapeutic love. Healing love is often more about witnessing (making the other person feel "seen") than about rescuing.[22]

Moreover, oxytocin, the "cuddle hormone," in some ways is itself as remarkably healing as the love that it undergirds. Over the long term, oxytocin exerts effects opposite to the negative fight-or-flight emotions. During prolonged periods of fear, anxiety, and depression, pain thresholds are lowered and cortisol levels and blood pressure can be chronically and deleteriously elevated. In contrast, during periods of sustained oxytocin release, cortisol levels and blood pressure are reduced, pain thresholds are increased, and a calm, non-anxious state results.[23] A recent study of the cortisol elevation and post-stress anxiety involved in public speaking found that intranasally administered oxytocin and social supports each buffered the effects of stress, and they were most effective when given in combination.[24] No wonder love and compassion are valuable at the bedside of the sick.

The British psychiatrist Sir Michael Rutter presents perhaps the best scientific documentation that we have of the transforming power of love in human development. He and his colleague David Quinton carried out an instructive twenty-year experiment.[25] They studied ninety-one women who had been taken from dysfunctional families and raised in orphanages since they were two. Rutter and Quinton wished to discover who among the institutionalized children would become good mothers by manifesting the caretaking that they themselves had never received. Not surprisingly, they were collectively much worse mothers than the controls. However, among the institutionalized women, two predictors of successful motherhood emerged: first, the capacity to elicit admiring and caring relationships from grammar school teachers, and second, the good fortune to marry loving, caretaking men. Furthermore, Rutter and Quinton demonstrated that a supportive marriage was not a function of a woman's preexisting psycholog-ical stability. In other words, it was not a function of assortative mating (that is, being relatively more loving and therefore marrying someone lov-ing). Rather, the beneficial effect had to be credited to the loving marriage itself. The uncared-for girls, like Tom Merton and Bill Graham, became transformed through love.

In the Study of Adult Development, I examined the lives of unloved men rather than unloved women.[26] I reached the same conclusion as Rut-ter and Quinton. I selected 30 adolescents, out of a sample of 456 inner-city youths, whose childhoods were the most barren and the least conducive to continued adult development. In childhood each man had been cursed with the variables that child developmentalists have demonstrated *prevent* resilience. Moreover, the predictions of the child developmentalists were right. At age twenty-five, the lives of these thirty men continued to be dis-asters. But by age fifty or sixty, nine of those thirty men were leading suc-cessful and generative lives. As with the women in Quinton and Rutter's study, the most critical healing event was their having found a loving spouse. We do not learn how to love from religious education. We learn love from our genes, from our biochemistry, and from the people who love us and let us love them.

Successful human development involves, first, absorbing love, next, re-ciprocally sharing love, and finally, giving love unselfishly away. All the great religions, our friends, our families, our genes, and our brain chemistry conspire to guide us along this path. Always love multiplies like "a magic penny." As Shakespeare's Romeo exclaims to Juliet, "My bounty is as boundless as the sea, my love as deep; the more I give to thee, the more I have, for both are infinite." No wonder some regard God and love as syn-onymous.

6

Hope

❧

Human hope is the greatest power in life
and the only thing that defeats death.

—Eugene O'Neill[1]

ʕ̈ʔ

Chapter 2 told of mammalian evolutionary advance and of the adult separation cry, which conveyed faith that one's mother was no cannibal. Hope conveys a still further evolutionary advance. Hope reflects the capacity for one's loving, lyrical, limbic memory of the past to become attached to the "memory of the future." This capacity occurs within our most recently evolved frontal lobes. The relative expansion of our frontal lobes is the anatomic trait that most unambiguously separates *Homo sapiens* from other primates. Our capacity to anticipate, to mourn in advance, to plant seeds, and to plan for the future are all capacities based in our frontal lobes. Only an integrated brain can hope that agriculture can really work, that seeds planted in bleak spring will bear fruit next autumn. And that is the difference that hope makes.

The evolutionary capacity of *Homo sapiens* to hope and to "remember the future" as possibly better than the past went hand in hand with the re-markably creative change that took place in the Stone Age tool kit 150,000 years ago—and still takes place in the computers and robotics of today. To be a successful hunter-gatherer, you needed only to remember where food had been last year. Armed with such a memory of the past, Neanderthal hunter-gatherers could survive by making the same Stone Age tools and finding the same berries and roots for 400,000 years. Then, suddenly, mankind learned to experiment, to tinker with the hope of finding some-thing new. Our *Homo sapiens* ancestors tinkered with bone to create nee-dles, with last year's wheat to grow a more abundant harvest next year, and with ivory to carve fertility goddesses to make fecund next year a womb that last year was barren. To be a creative farmer, shaman, or artist—in other words, to put things in the world that were not there before—you needed the mental capacity to envision the future. You needed to be able to hope that planting would lead to harvest and that prayer and ritual would lead to babies. I suspect that it was the inexorable maturation of our species that led early *Homo sapiens* to place useful objects within graves and to become the first mammal to demonstrate hope that life, or at least memory, existed beyond death.

Suffering equals hope destroyed, and suffering is more than pain: it is loss of control, it is despair, it is the loss of hope. However, if the loss of hope transforms pain into suffering, the return of hope transforms suffering back again into manageable pain. Suffering is the loss of autonomy; hope is its restoration. And so the ritual springtime celebrations of Easter, of Exodus, and of Demeter bringing back Persephone from Hades transform despair into hope.

> *I danced on a Friday when the sky turned black;*
> *it's hard to dance with the devil on your back;*
> *they buried my body and they thought I'd gone,*
> *but I am the dance and I still go on.*
>
> *They cut me down, and I leapt up high,*
> *I am the life that'll never, never die;*

I'll live in you if you'll live in me;
I am the Lord of the Dance; said he.
—SIDNEY CARTER (1915–2004), *Lord of the Dance* (1963)

૭૩

To define hope will take this entire chapter. I can't do it in a sentence or even a paragraph. "Come off it!" readers may protest. "Words are all we have." But, of course, that's not true. Did not the Chinese sages remind us that one picture is worth a thousand words? Do not great editors plead, "Show me, don't tell me"? Thus, chapter 1 defined *spirituality* not by recourse to Noah Webster but by a prayer, a story, a song, and three exemplars: Mohandas Gandhi, Martin Luther King Jr., and Nelson Mandela. To define words like "love" and "hope," I need to harness your whole brain, not just your speech center—to harness your "heart," not just your intellect. I hope that when you finish this chapter you will *know*, not just be *thinking* about, what I mean by *hope*.

To begin with, I must define what hope is not. Hope must be distinguished from wish. Wishes are words and left-brain. In contrast, hope is made up of images and is rooted in the right brain. Wishing on a star takes no effort; as I have already noted, if wishes were horses, beggars would ride. Hope often requires enormous effort and shapes real lives. Hope reflects our ability to imagine a realistic positive future. As we watch two people make their marriage vows, their *faith* encompasses only what is past; their *love* allows them to take a sacramental step in the present; but it is through *hope* and only through hope that, together, they may imagine their future. Hope is emotional, energizing, and strengthening; wishing is passive, cognitive, and potentially weakening.

The efficacy of prayer in healing often hinges on the distinction between hope and wish. If in secret I petition God that I wish you would recover from cancer or wish that I might win the lottery, the efficacy of my good intentions may be no better than wishing on a four-leaf clover. If, on the other hand, you experience my prayers as love and a sincere effort to share with you my strength and hope, it is likely that your suffering will diminish, even if your cancer cells do not always die. "I have nothing to offer you," the Alcoholics Anonymous sponsor tells her pigeon, "but my experience, strength, and hope." And the pigeon feels held.

Nor is hope the same as trust and faith. The opposite of trust is mistrust, but the opposite of hope is despair. It is faith that enables a child to establish secure attachment to a needed and vital other. But it is *hope* that enables a child without loving parents to believe in the future. Without trust, we become vigilant and paranoid. Without hope, we become desperately depressed. The opposite of trust becomes "people may hurt me." The opposite of hope becomes "I am a doomed person, and no good will ever come to me." Paranoia and depression are two very different maladies. Those without faith have no past. Those without hope have no future.

With hope, we can envision growing from prior despair to future possibilities. In contrast, neither love nor faith encompasses a future tense. Thus, the developmental sequence of orphans may be: I have lost my faith, I hope that I shall find it again.

Hope arises from the involuntary mammalian need to function effectively in the face of fear and setback. We call this source of comforting emotion—which also encompasses heartfelt prayer—*hope*. Hope reminds us that tomorrow may be a better day. Our verb "to despair" comes from the Latin *disperare*, to be without hope. Just as despair is emotional, so is hope. Real hope is rooted in heart and song as well as in cognition. For example, the following words of hope bring soaring choral music—not cognitive "belief"—to awareness: "Deep in my heart I do believe that we shall overcome someday."

Just as faith, as in the case of Camus's priest, Father Rieux, can sometimes create hope, new hope can restore old faith. This is illustrated in the sequel to Eugene O'Neill's play about his mother. In O'Neill's autobiographical play *Long Day's Journey into Night*, it is clear that the mother in the play, Mary Tyrone, blamed her son—and almost every other relative she had—for her addiction to opiates.[2] Indeed, all his life, O'Neill had wondered if he really was to blame for his mother's addiction. As he searched back for clues to the cause of his mother's addiction, he could get only as far as his mother's pain at his own birth and no further. But what had gone on *before* Eugene's birth? O'Neill's biographers were better informed than he.[3]

Even before her marriage to James O'Neill (Eugene's father), it had been noted that Ella Quinlan seldom smiled. Later, having found herself unable to care for her first two children, one of whom died from neglect, Ella's despair (hopelessness) became worse. As she grew to depend on her mother to help care for her children, she also avoided further pregnancies. Her mother's death occurred when Ella was far away and could not attend her funeral. Shortly after this ungrieved death, Ella allowed herself to remain pregnant with Eugene. In the play O'Neill's mother says, "I was afraid all the time I carried Eugene. I knew something terrible would happen. I knew that I wasn't worthy to have another baby, and that God would punish me if I did." But in O'Neill's play, and one suspects in real life, Ella never mentioned her real mother or her fear that there would be no one to help her care for her new baby, Eugene. Her loss of her mother, her "higher power," may have been the real precipitant of Ella's postpartum pain—of her loss of hope.

In the play Mary Tyrone moves the source of her despair forward in time and reminisces that it all began just *after* Eugene's birth: "All he [the doctor] knew was I was in pain. It was easy for him to stop the pain." And later she describes her morphine as "a special kind of medicine. I have to take it because there is no other that can stop the pain—*all* the pain—I mean, in my hands." Remember, in baby animals opiates are the only drug that can quench the pain of a child's separation from her mother.

Early in *Long Day's Journey*, Mary Tyrone also tells us that she has lost her faith. Thus, she cries out, "If I could only find the faith I lost, so I could pray again!" Instead of acknowledging pain over the loss of her mother, Mary Tyrone clings to her wedding dress, the way Linus in the comic strip *Peanuts* clings to his blanket. "What is it that I am looking for?" she keens. "I know it is something I lost . . . something I miss terribly." As the play ends, she hallucinates, "I had a talk with Mother Elizabeth. . . . It may be sinful of me, but I love her better than my own mother. Because she always understands." But Mary Tyrone remains without hope. Hopelessness and clinical depression are one. Both can be fatal. At the end of the play, in a psychotic reverie, Mary Tyrone imagines the future. "I went to the shrine and prayed to the Blessed Virgin and found peace again because I knew she heard my prayer and would always love me and see no harm ever came to me so long as I never lost my faith in her." This is hope, not delusion.

In 1914, two years after the events in *Long Day's Journey*, the Harrison Act was passed, making the prescription of morphine by Ella's doctors illegal. To withdraw from her now illegal morphine, Ella O'Neill was providentially sent to live in the hopeful environment of a convent for six months. In the convent Ella O'Neill's hope came true. She found real nuns to love and to be held by. She found real surrogate mothers who were more nourishing than her security blanket wedding dress, her drunken sons and husband, and her autistic fantasies. Thus, in the convent Ella O'Neill not only could be dependent on an institution and find a surrogate for the mother whom she had been seeking, but could also find fresh hope.

By 1919 Ella O'Neill had learned to smile and hope. Drug-free for five years after leaving the convent, she could write to her son Eugene, two days after the birth of his son, "I am one of the happiest old ladies in New York tonight to know I have such a wonderful grandson but no more wonderful than you were when you were born and weighed eleven pounds and had no nerves at that time. I am enclosing a picture of you taken at three months. I hope your boy will be as good looking."[4]

She now followed the budding career of her son, the playwright, with pride, intelligence, and empathy.[5] The future had meaning once more. And that is the difference that hope—with an assist, of course, from faith, love, and sobriety—makes.

⸭

Almost fifty years ago, Topeka psychiatrist Karl Menninger observed, "The *Encyclopaedia Britannica* devotes many columns to the topic of love and many more to faith. But hope, poor little hope! She is not even listed."[6] He made this observation in an article that he wrote about hope for the *American Journal of Psychiatry*. Hope, to my knowledge, has not been explicitly discussed in that journal since. Optimists, like the "cockeyed optimist" in *South Pacific*, may be "immature and incredibly green." But hope is mature, and what hope sees is real. Thus, Karl Menninger also went so far as to write, "The hopes we develop are therefore a measure of our maturity."[7]

Like humor, creativity, and springtime, you cannot study hope objectively, or even rationally. Nor can you quantify the beauty of butterflies, or the grace of five-year-old children. Yet all are real. Perhaps of more importance, hope saves lives. The strength of a patient's hopeful religious commitment is a consistent predictor of survival after heart surgery.[8] As the Johns Hopkins neuropsychologist Curt Richter noted many years ago, if rats swim until exhausted and are then rescued, in the future they can swim much longer without drowning than can naive rats without a history of prior rescue.[9]

In psychologist Martin Seligman's laboratory, Madeline Visintainer reproduced Richter's experiment, only more dramatically.[10] She examined the survival of rats that had experienced inescapable shock, sometimes called learned helplessness, compared to rats that had been exposed to shock that they could terminate. (The helpless rats yoked to the empowered rats received shock only when the latter did.) Visintainer calculated how to inject rats with just enough cancer cells so that half the rats would be expected to die. She then injected cancer cells into one group of thirty rats that had experienced, through their own efforts, successful escape from painful shock. She injected another group of thirty rats that had experienced the same shock as the first group, but in a setting where they were powerless to escape. Instead of 50 percent, only 27 percent of the hopeful rats died of cancer, while 63 percent of the hopeless rats died.

In the Study of Adult Development, we have observed in a less precise fashion the same power of hope over mortality in humans.[11] The survival of inner-city men, controlling for IQ, parental social class, ethnicity, and multiproblem family membership, was very significantly enhanced by increasing years of education. In other words, the disadvantaged children (independent of privilege and parental education) who grew up convinced it was worth working for a future—the men who hoped—lived longer. And that is the difference that hope makes.

Admittedly, hope, like Heisenberg's electrons, grows more elusive the harder we try to focus upon it. Saint Paul tries to explain why: "We are saved by hope, but hope that is seen is not hope" (Romans 8:24). You can only hope for what is both uncertain and still lies invisibly in the future. Nevertheless, hope adds a desperately important ingredient to living.

To understand, you have to let the music of hope wash over you. One of the most popular songs of World War II was "(There'll Be Blue Birds Over) The White Cliffs of Dover," which was written in 1941 England just as the world looked darkest. The song reminded the English that someday, somehow, the endless air raids and the hopeless British defeats, in Belgium, in Norway, and in Africa, would have to end. But this song of bluebirds did not lie. In drawing attention to "someday," it pointed to the sense of shared community in hope's concept of "someday"—as in "we shall overcome someday."

Stephen Sondheim and Leonard Bernstein convey the same idea of hope and community in *West Side Story* when Maria and Tony sing against a backdrop of the murderous conflict between the Sharks and the Jets (between the Montagues and the Capulets, as it were, or between the Shiites and the Sunnis).

> *Someday, somewhere,*
> *we'll find a new way of living,*
> *We'll find there's a way of forgiving.*

But if you did not also know the music to these words, they would mean much less. They might mean no more than a Hallmark card. For the temporal lobes are the seat of past memory, of love, of music, of spirituality. The music of Beethoven's Ninth Symphony reminds us to hope, and it is no accident that Israel's national anthem is called "Hatikva" (Hope).

⫷

Hope is not cognitive; hope is not reasonable; hope is not corny. Hope is part of our emotional mammalian heritage.

Artist, child psychiatrist, and student of adult development Erik Erikson put the virtue of hope at the beginning of life as "the earliest and most indispensable virtue."[12] Hope became for Erikson the very foundation block of all human development. Hope was the sustaining impetus behind what Erikson named "basic trust," or what I call faith. Moreover, with time hope seems essential to almost all the eight stages of Eriksonian development. Hope is the cornerstone to the mastery of initiative; hope sustains adolescent fidelity; and hope catalyzes adult intimacy. By reaffirming the individual's confidence in the next generation, hope gives meaning to the flowering of mature generativity. Finally, by undergirding what Erikson calls "integrity" at the end of life, hope provides the promise of the future to us or to our survivors that allows us to die in peace. Hope springs eternal.

⫷

Hope is the deep visceral conviction that this too shall pass, that tomorrow, or at least the day after tomorrow, will be a better day, that if you are patient, winter is inevitably followed by spring. Thus, hope is not a mere cognitive defense mechanism; hope is a positive emotion. Hope is the very opposite of Gertrude Lawrence in *The King and I* whistling a happy tune to shift her attention away from her fear. Hope is certainly not Scarlett O'Hara's denial as she stares at Rhett Butler's receding back and mutters, "I'll think about it tomorrow." Hope looks death squarely in the eye; hope accepts the reality of AIDS, of chapter 13 bankruptcy, of lost loves. In AA alcoholics begin their "Twelve Steps" by, first, stoically admitting their own powerlessness over alcohol. They then come to hope that a power greater than themselves might restore them to sanity. This is no idle wish, for every AA meeting surrounds them, unlike any other place on earth, with other once incurable drunks who have been sane and sober for years. Sobriety happens.

Surprisingly, the greater the suffering, the greater the power of hope. In his book *Love Against Hate*, Karl Menninger tells the story of how in the dark hopelessness of the Buchenwald concentration camp the inmate physicians and engineers, through bribery and ingenuity—and hope—built, in secret, an X-ray machine.[13] Such a Herculean effort was far more than mere wish. With great effort and hope, and at great risk, they built a machine that they used to help other doomed inmates live. But since death seemed inevitable, why build an X-ray machine in a death camp? The answer was hope. Indeed, there is hard evidence that their hope was not just wish, illusion, or cockeyed optimism. The evidence rests on one simple, if beautiful, scientific fact. When Buchenwald was liberated, some of the inmate physicians were still alive to tell the American army doctors who helped to liberate them of their marvelous creation, of their indomitable hope.

But besides such heartwarming anecdotes, where is the evidence for hope? How can we know that death is certain and yet hope for life eternal? Perhaps because every year we learn anew that after winter comes spring. By throwing flowers on graves, we acknowledge that this grief, too, shall pass. In throwing flowers, we hope that the memory of our love will live forever. From every bleak December garden, there will always be a resurrection in the spring. Again, I am not talking metaphysics, just the biological facts.

If a child is dying of a fatal disease, it is sometimes pointless to help the child's parent to imagine that the child will live. That would be merely wish. Rather, the task may be to start to instill hope that a future narrative exists and that loving people still exist within that narrative. That is why two grieving parents, their only child dead in adolescence, founded a university and called it by their son's name, Leland Stanford Jr. They devoted the rest of their lives to developing their university as a tuition-free gift of hope to other people's adolescent children. Yes, I agree that many facets of the Stanfords' lives were not admirable, but their hope has proven a boon to many—even if Stanford tuition is no longer just twenty-five dollars a term.

Besides, Emily Dickinson chants to us:

> *Hope is the thing with feathers,*
> *That perches on the soul,*
> *And sings the tune without the words,*
> *And never stops—at all.*
>
> *I've heard it in the chillest land,*
> *And on the strangest sea,*
> *Yet never in eternity,*
> *It asked a crumb of me.*

ॐ

Hope is endowed with the same qualities with which Sigmund Freud characterized humor. Hope, like Freud's humor, "is a means of obtaining pleasure in spite of the distressing affects that interfere with it." Hope, like Freud's humor, "scorns to withdraw the ideational content bearing the distressing affect from conscious attention . . . and thus surmounts the automatism of defense."[14] You cannot have hope without the capacity to recognize the reality of loss. Indeed, unlike wish and self-deception, hope may be impossible without the willingness also to mourn. Thus, paradoxically, the frank acknowledgment of words like "cancer," "death," and "powerlessness" can sometimes lance boils of despair and restore hope.

Nor is hope the same as fantasy. Fantasy allows us to imagine what never was, and never can be. Fantasy merely gives the lonely a paper doll to call their own. The explorer Robert Scott, starving to death in his tent in the Antarctic, dreamed nightly of hot meals. But such imaginary meals provided cold comfort, and so he died.

Scott wrote to his wife from the Antarctic, "I think the last chance has gone. We have decided not to kill ourselves but to fight to the last depot. . . . Make the boy interested in natural history if you can. It is better than games. They encourage it at some schools."[15] When the letter was found, Scott's hope for his son made all England weep. Moreover, his son, Peter Scott, strengthened by his father's hope, learned natural history, matured, and became a brilliant painter of wildlife. No, hope is not fantasy. Hope does not usually cure cancer, nor does it feed doomed explorers. Rather, hope lets grandmothers plant acorns that will someday shade their middle-aged grandchildren. Hope lets the orphans of doomed explorers go on to life-affirming careers. Hope, you see, does not abolish grief; it only reminds us of the possibility that, as in winter gardens, the seeds of love may be successfully resown.

☙

Nor is hope dishonest. Deception and lies are something that we offer to others. But by definition a lie is something in which we ourselves do not believe. Always hope embraces truth. True, the playwright Jean Anouilh had his heroine, Antigone, refer to "your filthy hope, your docile, female hope; hope, your whore."[16] But that was when Antigone was in the throes of a major depression. She knew only despair.

Paradoxically, symbols of hope sometimes recall a hideous past. For hope is honest. One of the great symbols of our age—the destruction of the Berlin wall—permitted the rebirth of hope for millions. And so, remarkably, people have treasured bits of that hideous wall once scarred with desperate graffiti and hopeless barbed wire. Again, the miraculous transfer of Nelson Mandela from three decades in his Robben Island prison to the leadership of his nation still provides a symbol of hope to millions. In part, our hope gains strength because we recall rescue from our previous despair. Like Curt Richter's rats, we all swim a little longer if we have a memory of hope come true.

☙

We cannot give hope to another; we can only share our own. I remember once I feared that my own hope had been turned by my cockeyed optimistic naïveté into a cruel deception. I had referred a young and trusting surgeon who had come to me with a drinking problem to the local AA meetings in his small Massachusetts town. Despite his concerns about town gossip, I assured him of his safety and anonymity. He was compliant, and he trusted in my hope.

But what did I know. To my horror, on his very next visit to me he told me of having encountered the mother of one of his young patients at a local AA meeting. I was terrified. To make it worse, her daughter had experienced an imperfect surgical outcome at the young surgeon's hands. Now the mother would know that her daughter's possibly less than competent surgeon was also a drunk. I felt hopeless. Perhaps I had sabotaged a young trusting surgeon's career with my naive, blind enthusiasm in faith healing.

But what did I know. The daughter had had an appointment with the young surgeon the next day. Her mother came with her. During the visit the mother said little, but the surgeon trembled inside. Then, as she left, the mother silently, softly pressed a card into the young surgeon's hand. The card was not a summons to a malpractice hearing. The card contained only Reinhold Niebuhr's famous prayer. "God, grant me the serenity to accept the things I cannot change, the courage to change the things I can, and the wisdom to know the difference." She had respected the surgeon's anonymity and had forgiven him his trespasses. Perhaps I was guilty of optimism, but the surgeon was blessed with hope—a hope both invisible and lifesaving.

In 1785 Benjamin Franklin conducted perhaps the first controlled study of psychotherapy. He found that mesmerism worked if, when blindfolded, you thought you were being mesmerized but in fact were not. However, mesmerism did not work if you thought you weren't but in fact you were being mesmerized. Rather than branding mesmerism a hoax, Franklin in his wisdom wrote, "The imagination of sick persons has unquestionably a very frequent and considerable share in the cure of their diseases. . . . [We] are saved by faith . . . under the genial influence of hope. Hope is an essential constituent of human life."[17]

When I was a young psychiatric resident, a clinically depressed elderly patient asked me to give her medicine for a cold. Filled with callow science and hopelessness, I pompously and unempathically told her that if I had a medicine that cured colds, I would be rich. Understandably, she was furious, and forty years later I am still ashamed of my heartless arrogance. A prescription for echinacea or Professor Linus Pauling's hopeful vitamin C would have served her so much better than my heartless, hopeless "science."

· The next year I learned the power of hope firsthand. Until I was thirty years old, I had had a phobia of public speaking. In all my schooling, I had participated in only one school play. In the eighth-grade Christmas pageant I played Joseph, for Joseph, mercifully, had no lines. After graduating from medical school, however, I began to write research papers, which in turn involved public presentations at national meetings. What was I to do? I did not pray. Instead, ten minutes before every lecture I took a capsule of Librium—at the time the newest scientific remedy for anxiety. Librium worked like a charm. My fear vanished, and in its place was a well-known side effect of Librium—a slight slurring of speech. A triumph of science over faith? Not really. Seven years later, long after my phobia of public speaking had, thanks to my hopeful use of Librium, been completely extinguished, I discovered the scientific truth. The pharmacological effects of oral Librium do not even begin to take effect until an hour has passed! I had always taken my capsule ten minutes before a twenty-minute presentation. I had not just been consoled; I had been cured by hope and faith. Indeed, one study showed that when anxious patients were given sugar pills and told that the pills were sugar placebos and that sugar placebos were just what they needed, fourteen of the fifteen patients experienced significant subjective and objective improvement.[18]

Today up to 50 percent of the improvement seen with antidepressant drugs like Prozac and Effexor and as much as 90 percent of the improvement seen with minor tranquilizers like Valium and Xanax can be demonstrated to result from placebo effect. The sensible conclusion from such evidence should not be that modern psychiatry is superstitious, but that the faith, hope, and love that go into patient care remain of the utmost importance to modern medicine.

During the 1950s Jerome Frank, a professor of psychiatry at Johns Hopkins University, was among the first to study dynamic psychotherapy empirically. After years of thoughtful experimentation and control of relevant variables, Frank's prescription for effective group psychotherapy was the deliberate instillation of hope. In his eyes, the task of group psychotherapy was to raise the patient's expectation of cure and to reintegrate him or her into the community. "At Lourdes, pilgrims pray for each other, not for themselves. This stress on service counteracts the patient's morbid self-preoccupation, strengthens his self-esteem by demonstrating that he can do something for others and cements the tie between patient and group."[19] Such community involves the sharing of suffering with a sanctioned healer who is willing to talk about the patient's problems in a symbolic way. The common ingredients of such a program include group acceptance, an emotionally charged but communally shared ritual, and a shared belief system. Are places of worship any different? I don't think so. Hope is contagious.

On the one hand, as Howard Spiro, a wise Yale professor of internal medicine, warns us, humankind has achieved much against disease through technology and science and much less through faith or will or hope or even love.[20] Penicillin and vitamin B help everybody. In contrast, echinacea and Kundalini yoga are good only for true believers, and even then the "scientist" may note no improvement.

On the other hand, Professor Spiro tells us of a pastor suffering from Crohn's disease, a chronic inflammatory and sometimes fatal bowel disease. The pastor wrote:

> When you come into my hospital room you need to know . . . that I have Crohn's disease and three small bowel resections . . . that I am chronically ill, and am seeking healing not cure . . . that I am anxious about aging and how I will cope, that I long for one perfect day, only one symptom-free 24 hours . . . that God, faith, meaning, ultimate concern, love, salvation are the being of my being . . . when you come into my room . . . you need to know all this if you want to heal me and bear my rage about my disease that will never be cured, that my daughter has Crohn's disease and is only 33 years old, that she too has had

her first surgery . . . when you come into my hospital room . . . keep hope alive, it is all I have."[21]

But remember, hope is honest. Placebos don't work because they "fool" the patient. Rather, the placebo serves as the physician's communion wafer and sacramental wine. A prescription at the end of the clinic visit seals the contract between two individuals who are committed by faith and love to hope for the patient's recovery. Hope, like meditation, relaxation, and service to others, distracts the patient from his or her self-focus on pain.

⁂

How do we learn hope? Where does hope come from? How does it develop? I believe hope comes through our earliest experience with care. Curt Richter's rats could swim longer because they had been rescued.

Ponder who in your life taught you that you had a future. It is almost always somebody's mother. Every time that we take an aspirin as a placebo to go to sleep or to ease a sore throat, the sour taste of the aspirin tablet evokes a loving mother who decades ago lowered our suffering from a fever with the chemistry of aspirin. Don't get me wrong; aspirin is an effective, scientific medicine. It lowers fever and lessens pain from inflammation. Everyone feels better and sleeps better with less fever and pain. But years after aspirin once scientifically helped us to sleep, the same little white tablets with their sour taste beget hope and bring back the memory of our mother's comfort even though she is far away. Thus, aspirin may help us to sleep even though our insomnia springs from worry or jetlag—not fever.

Coretta Scott King told a story about Martin Luther King's grandmother that helps put the evolutionary sources of hope in perspective. Where did the hope come from that allowed Coretta Scott King's husband to tell a throng of 250,000 rapt listeners about his wonderful dream of "knowing that we will be free one day."

In Coretta's words, "Martin would tell me of his grandmother's wonderful spiritual qualities and also of her soft heart. When Daddy King would whip Martin for something he'd done, Martin would take his punishment without a word, determined never to cry. . . . But in the background always, was his Grandmother Williams, tears streaming down her face, unable to bear the punishment."[22] Hope comes from viscerally feeling, not cognitively knowing, that we matter, that we shall overcome someday.

Grandmothers, in their wisdom, know a four-word mantra of hope that, in their naïveté, new parents can rarely conjure up, but without which new parenthood would be unbearable. The four-word mantra is "This too shall pass." I learned this mantra from my mother a week after her grandson, my son, was born and I had been fretting that he would never stop crying. But we cannot learn hope without experience and without models. We must see seeds grow before we can believe in sowing.

After having a vivid dream in 1969 about his own mother, Mary, who had died long before when he was only fourteen, Paul McCartney felt much as I do. Waking from the dream, he wrote the immortal lines:

And when the night is cloudy, there is still a light that shines on me,
Shine until tomorrow, let it be.

7

Joy

⚜

Joy and woe are woven fine,
A clothing for the soul divine;
Under every grief and pine
Runs a joy with silken twine.
It is right it should be so;
Man was made for joy and woe;
And when this we rightly know,
Safely through the world we go.

—WILLIAM BLAKE, *"Auguries of Innocence"* (1863)

⚜

Students of the primary emotions often keep different lists. But joy, along with fear and anger, is on almost everybody's. Nevertheless, of all primary human emotions, joy is the one least studied. Perhaps the power of joy sometimes frightens us.

Pierre Teilhard de Chardin was the very model of a Jesuit Darwinian; he considered joy the most infallible sign of the presence of God. Antonio

Damasio is the very model of a modern neuroscientist; in 2003 he published *Looking for Spinoza*—perhaps the most sophisticated treatise on joy to be found. Damasio concludes, "The current scientific knowledge regarding joy supports the notion that it should be actively sought because it does contribute to flourishing."[1]

How can we define joy? Consider for a moment a gaggle of geese, a flock of sheep, a pride of lions, and a congregation of Methodists. What is the difference between how we imagine these honorable gatherings and how we imagine . . . well, how we imagine an exaltation of larks! An exaltation of larks makes us look up, not down. An exaltation of larks, the word "Hallelujah," and joy—all convey something wonderful, something limbic, not lexical.

Consider the definition of the word "Hallelujah." Hallelujah is Hebrew for the Christian exclamation "Praise ye the Lord." Hallelujah is Hebrew for the Muslim exclamation "Allah is Great." For joy is ecumenical. Joy is looking up. Hallelujah in any language means joy, and joy in any language means reconnection with a power greater than ourselves.

Cross-culturally, spiritual joy is widely valued. Joy is a common accompaniment of all "white light," "near-death," and mystical experience. An Eskimo shaman writes,

> I sought solitude, and here I soon became very melancholy. I would sometimes fall to weeping and feel unhappy without knowing why. Then, for no reason, all would suddenly be changed; and I felt a great, inexplicable joy, a joy so powerful that I could not restrain it, but had to break into song, a mighty song, with only room for the one word: joy, joy! And I had to use the full strength of my voice. And then in the midst of such a fit of mysterious and overwhelming delight I became a shaman, not knowing myself how it came about. But I was a shaman. I could see and hear in a totally different way.[2]

While driving, a Western musician described a similar experience to a psychologist via a tape recorder that he happened to have in his car. "I guess I've just had the kind of experience that Saul must have had on the road to

Damascus. . . . I was just moving along and, wham, I went all goose bumps and all the hairs on my arms and legs just started standing on end, and I was just kind of full of electricity. . . . I'm starting to cry again. . . . Which is just such an amazingly joyful experience for me."

In a narrative written fifteen years after the recording was made, the same musician reminisced:

I had a mystical experience and didn't talk about it for more than 15 years. . . . All of a sudden, out of nowhere, this wave of spiritual electricity washed over me. My body and the car and the landscape and everything started turning into smaller and smaller and smaller pieces. [Such language is equally consistent with both religious experience and temporal lobe seizures.]

I can't find the words to tell you the ecstasy and the peace of those moments. . . . The message that needs to be shared is the same message that came from the thirteenth century mystics. One of them observed that the reason we can't dwell for very long in that space is that if we remained there long, the experience of the love of God would annihilate us with joy. . . . I was afraid of what people would think of me. Maybe they would think I had gone over the edge or had been converted to some New Age religion. So I just kept it to myself. What a strange thing—that we keep the most transforming experiences of our lives to ourselves because we are afraid of what people will think.[3]

⁂

Joy is not easy to talk about. Joy can feel too intense, too private for others to bear. The Victorians, before Freud, felt that way about sexual excitement. Our joy often seems private, and yet, paradoxically, joy also feels like the most intimate connection. Unlike young children and golden retrievers, grown-ups are embarrassed by strong emotion. In the case of joy this is a pity, for joy is an uplifting, a rebirth, a phoenix rising in triumph.

The Lord of life is risen today,

Sing songs of praise along the way.

Let all the earth rejoice and say "Hallelujah."

Good Christians all rejoice and sing!

Now is the triumph of our king!

—CYRIL A. ALINGTON, *"Good Christians All, Rejoice and Sing"*

Hallelujah! The apostles had thought that Christ's death would be the end of everything, and then suddenly their lives had just begun. Two thousand years later Christians still greet Easter at daybreak with joy. Similarly, more than three thousand years after the Exodus, Jews feel joy in conducting a Seder at sundown. Centuries pass, the reasons differ, but sources of joy, unlike sources of happiness, never grow stale.

Many are familiar with the American poem "Casey at the Bat." Certainly, it is well known that there was no joy in Mudville when mighty Casey struck out in the ninth inning with the bases loaded. But had Casey actually hit a home run on that fateful day, then Mudville, like the 2004 Boston Red Sox, would have triumphed. And in 2004 Boston was filled with joy—not happiness, but joy. What does triumph have to do with joy?

Joy is God's—well, somebody's—infinite generosity. No matter how old or jaded we become, we never yawn with the first crocus of spring. And if we can but pause and focus on the power and the glory and the wonder—and the triumph—of a beautiful sunset, then night too might lose its sting.

Maybe joy and triumph are connected. Maybe that is why joy, like triumph, seems dangerous. Well and good. But why do we fear triumph? Why do we fear joy? Why does the triumph in joy feel doubly perilous? We are almost all afraid that after one shining moment of joy, the ax is gonna fall. As Emily Dickinson reveals:

I can wade grief, . . .

Whole pools of it,—

I'm used to that.

But the least push of joy . . .

Breaks up my feet,
And I tip—drunken.

In the Greek myth of Icarus, the young lad has equipped himself with a splendid pair of waxen wings. When he rises up, as larks do, flying triumphantly, flying joyfully toward the sun, does not his cautious father, Daedalus, warn him that the sun will melt his wings? And so our last view of Icarus is always one of his falling, chastened, to his death. How puritanical, how sad. What a waste of joy. After all, the sun is 93 million miles away, and air grows cooler as we ascend. Flying high does not melt wax wings. It makes them stronger. It is our forbidden, triumphant joy at soaring, not any realistic danger of falling, that seems so perilous that humans perversely forbid joy to each other. If we feel too much joy, we fear that we may burst.

Joy is fundamental to human nature, but in twenty-four brilliant volumes covering almost every facet of human psychology, Sigmund Freud managed totally to ignore joy. But then, Freud also mistrusted the "oceanic" feelings of spirituality and music. Freud utterly failed to appreciate the importance of joy. He mistrusted any emotion that threatened rational cognition.

Joy happens. But joy, like the light from Moses's burning bush, seems often too overwhelming to contemplate alone. Indeed, we are told by one of the few psychoanalysts brave enough to ignore Daedalus and to discuss joy, "In terms of the specific goals of parenting, one of the parent's tasks is to facilitate the infant's experience of joy."[4] If, as Rodgers and Hammerstein suggest in *South Pacific*, "You've got to be taught to hate and fear," you also have to be taught to bear joy. The task of good parents is to be attuned to their children's joy and not hold them back.

When we remember the Israelites passing through the Red Sea dry shod, and the Red Sea closing behind them, drowning their oppressors while granting the Israelites triumph, we can all experience joy—the joy of Icarus flying in triumph toward the sun. The ax did not fall, only triumph—triumph after all seemed lost. And so for three millennia every spring the menorahs of Passover convey joy.

Ideally, triumph should never be at someone else's expense. Thus, Moses, like Lincoln, when he led other people's slaves to freedom, was not stealing; he was triumphantly returning a stolen personal freedom.

Why do I turn to Passover, to spring, to Easter hymns, to express the passion of joy? Why won't words and science do? Neuroscientists dissect the brain with care. They can—sort of—locate centers for grief, pleasure, anger, and fear. But neuroscientists have not located joy, for joy is more complex than a mere pleasure center. Joy, like love, is the comfort of attachment and of real relationships. Joy involves much more of our central nervous system than just the septal area and nucleus accumbens, which serve the pleasure of cocaine or heroin addiction, more than the hypothalamic centers motivating sex and hunger or the amygdala nuclei that ignite anger and fear. So I need music and song, the product of our integrated brain, to fully articulate joy.

However, it is far easier to talk about happiness than joy. Joy is all about connection with others; happiness is all about drive reduction for the self. Happiness allows us to run from pain, while joy, as William Blake alerts us, allows us to acknowledge suffering. Indeed, sometimes joy can let us run toward pain. Happiness is a state of mind, an intellectual appraisal, a level of satisfaction, but happiness, unless paired with excitement, is not a basic emotion, for happiness is largely cognitive. That is why social scientists and economists love happiness. Happiness is tame. In contrast, joy is a primary emotion. Joy is perceived subjectively in our viscera. Joy is connection to the universe. Happiness is giggling at a Tom and Jerry cartoon. Joy is laughing from the gut, and we often weep with joy. Happiness displaces pain. Joy encompasses pain.

Joy is spiritual; happiness is secular. There is all the difference in the world between the apostles returning to Jerusalem with great joy and, say, a celluloid Fred Astaire tap-dancing up Fifth Avenue and wishing Judy Garland a "Happy Easter." For joy is not happiness—joy is connection.

On the written page, spring offers the most powerful metaphor I know to express the phenomenon of joy. For some people, Easter is the public, unequivocal acknowledgment that the son (sun) is indeed risen, that days will be longer than nights, that Persephone will return once more from Hades, and that after winter's discontent we are loved once more by nature and by spring.

Joy is different from the excitement of a romantic tryst or an adult "happy meal" at some three-star restaurant. Joy is not a gourmet dinner, nor is joy winning the lottery. Joy is watching a parched Texas field turn green after three years of drought. We feel happiness at make-believe movies; we feel joy at reunions in real life. Excitement, sexual ecstasy, and happiness all speed up the heart; joy and cuddling slow the heart. Stimulate the primitive lateral hypothalamus and you produce excitement and arousal of the sympathetic nervous system. Stimulate the limbic septum and the parasympathetic system is aroused and the organism is calmed.[5] Mammals will work to stimulate both areas. Both eros and reunion are equally sweet, but a loving smile soothes us; flirtation excites us. One might say that joy, like love, is part of the bonding process. As the widely popular French philosopher Comte-Sponville puts it, "Love exists only as joy, and there is no joy other than love."[6] But why?

The returning human face, like the returning sun, is an innate releaser of joy. Joy is not just happiness. Joy is often reunion. Happiness and excitement are for anniversaries, like Bastille Day, the glorious Fourth, or a "surprise!" birthday party. It lasts but for a day. Joy is how our parents felt on the day we were born, for joy lingers. Unlike happiness, joy is not all about us. We feel joy when we learn that the operation on our dying child was a miraculous success.

Excitement and happiness are associated with first glimpsing the flashing, but transient, neon lights of Las Vegas or Broadway. Joy is associated with the light of an ineffable sunrise, for a sunrise is real and so are clouds turned to flame by sunset. As one writer notes, "Reckless driving, gambling, needless financial risk taking, and for some mindless violence become activities that can generate, however fleetingly, a sense of excitement that is only a pale substitute for the ability to enjoy life."[7] For both lovers and addicts, the search is exciting and is driven by dopamine and norepinephrine. For both lovers and addicts, being united with the object of the quest is calming. For the addict, the quest is rewarded by heroin from without. For the postcoital lover, the quest is rewarded by endorphins and oxytocin from within.

Happy laughter comes from the sudden, unexpected release of danger, as after any good joke. Thus, emotional happiness comes from a sudden discharge or reduction of tension. Indeed, laughter often reflects both excitement and surprise. As such, happiness does not require connection, whereas joy comes from the smile of another. Alone on a desert island, we can laugh ourselves happy watching the Marx Brothers or *Seinfeld* reruns. We feel joy—and tears—when our rescuers arrive at last. Even those of us never rescued from a desert island have all experienced tears of joy, tears of connection. As William Blake observed, "Under every grief and pine runs a joy with silken twine."

Beethoven, one suspects, knew very little of happiness, but he knew joy. In Beethoven's opera, his hero, Fidelio, escapes from prison into the bright light of day and achieves, at last, reunion with his beloved Leonora. The music of Beethoven's opera puts joy into our soul, but only because the sorrow and pain of Fidelio's imprisonment still remain in mind. Yes, joy and woe are woven fine.

Happiness is often produced by denial. When we finally notice that the clown's real mouth turns down, not up, we may feel cheated, for he was only pretending. Joy includes recognition of longing, of both coming and going, of weeping followed by reunion.

> *And it came to pass while he blessed them,*
> *He was parted from them and carried up into heaven.*
> *And they worshiped him, and returned to Jerusalem with great joy.*
>
> —LUKE 24:51–52

⁂

What is the evolutionary purpose of joy? What has allowed the emotional intensity of a Seder to endure for more than three millennia? What is the purpose of an exaltation of larks when my dying parent, or my lost child, or my Redeemer, really does return? In short, what is the purpose of a primary neural reward system dedicated to separation and return? It is probably not rocket science to suggest that loving, hardwired parental care has provided a decisive competitive edge for the survival of the children of great apes and *Homo sapiens*. Since children will wander off, a powerful reward system is needed to retrieve them from freeways and from tigers—especially if it takes ten to twenty years for them to grow up.

In short, joy is the motivational system that reinforces return. Joy, like a mother and an infant smiling, has nothing to do with drive reduction, only community. Indeed, it would be hard to imagine the creation of a healthy community without the smiling response. One of the tests of a religious community is whether its residents feel emotional incarceration or joy. When religious gatherings for tens of thousands of years have cemented human community, they have survived. Oppressive cults have much shorter lives.

> *When we've been dead ten thousand years*
> *Bright shining as the sun*
> *We've no less days to sing God's praise*
> *Then when we'd first begun.*
> —JOHN NEWTON, "Amazing Grace"

In infant development the distress cry comes first—the cry to have hunger and pain relieved and drives reduced. At two months of age, infants develop the smiling response, crude at first but by six months a charismatic magnet, elicited specifically and most powerfully by the mother's face.[8] Indeed, even at two months the infant smile is unrelated to drive reduction; it is specifically released by the joyful mutuality of eye contact. Developmentally, the child's smile, the kitten's purr, and the puppy's wagging tail emerge at the same time. These social responses are elicited by and in turn elicit positive emotion. They all occur when the infant brain's more primitive limbic system becomes effectively wired to the forebrain. Private instinct evolves into social bonding. Narcissism evolves into love. Historically, as soon as human beings were capable of becoming civilized, the dog domesticated them with a wagging tail, the kitten tamed them with a purr, and the child enslaved them with a smiling face.

But there is another reason besides reunion that natural selection supported the emotion of joy, and that is to reinforce play. In human play, happiness and joy are both involved. Limbic, rough-and-tumble play, characteristic of children in every culture, elicits both joy and happiness. Our own happy play at games of chance and our own happy flirtations are akin to our laughter at someone else's pratfall. Unempathically, our own play makes us happy. Play, however, is also all about survival. If procreation is rewarded with the fleeting feeling of orgasm, so play is rewarded by the more enduring emotion of joy. Play teaches us to tolerate risk. The infant plays peekaboo: Mother is gone, and then she returns—joy. In rough-and-tumble play, wolf cubs, small boys, and mighty Casey all play to win, but they also learn how to lose. Tribal social cohesion involves learning how to lose and how to win—gracefully. The joy of risky play is the child's reward for taking all those chances.

With play we learn how to court, to keep house, to cuddle and put our dollies to bed, and how to exercise our brain without consequences. There is so much that children have to learn. If they had to practice over and over again—without joy—learning would seem like the dullest part of school. Instead, joy helps to develop the talents we were born with. But to learn social survival skills we do not need professional teachers. Play, reinforced by joy, is quite enough. Oh, and parents and siblings help too.

While the neurophysiology of the distinct neural circuits undergirding play and the emotion of joy has not yet been clarified, there is no question that in mammals play is hardwired. The emotion used to communicate joy, laughter, is inborn, not learned. Blind and deaf children laugh readily. Reunion in chimpanzees is accompanied by sounds homologous to human laughter. As aforementioned, rodents without their neocortices can provide maternal care. Likewise, they can also still play. The limbic system is brain enough to play and to raise babies.

Rat pups, deprived of play through temporary isolation, will rush to play as soon as they get a chance.[9] Play not only enhances social bonding but depends on prior social bonding. Being tickled by or dancing with friends brings joy; being tickled by or dancing with strangers may seem painful or just drudgery. We need to feel secure before we can play.

Play depends upon a climate of positive emotion. Fear, sadness, hunger, and anger all inhibit play; so do drugs like epinephrine (adrenaline) and amphetamines that stimulate the sympathetic nervous system. Opiates and, under certain conditions, acetylcholine, the major transmitter of the parasympathetic nervous system, enhance play.[10] Testosterone—so important to fighting and sexual dominance—somewhat reduces play.

Rough-and-tumble play, hardwired in all young mammals, can be a source of true joy because it brings empathic connection. Adults no longer roughhouse, but as we grow older, rough-and-tumble play is replaced by sport, singing, and especially dancing; all are often accompanied by both joy and happiness. Rhythmic exercise becomes dancing only by the addition of two crucial ingredients—joy and another person. It takes two to tango.

Joy is also found in communal meditation. Thirteenth-century cathedrals reflect human community as few other structures can, and it is the rare visitor who does not experience joy as well as awe when entering Chartres or seeing Stonehenge for the first time. For a moment we become connected to the unifying joy of strangers worshiping together eight hundred or four thousand years ago.

৶৳

Joy is not only different from happiness. Joy is different from pleasure. The affect of joy is very different from the pleasure of sex. Joy goes beyond, far beyond, Freud's pleasure principle. Freud had confidently maintained that the purpose of human lives, as evidenced by their behavior, "can hardly be in doubt. They strive after happiness . . . this endeavor has two sides, a positive and a negative aim. It aims on the one hand, at an absence of pained displeasure, and on the other, at the experience of strong feelings of pleasure."[11] What did Freud know. The long-term truth of the matter was that Freud's moments of pleasure from chain-smoking cigars brought him years of cancer-induced, lingering pain. Yet by empathically sharing the pain of his patients, Freud found a source of contentment, and quite possibly joy, until he died. He just didn't write about it. In myth, but not in reality, psychoanalysts were not supposed to feel love for their patients or joy when the patients returned to the consulting room.

Consider the facial dance of joy that goes on between a smiling infant and the infant's mother returning the smile. First, social smiling, then peekaboo—separation and reunion. Satiation does not occur. Pleasure, like a three-course meal, usually reflects drive reduction. Once hypothalamic pleasure is achieved, we become sated. In contrast, joy, unlike coitus, does not have a refractory period. After all, a just-fed, clean-diapered, and well-slept infant can smile at her mother with contagious joy, and that smile can make the mother smile and feel joy in return. The human smiling response is hardwired. Connection, reunion, community, and joy. Joy is how "selfish" genes unselfishly share. It's win-win all the way around.

Finally, a sense of mastery, another positive emotion, is also different from joy. Mastery, like orgasm, pleasure, or happiness, is a profoundly satisfying experience. But mastery occurs only from our own efforts. Mastery is taking our first step, or riding our first ten feet on a bicycle, or getting our computer to download from the web for the first time. Our pulse speeds up. We are excited. We are empowered. Mastery, like contentment, almost always grows out of cognitive experience. When Archimedes shouted, "Eureka!" it must have been an exciting, not an oceanic, experience. Connection has nothing to do with it. All by himself, Archimedes had discovered that his body displaced its own weight in his bath.

Mastery lets me know I can. Mastery is all about me. Joy is watching our child take her first step, truly a small miracle. We had nothing to do with it, and our pulse does not accelerate. When at the close of La Traviata Alfredo and Violetta are joyfully—and tearfully—reunited, the musical tempo is very different from the excited, pounding musical tempo at the end of Bolero.

By lumping three positive emotions (contentment, excitement, and joy) together as "pleasure," Freud obscured our ability to build a satisfactory theory of affects. In a letter to Freud, the novelist Romain Rolland suggested that the "oceanic feeling" associated with joy, not a cognitive belief in God, was the true source of religion. Freud responded that he could not discover any such oceanic feeling in himself and could not convince himself of the primary nature of such a feeling.[12] "The underlying tone of Freud's discussion of religious experience is to dismiss it as some kind of regressive aberration."[13] If Freud could not acknowledge joy, no wonder he was such a pessimist. What an irony it is that in German *Freude* means joy.

Among social scientists, the Princeton psychologist Sylvan Tomkins has been the most successful in giving the affect of joy equal status as a primary emotion with grief, anger, and fear.[14] Indeed, Tomkins, a brilliant and influential student of the primary emotions, provided us with the most scientific and clinically sensitive discussion of joy that we had until Antonio Damasio. Tomkins suggests that the affect of "enjoyment-joy"—one of his nine basic affects—is very different from his affect of "interest-excitement." While excitement is easy enough to induce in oneself (through drugs, roller coasters, or skiing black diamond trails), joy is much more difficult to create alone. Tomkins points out that dynamic psychology in general and Freud in particular had each tended "to limit themselves to the ramifications of the affects of fear and anger and to the hypothalamic drives of sex and hunger."[15] Thus, Tomkins has to remind psychologists—Tomkins has to remind us all—that we cannot understand human beings unless we understand joy and how joy comes to be.

Tomkins suggests that joy often binds us to people who have first produced and then reduced pain. Certainly, without the pain of farewell there can be no joy in reunion. Without the pain of disapproval, there can be no joy in forgiveness. Without the pain of captivity, there is no joy in exodus.

Thus, just as hope, love, forgiveness, and compassion are all connected with suffering, so too is joy. Terrible things happen in life, and positive emotions do not deny them. Nevertheless, like positive emotion in general, joy can be an anodyne to suffering. Theological historian Karen Armstrong acknowledges this in her revealing autobiography:

All the world faiths put suffering at the top of their agenda. . . . If we deny our own pain, it is all too easy to dismiss the suffering of others. . . . Paradoxically, what I have gained from this identification with suffering is joy.[16]

In calling religion "the opiate of the masses," Karl Marx was as dismissive of oceanic joy as Freud. Both Freud and Marx failed to understand that opiates are what you do if you are without community—religious or otherwise. Opiates are the lonely human's autistic connection; opiates are the lonely human's religion. Freud and Marx both failed to understand that joy, the soothing process inherent in spiritual communion, is a major source of the very community building that both of them held dear. True, for the modern physician the opiate receptors in the brain are there to diminish pain, and their artificial stimulation by morphine can reproduce a fleeting oceanic sense of union akin to real joy. But as the epidemiology of heroin abuse illustrates, opiates are an ersatz comfort and appeal only to the spiritually and communally disenfranchised. C. S. Lewis points out that addictive pleasure and joy are very different from each other. They have but one thing in common: "the fact that anyone who has experienced it will want it again."[17] Joy is not a substitute for sex, but sex is very often a substitute for joy. More important, joy and pleasure differ because joy is never within our own power to induce, and addictive pleasure always is.

Tomkins goes on to suggest that implicit in Freudian theory "is a hidden—indeed rather puritan—value judgment that the early communion between mother and child is to be transcended in development." If maintained, Freud suggests, such early communion must be labeled infantile, or worse yet, perverse. Tomkins disagrees. "This we take to be a blindness to the enduring positive and universal values for human beings. It reflects a puritanical prejudice against dependency per se and an insensitivity for a type of communion in which separateness is transcended through complete mutuality."[18] Like love, compassion, and forgiveness, it is hard to distinguish deep joy from spirituality.

Many of us sneer at the idea of a clinging adult. God forbid that any adult be allowed to experience dependence on a higher power. But in truth, it is through remembrance of past clinging experiences in childhood that we experience joy in spiritual communion. "Break this bread in remembrance of me." It is the prospect of being allowed to cling—with full social approval—that leads many to feel such joy on Easter morning. It is in commemoration and reaffirmation of earlier clinging that at Easter we can receive comfort in the remembered arms of a resurrected, if metaphysical, savior.

> *And He walks with me and He talks with me*
> *And He tells me I am His own.*
> *And the joy we share as we tarry there*
> *None other has ever known.*
> —C. Austin Miles, *"In the Garden"*

Finally, why is joy so often linked to pain? Because joy is grief inside out. Consider funerals. There is no happiness at a funeral. Death takes all happiness away. But at funerals there are wakes, and at wakes there is humor, there is remembrance, and there is joy. Why? The joy at wakes comes both from the reunion with living relatives whom one has not seen for years and from remembering and celebrating the life of the departed. And so with tears of remembrance running down our cheeks, we are reunited with our remembrance of past love. And love remembered no longer lives in yesterday. Remembered love lives triumphantly today. At wakes love is often resurrected like the first crocuses of spring that triumph over snow.

> *Fields of our hearts that dead and bare have been:*
> *Love is come again, like wheat that springeth green.*
> —John Macleod Campbell Crum, *"Now the Green Blade Riseth"*

Once humans discovered that autumn harvests must begin with spring planting, "the wheat that springeth green" domesticated humans into settled communities. Always the affect of joy was associated both with the planting and with the harvest. If God did not exist, we would have had to invent Her, if only to explain our joy and gratitude as the grapes and olives were picked and the wheat threshed.

Like wheat that springeth green, joy over pain is triumphant. When Friedrich von Schiller wrote in his "Ode to Joy" the words "Brothers, beyond the stars surely dwells a loving father," his mere words do little for us. Perhaps Schiller had a kind dad. When Beethoven put Schiller's words to soaring, triumphant, oceanic music, we finally got it. Indeed, both Beethoven and Schiller were responding to pain within and beyond themselves when they created odes to joy. Before Schiller wrote his poem, he had just helped to prevent a young man's suicide. Beethoven most certainly did not have a kind dad, and his attention to joy possibly prevented his own suicide.

Beethoven had grown up the traumatized child of a physically abusive and alcoholic father. At age thirty, Beethoven, depressed and suicidal due to his increasing deafness, had written, "Oh, if I were rid of this affliction, I would embrace the world." In his diary he had cried out, "Oh Providence, grant me at least one day of pure joy—it has been so long since real joy echoed in my heart."

If his deafness got worse, Beethoven's diary had hinted he would kill himself. But the recovery of his hearing was not to be. Over the next twenty years little happened in Beethoven's life to make him happy; his deafness became total. And yet even stone-deaf, he could still believe in reunion and connection. "Be embraced, all ye millions," his chorus sings, "with a kiss for all the world. Brothers, beyond the stars surely dwells a loving father." We feel Beethoven's pain; we feel his joy. But it is so much easier to sing about joy than to talk about it.

No, there is no easy definition of joy. Go and experience it for yourself! Put this book down and listen to the last movement of Beethoven's Ninth Symphony. Perhaps then you will hear what cannot be put into words.

8

Forgiveness

༝

Without forgiveness there is no future.

—Archbishop Desmond Tutu

༝

Forgiveness is not some bleeding-heart, Sunday school platitude. Forgiveness, too, is based on mammalian evolution, realpolitik, and social Darwinism. But what exactly is forgiveness? Forgiveness is "a willingness to abandon one's right to resentment, negative judgment and indifferent behavior towards one who unjustly injured us, while fostering the undeserved qualities of compassion, generosity and even love toward him or her."[1] Surprisingly, peace of mind comes more in forgiving others than in being forgiven. A paradox.

To forgive, you have to be able to manifest two of the most recently evolved skills of *Homo sapiens*: empathy and the capacity to envision the future. Consider how in 1919 patriotic France, loving and feeling grief for over a million of her sons who had been slaughtered in their own fields by "barbaric Huns," constructed the "just" Versailles peace treaty. The treaty was designed to produce reparations for the impoverished French people and also to so weaken Germany that she could never make war again. No loving parents could do less for their own children. Nevertheless, seeking mercy for their own and vengeance toward the enemy—but no more vengeance, mind you, than justice (and retaliation for the harsh German peace terms after the 1876 Franco-Prussian War) required—led inexorably to World War II. Without the "just"—and shaming—Treaty of Versailles, it is unlikely that Hitler and the Holocaust could have occurred.

What went wrong? In pursuing justice, the Allies did not employ empathy, nor did they envision the future. The Germans, rather than sign a forced document of crippling reparations and a humiliating admission of total responsibility for the war, agreed to say that they were sorry and to send their own citizens to rebuild Belgium and France.[2] The loving and just France said, "No." Such an act of tangible reconciliation and reparation would have deprived Frenchmen of jobs. In 1919 forgiveness seemed an unaffordable luxury.

After World War II, the Marshall Plan was not remotely just, but it was both empathic and future-oriented. Compared to the Allies, the Germans had behaved much worse in World War II than they had in World War I. But General George Marshall was one of the most mature statesmen the United States has ever known. The Marshall Plan was built on the paradoxically altruistic *and* utterly selfish belief that bread cast upon the waters would return tenfold. The plan was not the product of do-gooders as much as it was a Machiavellian effort to defeat communism. But that did not matter, for as Anna Freud explains, altruism, a very mature coping strategy, "comes from the badness, not the goodness in our hearts."[3] It is enough that the Marshall Plan was empathic and envisioned the future. By forgiving and by expressing faith in the brotherhood of nations, the Marshall Plan helped to make the European Community possible.

In many ways the Marshall Plan took a line out of Lincoln's forgiving second inaugural address: "with malice toward none; with charity for all." However, the Marshall Plan was very expensive. Providing brand-new steel mills for Germany and Japan created massive unemployment in the old-fashioned steel mills of Gary, Indiana, and Pittsburgh, Pennsylvania. But forgiveness is for the future, not the present. Judged by scientific historical criteria, the Marshall Plan proved a stunning success. There has been inter-national peace in Europe for a record-breaking sixty years. If you think for-giveness is expensive, try vengeance.

In the view of the spiritually aware University of Pennsylvania neuro-radiologist Andrew Newberg, for both animals and humans "the evolution of forgiveness behavior is profitable for social groups in that it cuts off pro-gressively escalating revenge behavior."[4] In order to forgive, however, we must give up a rigid sense of self. Forgiveness allowed the Athenian patriot Aeschylus—a tough-minded writer of tragedies and veteran of the bitter Persian wars—to depict Athens and Persia as sisters. Subjectively, the ex-perience of forgiveness when it occurs is not just the emotion of being re-lieved of a burden, but also a joyful eureka sense of having solved a problem. Suddenly, the fight-or-flight response of vengeance is replaced by the calm-ing vision of green pastures and still waters of peace.

We are calmed by the vision of forgiveness, even if we are not directly involved. For example, the authority and popularity of the Dalai Lama has been enhanced by his astonishing suggestion to Americans outraged by the Chinese seizure of his homeland of Tibet: "We must pray for the Chinese." Our response to such advice is not cognitive but visceral. Against our bet-ter judgment, we are calmed. In contrast, both the security and visceral well-being of the United States and Israel have been steadily eroded by their pursuit of vengeance toward acts of terrorism without calculating the long-term consequences of such a response.

ॐ

Like hope and joy, forgiveness is another positive emotion that society has been reluctant to study. Just consider the number of law school courses that are given on criminal law, tort law, and divorce law for every course offered on forgiveness or even mediation. In psychological literature over the last century, journal titles were more than four times as likely to contain words like "revenge," "retaliation," and "retribution" than words like "forgiveness" and "forbearance."[5] Almost since its inception, psychoanalysis has been fascinated with the dynamics of shame and revenge, but psychoanalysis has to-tally ignored the dynamics of forgiveness.

So where do we begin to understand its workings? The bad news is that, like trying to be funny, the harder we cognitively try to forgive, the harder it becomes. We are not in conscious charge of forgiving or of being forgiven. Forgiveness, love, tears, and laughter cannot be commanded; they are little miracles that command.

Forgiveness imposed by religious duty increases blood pressure; forgive-ness mediated by empathy and love does not.[6] Nursing the hurt, savoring the grudge, increases blood pressure and speeds the pulse; this cardio-toxic effect is not seen when the victim empathizes with the transgressor and en-visions forgiveness.[7] Instead, the parasympathetically mediated slowing of the heart rate and lowering of blood pressure that accompany forgiveness reduce cardiac risk.[8]

Forgiveness is more emotional than cognitive. For three thousand years, the peoples of the Middle East have enjoyed excellent cognitive teaching about forgiveness. Three millennia ago, a Sanskrit maxim was forged: "Forgiveness is the ornament of the brave." Two and a half millen-nia ago, the Book of Leviticus (19:18) directed, "You shall not take ven-geance or bear a grudge against your neighbor. Love your neighbor as yourself." Two thousand years ago, a young Palestinian Jew gave us the daily reflection on forgiveness found in the Lord's Prayer, and from the cross he cried, "Father, forgive them, for they know not what they do" (Luke 23:34). Thirteen centuries ago, the wisdom of Allah as recorded in the Qur'an by Muhammad used the word *qhafara* ("pardon/atone") 234 times.[9] Neverthe-less, for the last half a century, in Palestine and in Israel, such wise advice has been ignored. Every time an innocent victim has died in the Israeli-Palestinian conflict, the other side has tried to collect an uncollectible debt by killing yet another innocent victim. However, we all have trouble with forgiveness; let us look in the mirror before we cast stones.

Tragically, too often it is oppressive parents who try to extract apologies from rebellious children instead of the other way around. All of us some-times forget that it is especially hard for the weak to forgive until the pow-erful have said they are sorry. Not until the twentieth century, when three heroic, colonially abused young men—Mohandas Gandhi, Martin Luther King Jr., and Nelson Mandela—modeled forgiveness did the powerful finally get it. Recently, a Christian pope, John Paul II, could apologize to Africans for the Church's role in slavery, to Jews for the Church's role in fifteen hundred years of persecution, and to the Islamic world for the Crusades.[10] And yet there are still those who criticize Pope John Paul II for letting down the side. In the past being powerful meant never having to say that you were sorry.

Forgiveness is a function of cultural maturity. Indeed, it is only toward the end of the twentieth century that the examples set by Gandhi, King, and Mandela allowed forgiveness to capture the attention of social science. Only in the last two decades have there been research studies affirming the long-range practicality of forgiveness. And we still have great difficulty formulating how to make forgiveness happen.

For example, nineteenth-century Christians in England and America paid lip service to forgiveness on Sunday mornings, but during the rest of the week they could not even forgive victims, let alone transgressors. Citizens were legally hanged for attempted suicide. Victims of rape were condemned for seductiveness. In the United States, a nation dedicated to the preservation of individual liberty, slaves who tried to escape to freedom were mutilated rather than applauded. More self-defeating still was the fact that whenever Christian nineteenth-century creditors wreaked vengeance on debtors by imprisoning them, they were guaranteeing that reparation could not take place.

The evolution of forgiveness has taken a long time. Forgiveness began with the evolution of the unique mammalian capacity to play and to nurture young. The mammalian world is filled with gestures of appeasement to deflect vengeance, but at the same time mammalian play is filled with minor injuries accepted with good humor. You can pull a puppy's tail, but not a rattlesnake's. In rough-and-tumble games throughout the animal kingdom, and in mother-pup relationships, forgiveness is hardwired. Forgiveness produces an upsurge of warm feelings for the forgiver, and as the Marshall Plan illustrated, the very hard work of atonement and pardon is contagious and binds up the wounds of families and the wounds of nations. Some even believe that it was the "blood of the martyrs" (the early Christians suffering and forgiving their tormentors) that catalyzed the rapid spread of Christianity in the third and fourth centuries CE.

However, in play and in raising infants, you are likely to feel a little bit safe. Suppose, however, you do not feel safe. How is forgiveness possible then? Now we come to the sticking point. The outside world is often very dangerous, and forgiveness practiced as a means of social policy, however practical, remains very difficult. Abraham Lincoln and General George Marshall were dealing with thoroughly defeated, and closely related, adversaries. They both felt pretty safe. In contrast, Donald Rumsfeld and Osama bin Laden both made the other side feel very unsafe, and they both felt very unsafe themselves.

In adolescent youth and in adolescent nations, vengeance is necessary to promote identity formation. Allegiance to the faulty math of zero-sum games strengthens the sense of self and, by extension, the morale of every football team. If they lose, we win. Why play if you don't keep score? Identity and winning are important. Nevertheless, our capacity for forgiveness goes steadily up as we mature, and the importance of winning and being terminally unique declines.[11] The wise and forgiving middle-aged Nelson Mandela who left Robben Island after three decades of imprisonment was not the same feisty, vengeful youth who had entered.[12] The difference that age brought to Mandela was that when he entered prison he was bent upon setting his people free. When Mandela left prison, he was dedicated to setting both his people and their oppressors free.

In old age we must all make peace with the world, however unjust. Eventually, we must learn to surrender the right to get even, lest the sins of the father become the legacy of the children. Thus, the transformative miracle of forgiveness is more likely to occur with maturity. At least two studies have demonstrated that forgiveness increases steadily from age three to age ninety.[13]

We might remember the forgiving words of Malcolm Fraser, a wise former prime minister of Australia. On Australia's Sorry Day, for the first time in history, a nation publicly apologized for the genocidal behavior of its ancestors. Empathically, Fraser pointed out that "the current government is unwilling to apologize, believing that it carries with it a connotation of guilt, and because this generation of Australians is not guilty of what was done in earlier times. Of course it is not. But an apology in its broadest sense does not carry any connotation of guilt; it means I regret what happened. It should not have occurred; it was wrong."[14] Those whose acts we condemn have often lived in a different time from us, in a different maturational space, and with different ideas.

ध्रे

In order to better understand the positive emotion of forgiveness, psychology, religion, political science, and humanity in general must ask, and then answer, four crucial questions. First, what goes on in the heart and mind of the wounded person during trespass, and then what happens during the transformative act of forgiveness? Second, does forgiveness depend on the person, on the situation, or on the facilitation of forgiveness by a healer? Third, when and under what conditions is it helpful to revisit the experiences that occurred during traumatic trespass in order to promote forgiveness?[15] Fourth, what are the psychological ingredients that make successful reconciliation and forgiveness possible?

Before addressing these four questions, let me identify six things that forgiveness does not mean. First, forgiveness does *not* mean toleration of wrongdoing. The forgiving know no hatred of any man, yet their indictment of injustice can be ferocious.[16] There is a critical difference, however, between anger at trespass and vengeance. Anger at trespass can be highly adaptive. Israel's assertive victory in the Six Days' War was lifesaving. But thus far Israel's efforts to avenge each and every suicide bombing have only increased the likelihood that yet another will occur. Second, to forgive does *not* mean to forget. We must remember that hot stoves are dangerous. Museums of the Holocaust are valuable. Third, to forgive is *not* to surrender our right to justice; wise justice, however, remembers that two wrongs do not make a right. Fourth, forgiveness does *not* remove pain that is past. Forgiveness only removes pain in the future. Fifth, forgiveness does *not* mean we excuse the wrongdoer, only that pardon provides a chance for the wrong-doer's behavior—and, sometimes, our own pain—to improve in the future. In 1919 the Germans should have been allowed to rebuild France. By way of comparison, the long-term effects of Germany paying voluntary repara-tions to Israel have turned out far better than many people expected. Fi-nally, forgiveness does *not* mean that we encourage repetition. Indeed, there is a place for punishment, but we cannot acquire a scientific understanding of its efficacy without long-term follow-up. Enforcement of traffic fines *does* reduce inconsiderate parking. But in the United States there is scant evi-dence that draconian mandatory sentences for drug sales reduce either drug sales or narcotic addiction.

డిఓ

My first question was: what goes on during trespass in the hearts and minds of the wounded victim and the perpetrator? To answer this question, let me again use examples from my own life. I was three years old and a perpetra-tor. Climbing the stairs, I carelessly banged my knee against the banisters. In pain and with unmitigated and unrepented evil, I took the hanger I was holding and struck an innocent passerby, my mother, on the head. Vengeance is mine, saith the three-year-old. To angry bombers the venge-ful destruction of Dresden in 1945 or the World Trade Center towers in 2001 could not have felt sweeter.

I was in pain, and somebody else should jolly well pay. Striking my mother felt wonderful. My mother understood. The mirror cells of her in-sula and anterior cingulate allowed her to comprehend my pain and my primitive nervous system. Thus, she forgave me. Besides, her frontal lobes helped her to think into the future. What would punishment have accom-plished?

In the next example, I was the innocent victim. At the end of a lecture to undergraduates, a student verbally assaulted me. Angrily, she complained of a B-minus on her hour exam. I hated her. She had received an honor grade, and it counted for only 20 percent of her final grade. Besides, there were other more worthy students waiting to ask their important professor important questions about his important lecture. I was twisted inside with righteous, self-centered indignation. Projecting, I condemned her silently as a narcissistic twit. But as a physician, I had been trained to take the cotton out of my ears and put it in my mouth. So, despite my reptilian rage, I listened to her next sentence. "This morning I was turned down by my fourteenth medical school." Suddenly, by understanding her pain, I forgave her. Empathy replaced paranoia. Suddenly, it was all about her, not me. By forgiving her, the twists left my insides. My inner transformation was analogous to the well-known psychology book illustration of the ugly old hag who, through an abrupt shift in the viewer's gestalt, becomes transformed into a delicate young woman. Forgiveness is like that. I got the same endorphin rush that we saw in chapter 2 accompanies generous giving.

৩৪

Let me now address the second question: does forgiveness depend on the situation, the person, or the healer? Sometimes the situation is all-important. The situation was very important in facilitating the Marshall Plan. After the war America needed Japan and Germany as allies. Besides, for America, in 1946 forgiving Germany was easier than forgiving had been for France in 1919. World War II was ultimately fought on German, not American, soil. American civilians had not suffered, and many American soldiers were of German ancestry. Germany had not defeated America forty years earlier. For Americans, vengeance would have been far less sweet than it was for the French in 1919.

Forgiveness means replacing projection with personal responsibility. It was easier for Americans to observe, in the words of Pogo, Walt Kelly's famous cartoon possum, "We have met the enemy and they are us." Also in 1947 Americans were safer than the French were in 1919. The United States had the atomic bomb.

In effecting forgiveness, the individual is as important as the situation. On January 30, 1956, Martin Luther King Jr.'s house in Montgomery, Alabama, was bombed. His wife Coretta described what happened next.

> The situation outside the house was tense and dangerous. Many were armed; even the little boys had broken bottles. . . . At that point Martin walked out on the porch. His own home had just been bombed, his wife and baby could have been killed. . . . He held up his hand, and they were suddenly silent—the crowd of angry men and women, of excited children and sullen frightened policemen—all were absolutely still. In a calm voice Martin said, "My wife and my baby are all right. I want you to go home and put down your weapons. . . . We must love our white brothers, no matter what they do to us. . . . We must meet hate with love. . . ."
>
> After that the crowd began to thin out, and the people went back to their homes. A white policeman's voice was heard in the crowd saying, "If it hadn't been for that nigger preacher, we'd all be dead."[17]

Due to a single deeply spiritual individual, a transformative miracle had taken place—one that included faith, hope, and love. One that depended on both the forgiver and the forgiven understanding past, present, and future. Always, revenge is rooted only in the past. Perhaps one reason that prayer is so important to forgiveness is that prayer helps to root us in the future. We know better than to pray over spilled milk.

This vignette illustrates two important transformative facets of forgiveness. First, forgiveness can be achieved by deep meditation and prayer. Andrew Newberg has found that in deep meditation the boundaries between self and the universe are erased in favor of a subjective sense of union with the other.[18]

The second transformative facet of forgiveness is that it is contagious. If the vengeance of the Treaty of Versailles begot still greater vengeance in the Germans, just so the loving positive emotion of King's forgiveness evoked gratitude and warm feelings—even empathy—in his "redneck" adversaries. I suspect that forgiveness survives as a sociobiological tendency in our species because of the lives it saves.

Contrast the provocative, dangerous behavior of Ariel Sharon when, shortly before being elected prime minister of Israel, he insisted in 2000 on visiting the Muslim Temple Mount in Jerusalem, and the vengeful response of the Hamas organization that ended the nascent peace process, to the behavior of two other individual Palestinians. In 1948 a Jewish refugee family was assigned a house with a lovely garden in Ramalah, a town near Tel Aviv. They were told that the property had been abandoned. Twenty years later, after the Six Days' War, its former owner, Bashir, appeared at the door. He informed them that his family had not abandoned the house. Rather, in 1948 they had been forcibly deported to Gaza. Later, Palestinian Bashir took part in a bomb attack that killed several Jewish civilians. Bashir was imprisoned for fifteen years. In 1985, when Bashir was released, the owners sought him out and offered to sell their house and give him the money— not to try to effect justice but to acknowledge suffering. "I don't want the money," said Bashir. "I would like to see the property turned into a kindergarten for Arab children, so they can enjoy the childhood I could not have."[19] In 1991 the house became the first Jewish-Arab cultural center in Ramalah and a summer peace camp for one hundred Arab and Jewish children. It is the only such center in Ramalah where Arab children are taught in Arabic.

Since we cannot collect bad debts, personal relief often lies only in creative forgiveness. And since in so many tragedies—as in World War I and in Palestine—who is the victim and who is the transgressor is unclear, it always helps if forgiveness is a two-way street.

ॐ

My next anecdote illustrates the importance of the healer in forgiveness and addresses the third question: when is it safe to facilitate forgiving transformation in a victim and address the painful past? Answer: only when the victim, like Coleridge's Ancient Mariner, wants to tell his story—and then slowly. Harvard psychiatrist and trauma specialist Judith Herman cautions us that the listener must act as a witness or midwife to the memory of the transgression.[20] The listener must not, as happens too often, try to be a rescuer or, after a rejected rescue, become yet another victim. Not only must the witness offer empathy, but often the witness must share responsibility for bearing the burden of the pain.

As we saw in the last chapter, Eugene O'Neill grew up as a severely neglected child with an often absent, alcohol-abusing father and an opiate-dependent mother. For years O'Neill sought vengeance. His high school principal had predicted that the angry young O'Neill would die in the electric chair—not win a Nobel Prize. As a young adult, O'Neill vengefully chopped off the legs of his mother's furniture with a machete, and he grossly neglected his own children.[21] Vengeance is mine, saith the three-year-old.

The seeds of O'Neill's forgiveness toward his family were not sown until twenty years later, for to forgive we often need a witness to our pain. At that time, for six weeks, O'Neill saw a "research psychoanalyst," Gilbert Hamilton, who was studying marriage. During those six weeks Dr. Hamilton served O'Neill as a willing witness, and O'Neill learned how to talk about and remember the truth about himself. During these six weeks he made the autobiographical notes that fifteen years later would provide the outline for his great and forgiving play Long Day's Journey into Night. As I have already suggested, forgiveness does not happen overnight. In O'Neill's case it took thirty-five years.

More than ten years later, as he finally began to write Long Day's Journey into Night, O'Neill experienced no less pain than when he told his life story first to Hamilton and later to his wife Carlotta, but now, after years of incubation, there was greater resolution. Carlotta recalled O'Neill's agony while writing and remembering. "At times I thought he'd go mad. It was terrifying to watch his suffering."[22]

In 1940, as an anniversary present, O'Neill dedicated Long Day's Journey to Carlotta, his witness:

Dearest: I give you the original script of this play of old sorrow, written in tears and blood. A sadly inappropriate gift, it would seem, for a day celebrating happiness. But you will understand. I mean it as a tribute to your love and tenderness which gave me the faith in love that enabled me to face my dead at last and write this play—write it with deep pity and understanding and forgiveness for all the four haunted Tyrones.[23]

Sometimes a third party or a therapist is crucial. The third party, as in Alcoholics Anonymous, can share personal experience, or a therapist can serve as a witness, or a reconciliation team can serve as a neutral mediator. Since justice is often not possible, the third party can also help the victim to mourn what cannot be restored. Good tort lawyers often make things worse, for a $1 million settlement can hardly make up for the loss of a child to a terrorist or a drunk driver. Healing occurs only through forgiveness.

۞

My fourth and final question is: what are the psychological ingredients that make possible successful reconciliation and forgiveness? Instilling faith, hope, love, and joy in victims is often beyond our reach, but we can try to be facilitators of their acts of forgiveness. If we are to facilitate this process, however, we need to understand the dynamics of forgiveness.

First, we must realize that to take away the prospect of vengeance from the recently wounded is as fruitless as snatching a pack of Camels out of the hands of an active smoker. Indeed, vengeance is so delicious that sometimes an act of forgiveness can be perverted to do revenge's bidding. Too rapid, too superficial forgiveness may reflect an aggressive need to dominate through moral superiority. The witty, but not always charitable, Oscar Wilde advised, "Always forgive your enemies. Nothing annoys them so much." Before real forgiveness is possible, both observer and perpetrator must go way down to feel the depth of the pain.

Vengeance, like smoking, gambling, and eating too much chocolate, always feels good at the time. Regret comes later. At the beginning, therapeutic intervention must be to redirect rage away from the perpetrator, usually kept out of range, and toward the empowerment of the victim, for from an evolutionary standpoint anger, like other passions, is an asset to survival. Thus, castration of the rapist is rarely possible or even helpful, but joining an angry "Take Back the Night" march and helping other rape victims to assert themselves in a court of law are often both possible and salutary. To be most effective the anger must be harnessed to serve the future and to empower the victim, not to immolate the perpetrator. In AA, to help a sponsee abandon suffocating resentments for the fresh air of forgiveness, the sponsor may advise, "I guess there is nothing left to do but pray for the son-of-a-bitch!"

Forgiveness involves a still deeper issue than forgiving bad debts.[24] When we are trespassed upon, we feel shame as well as violation. We feel shame at having been at the mercy of another's power. If that person will not relinquish that power by making some apology and reparations, we must attack. Shame, of course, is even more painful than trespass, and we protect ourselves against shame by rage, righteousness, and seizing power. Thus, another form of vengeance is to invoke Talion (an eye for an eye and a tooth for a tooth) law and shame the transgressor. And again, such shaming only evokes further retaliation. Seeking revenge, rage, righteousness, and power are all good defenses, but such defenses are neither empathic nor future-oriented.

Always, forgiveness must be shown and not told. The psychodynamics of forgiveness and reconciliation are better gained from witnessing acts of forgiveness than from reading books. A recent study found that informal therapeutic groups, such as prayer groups, self-help groups, and men's and women's groups, led to increased forgiveness in 61 percent of 1,379 individuals.[25] To facilitate the delicate process of reparation, reconciliation, and forgiveness in alcoholic families, family therapists will learn much from attending multiple open meetings of Al-Anon (twelve-step groups for the relatives of alcoholics). And perhaps the training of every psychotherapist and mediator should include a careful study of South Africa's Truth and Reconciliation Commission. The goals of that commission were fourfold: (1) seeking the truth about what happened, not denial; (2) restoring human and civil dignity to the victims; (3) striving for understanding and forgiveness—not punishment—of the perpetrator; and (4) seeking reparation from, not vengeance against, the perpetrator. By focusing on patients' past grief and anger, psychotherapists, like me, often inadvertently foster the emotions of resentment and self-pity—the enemies of forgiveness. In our rush not to be Pollyannas, we forget that by helping our clients rehearse the emotions of gratitude and forgiveness, we might provide exercises that could lead to liberation from an emotional prison whose four affective walls are envy, jealousy, resentment, and revenge.

ॐ

Always, such a shift in attention relieves pain. With chronic resentment comes injustice collecting, paranoia, profound unhappiness, unpopularity, and twisted guts. With forgiveness comes empathy, altruism, future-mindedness, gratitude, and peace of mind. Forgiveness, an emotion with humble roots in mammalian play and in the evolution of social cooperation, has evolved to inspire awe in all of us. The wonder is that it took Gandhi, King, and Mandela to draw forgiveness to our scientific attention.

The relief of guilt is not the only point in seeking forgiveness. Guilt is rooted in the past; forgiveness is in the future. Joy does not just come when we feel that others forgive us. Rather more important, the greatest joy of forgiveness comes when we forgive the other. Only then are we freed from the oppressive swamp of resentment and from the painful bile that burns our insides as we thirst for revenge. Always, forgiveness shifts attention from the personal to the awesome.

As is clear from the examples I have chosen, the transformation of vengeance into forgiveness is a slow process. It cannot be rushed. As is true for relief from any addiction, appeal to the victim's spirituality helps, but temporary relapse into bitterness is common.

Nevertheless, it is well to remember that forgiveness is possible even for those who lived under far less forgivable regimes than the oppressive colonial democracies experienced by Gandhi, King, and Mandela. In 1945 a scrap of paper was found in the Ravensbrück concentration camp. It contained a prayer:

> O Lord
> Remember not only the men and women of good will,
> But all those of ill will.
> But do not remember all the suffering
> They have inflicted upon us;
> Remember the fruits we have bought
> Thanks to this suffering—
> Our comradeship, our loyalty, our humility,
> Our courage, our generosity, the greatness of heart
> Which has grown out of all this;
> And when they come to judgment,
> Let all the fruits we have borne
> Be their forgiveness.[26]

9

Compassion

۞

Basic human nature is compassionate.

—Dalai Lama

۞

In the academic world, respectable careers are to be made in the fields of glorifying "selfish" genes, studying depression in ever greater detail, and deconstructing tender literature. In such a world, the scientific study of compassion is very new. Indeed, sometimes academics have as much trouble with compassion as they do with love and joy. In a dialogue with the Dalai Lama, Anne Harrington, a Harvard professor of the history of science, provocatively led her witness: "I am struck by the fact that historically the more deeply our sciences have probed reality, the less relevant concepts like 'compassion' become."[1] In response to her tongue-in-cheek question, the Dalai Lama, himself a persecuted refugee and a victim of colonial oppression, countered, "When I say that I believe human nature to be fundamentally good and compassionate, I base this belief on empirical observation."

I would heartily agree. The empathic human response to pain and its accompanying positive emotion, compassion, do not have to be taught. We have evolved to be compassionate. Unlike the evangelical church pastor and bestselling author Rick Warren, I do not presume to know who God is. But we have both arrived at rather similar conclusions that love and compassion come not from free choice. Warren writes: "God was thinking of you long before you ever thought about Him. He planned it before you existed, without your input. You may choose your career, your spouse, your hobbies and many other parts of your life, but you don't get to choose your purpose."[2] I would express the involuntary nature of compassion only slightly differently. The generous offers of help that accompanied the World Trade Center catastrophe on September 11, 2001, and the flooding of New Orleans after Hurricane Katrina in 2005 did not just reflect free will but are part of our psychobiologic makeup. In the last decade, for the first time in history, disasters in hitherto unknown locations on the globe have evoked compassionate response from the entire world. Today prosperous nations now almost universally worry about tidal waves in remote Ache, famine in remote Niger, and earthquakes in remote areas of Pakistan.

This book asserts that both biological and cultural evolution have brought nonrelatives—not just siblings—together to help each other and help transform a dangerous, tribal, clannish world into a safer, unitary hive. But why now? Clearly, for most of the last two thousand years cultural memes espousing unselfish love have not been enough. But over the last several decades cultural evolution, assisted by greater safety in the First and Second Worlds, has reduced, although not eliminated, the survival value of negative emotions among nations. Through increased longevity, democracy, sexual equality, and literacy, and through advances in public health, communication, and food production, opportunities for expressing the future-oriented positive emotions have increased. Such increased safety has allowed humanity to pay attention to the spirit rather than just to the compassionate words of the world's great religions. Despite headlines emphasizing conflict, the world's populations have become more compassionate toward each other. For example, a fact left out of the news in the United States was that, after the 2001 destruction of the twin towers in New York, hundreds of thousands of Iranians demonstrated in Teheran to declare that such a wanton act of terrorism was incompatible with Islamic principles.

However, headline writers prefer bad news, and thus the negative, suicidal anger of twenty Islamic extremists trumped American awareness of the compassion of hundreds of thousands of our alleged enemies. Nevertheless, the distortions of yellow journalism and of power politics do not disprove the Dalai Lama's assertion that humans are basically compassionate.

If we are hardwired to find danger more interesting in our newspapers than loving-kindness, we are still hardwired for public compassion when society offers us the chance. To facilitate infant survival, genetic evolution has created in humans the impulse to separate kinfolk from their pain. Cultural evolution and the maturation of Piagetian formal operations during adult development have generalized this impulse to help strangers survive. However, it is a pity that the impulse of one person to comfort another is studied less than almost any other major topic in general science.

⚜

Let me first define compassion and then discuss the evolution of compassion in human beings. Compassion, like love, is a hallmark of all the world's great religions. But love and compassion are very different. Love is the desire to join with someone who is appealing; compassion is the desire to separate someone, even if unappealing, from his suffering. Few enjoy receiving the sympathy and pity that come from being loved as much as they do the empathy that comes from receiving compassion and that allows us to feel seen. If it is a blessing to be loved, it is also a blessing to be "seen," a blessing that derives from the evolution of primate mirror neurons as much as from anywhere else.

For a couple of decades "mirror neurons" have been identified in primates but not in other mammals. Mirror neurons are thought to facilitate the phenomenon of learning behavior by observation rather than by motor rehearsal. This phenomenon is commonly referred to as "monkey see, monkey do." Even more recently, in 2004, neuroimaging by fMRI in humans revealed that mirror neurons might serve another purpose besides facilitating social imitation. While witnessing a loved one's pain, the mirror neurons arouse our own limbic emotional centers for pain so that we can literally feel another's pain. However, our neocortical analytical centers, which would make us flinch were the pain our own, are not aroused. Put differently, when witnessing another person burning his hand, the mirror neurons in our own limbic insula and anterior cingulate "light up" on the neuroimagist's screen as if the burned hand were our own. But the cells in our neocortical motor centers (for example, "I feel a burning in my left hand that prompts me to pull it away") remain quiescent.[3] Of equal interest is that the degree of heightened mirror cell brain activation in one individual while witnessing another's pain correlates significantly with the same individual's scores on pencil-and-paper tests that assess empathy.[4] Thus, the mirror neuron network integrating the insula to the rest of the limbic system appears to be one key to emotional intelligence.

Love and compassion are different. Love is based on attachment, and so the loss of the loved one produces the very self-absorbed suffering and grief from which the Buddha tried to protect us by teaching detachment. Snatch a loved object away from its lover, be it a toddler's lollipop, a mother bear's cub, or a patriot's freedom, and the result is a flood of all-about-me negative emotion and protest, anger, grief, and terror. The loss of a loved one, no matter how unselfishly loved, produces pain and self-absorption. That is how the brain is wired. In contrast, the "pain" of compassion, based on empathy and not sympathy, focuses us inexorably on the other. Compassion and empathy allow us to hold the other benevolently in mind and even to run toward another's suffering.

A caricature of the difference between love and compassion can be illustrated by the following thought experiment. Imagine yourself on a bicycle. A passing car sideswipes you and throws you from your bike. Your leg is badly broken. Who do you hope will be in the next car to come along, your mother or a paramedic? Both would "feel your pain." But fueled by her great love, your mother would be immobilized by her pity, her sympathy, and her own pain. In contrast, the paramedic would empathically understand your suffering and would then dispassionately splint your fractured leg so that you could be moved with the least pain. The paramedic would accurately "see" your fracture and "know" the procedures that would protect you from needless further pain. It would not diminish the paramedic's compassion that he had already attended to three other accidents that morning. It would not matter that his professional compassion was "paid." Perhaps he passionately serves others not only to make a living but also in part to escape his own suffering resulting from his wife having been killed the year before by a drunken driver. Compassion, like love and forgiveness, benefits the giver and receiver equally. Compassion, like love and hope, is a good biological trick.

The grieving widow does not wish for a sympathy card per se as much as empathic sentiments like, "I remember your husband's gift for making people laugh," or, "It would give me great pleasure if I could look after your garden for the next two weeks." Psychoanalysts, fortune-tellers, shamans, and hypnotists are all healers in part because not only do they care for and make us feel like the focus of attention, but their empathy makes us marvel that someone can read our minds. We all wish to be "seen" and not pitied.

But it is not enough to feel another's pain. To feel compassion is not only to resonate with another's pain but to do something about it. My three-year-old granddaughter was weeping for reasons that her mother and I dismissed as self-absorption. Nevertheless, her one-year-old sister rushed to comfort her. My one-year-old granddaughter did not keen, "I feel your pain"; instead, she threw her arms around her sister. In his empathic play, Aeschylus so crafted his compassion for the Persians that other Athenians could resonate with it and could clap, not jeer him, when he called Athens and Persia sisters.

I know the bright young grandson of fundamentalist Christian missionaries to India. In the 1970s he had traveled himself to India so that he could rid himself of his grandparents' rigid dogma and become a Hindu. Five years passed, and he found himself on a hilltop in Central America meditating and praying for the villagers on the next hill, who were being shelled by the reigning dictator's military forces. Suddenly he had an aha! insight and recognized that his prayers, however loving and unselfish, were accomplishing nothing. Almost immediately, he returned home. With conviction, compassion, and foresight, he went first to law school, then briefly to Wall Street to finance his future. Then he returned home to work in the public sector. He won office by an astonishingly wide margin, and for years he has served idealistically, but effectively, in his home community. Real compassion leads to action, not just prayer.

⁂

Besides mirror cells, another source of empathy is the so-called mature involuntary coping mechanisms written about in the diagnostic manual of the American Psychiatric Association, *The DSM-IV*. Human beings deploy a variety of coping mechanisms—some healthy and some not so healthy—as inborn aids to self-soothing and resilience.[5] The neurobiology of these mechanisms, sometimes called ego mechanisms of defense, is unknown, but we do know that these mechanisms are not under conscious control. On the one hand, the misfits, those with "character disorders," the jerks and the villains of history, have tried to adapt to life's difficulties with narcissistic, unempathic, and involuntary mechanisms like projection: the test was unfair; the devil made me do it; my misery is all your fault. Another such mechanism is autistic fantasy: I can love only what I see in the mirror; I want a paper doll that I can call my own; I feel safe only when I play by myself. A third such self-absorbed defense is the tantrum: hissy fits and violent acts that create self-satisfying "shock and awe." Still another mechanism is dissociation (sometimes called neurotic denial). For example, Scarlett O'Hara's "I'll think about it tomorrow," *Mad* magazine's Alfred E. Neuman's "What, me worry?" and Louis XV's "Après nous le déluge" are all self-centered solutions that work fine over the short term but are profoundly annoying to others and, in my own prospective study of human lifetimes, have proved disastrous to adaptation over the long term.[6]

In sharp contrast to these mechanisms are the empathic, but equally involuntary, mature coping mechanisms that, like compassion and empathy, are essential to human resilience. The most self-evident of these involuntary mechanisms is altruism: the Golden Rule, for example, or "Ask not what your country can do for you; ask what you can do for your country." The second involuntary mechanism is humor: the deeply unhappy Marilyn

Monroe, Charlie Chaplin, and Woody Allen empathically facilitated laughter in others. Humor involves not taking ourselves too damn seriously and also gauging the other's state of mind with precision. Without empathy, the comedian becomes a jerk.

A third adaptive involuntary coping mechanism is sublimation. Artists are artists, and not just doodlers, because they can empathically understand that beauty is in the eye of the beholder, not just their own, and that truth, not self-comforting delusion, is beauty. Ludwig von Beethoven and Eugene O'Neill alleviated their own misery by transmuting it into exactly what a waiting world wished to hear and see. The men and women who deploy the largely involuntary compassionate and empathic coping mechanisms of humor, altruism, and sublimation enjoy far happier lives than those who deploy the less mature and more self-centered coping mechanisms.[7] But when asked for the causes of their behavior, the experts at empathy and the exemplars of compassion explain that they do not act through conscious, morally reasoned planning, "but because to do anything else would be impossible."[8] They often remain unconscious that they once suffered the very pain they are trying to relieve. Such transformations of human pain into empathic connection reflect human neurobiology at its most glorious.

Like forgiveness and love, compassion cannot be commanded; fortunately, compassion commands. Involuntarily, our empathy and compassion are aroused by an infant's separation cry. The iconic photograph of a naked little girl, hideously burned by American napalm, screaming and running in isolated terror along a Vietnam street, may have done as much to turn Americans against the Vietnam War as any fifty editorials. Who would not selflessly respond to an abandoned child by the side of the road? You see, Darwinian evolution intends us all to be Samaritans.

Healing as a vocation has traditionally relied on compassion as a guiding principle. In the sixteenth century Paracelsus wrote, "The true physician is known by his compassion and by his love for his neighbor. The art of medicine is rooted in the heart. . . . No one requires greater love of the heart than the physician." But although Paracelsus might not have admitted it, he was writing about all healers, not just about my-son-the-doctor. Mothers, nurses, and little girls caring for orphan baby birds are all "true physicians." And he was using "love" to mean *compassion*, not *attachment*.

Compassion also facilitates cure. Placebos have no direct power except through past trust in mothers and doctors and the time-present experience of another's compassion, both of which are biologically active. Indeed, a promise of cure in which we have faith may bring more comfort than a scientific cure against our will or one with which we do not comply. Despite doctor's orders, very few patients take all the pills prescribed to them in the time allotted. However, they are more conscientious if they believe that their doctor cares. Thus, empathy, even if it does not cure, still facilitates, through increased compliance, the power of science to cure. Or as Yale professor of medicine Howard Spiro asserts, "The placebo effect affirms the power of community, the miracle that one person can help another simply by trying."[9]

Placebos, like compassion, epitomize the power of human relationship. I once asked an AA member what he did when he got the urge to drink alcohol. He said, "When you walk into the phone booth, put a quarter in the slot, and call your sponsor, you know you're not going to drink." With his quarter came community and with community came compassion and a shield against relapse. He had an abiding faith that somebody else would care.

Very recent neuroscience has provided evidence to support my armchair assertions. Compassionate gentle touch releases endorphins, our brains' endogenous opiates. Placebos often do the same. Thus, compassion relieves suffering with pharmacology as well as with care. In Parkinson's disease, an illness long known to be responsive to placebo administration, there is in vivo evidence that placebos release substantial quantities of dopamine.[10]

Dopamine is the neurotransmitter whose relative absence causes the pathology in parkinsonism.

In 2005 Rachel Bachner-Melman and her colleagues reported on a study of 354 families. A questionnaire measuring "the propensity to ignore one's own needs and serve the needs of others" correlated with the presence of dopaminergic gene variants consistent with their hypothesis that "the genetic architecture of altruism in humans is partly built from genes that drive an altruistic behavioral pattern regardless of kin considerations."[11] As noted earlier, the very dopaminergic brain assemblies that the drug addict short-circuits to obtain a transient high probably evolved to make prosocial behavior rewarding.

In 2006, only a year later, neuroscientist Jorge Moll and his colleagues at the National Institute of Neurological Disorders studied the neurophysiology of those making charitable donations and supported this hypothesis.[12] Their fMRI study brought much of the recent brain research on both altruism and attachment into a coherent perspective. In a series of ingenious experiments, the investigators examined the brain function of nineteen subjects making decisions about whether to donate significant sums of money provided by the experimenters to organizations of which the subjects approved or whether to keep the money for themselves.

The mesolimbic, dopaminergic reward system (popularized by recent studies of drug addiction) is activated by seeking sex, drugs, food, and money. These same centers were activated when Moll's subjects made a charitable donation at the expense of their own pocketbooks. In other words, our brains are designed to obtain pleasure from caring for unrelated others as well as for ourselves. In addition, the same giving behavior activated the *Homo sapiens* anterior prefrontal cortex, especially when the altruistic choice prevailed over the selfish choice. This is the same ventromedial prefrontal cortex that, when obliterated in Phineas Gage by the famous tamping rod, also destroyed his capacity for tact, tender feelings, social embarrassment, and compassion.[13] This is the same paralimbic mammalian cortex that is "primitive" (only four layers) in contrast to the more recently evolved, six-layered neocortex of *Homo sapiens*.

Moll and his colleagues speculate that the linking of the uniquely

human anterior frontal cortex with the more primitive mammalian limbic reward system "might have emerged through similar gene-culture co-
evolution mechanisms."[14] Combine these findings with the greater number
of spindle cells mediating a sense of fairness in humans and the fact that
oxytocin induces trust in investors (chapter 5), and we begin to have a coherent case for prosocial compassionate evolution.

ॐ

Over the last 200 million years, the genetic evolution of the human hypothalamus, with its capacity for the four Fs—fight, flight, feeding, and fornication—has rendered our selfish "drives" only modestly more sophisticated
than an alligator's. Human capacity for negative emotions like fear, disgust,
and rage has probably not evolved much beyond that of a cornered rat. In
contrast, our capacity for the future-oriented positive emotions, like altruistic responses to the suffering of strangers and compassion, continues to
evolve. Human beings, for better or for worse, remain a work in progress.

The genetic evolution of the higher primate's limbic spindle cells and
mirror cells leading to empathy has taken millions of years. The cultural
evolution of almost universal admiration for compassion in both the New
Testament and in the Buddhists' Pali Canon has taken only two thousand
years. The compassionate creation of the first Islamic and monastic hospitals only fifteen hundred years ago has proven as useful to human survival
as a clever brain per se. The Benedictine Rule states: "The care of the sick
is to be placed above and before every other duty." In contrast, the selfish
but very "fit" and scientifically advanced Nazi Third Reich deliberately
killed the chronically ill and believed that a society's resources should be
devoted to the genetically healthy and to tribal conquest. In order to decide
whether a Nazi or a Benedictine faith tradition is better suited to Darwinian survival in a postmodern world, we must not depend on softhearted
"liberals" battling the sharp wits of Charles Krauthammer, Ayn Rand, and
Ann Coulter. Instead, we need to depend on science—on empirical, long-
term follow-up. The Nazi order lasted barely a decade, but after fifteen hun-

dred years the Benedictine Order is still alive and well. The brilliantly rational, but spiritually challenged, French Revolution lasted no longer than the Third Reich. At last, Darwin's ungrateful geology professor, Adam Sedgwick, who complained that Darwin was immoral (see chapter 3), can rest in peace. Empirical follow-up of Darwin's survival of the fittest theory appears to be more "moral" than he suspected.

Although it may not always seem that way, the cultural evolution reflected by the invention of the hospital continues. In 2006 two times as much of the American GNP was devoted to health care as to defense, and the ratio is still higher in other Western countries. This was not true two hundred years ago, let alone two thousand. The evolution of that very Franciscan and compassionate "instrument of peace"—the universally prestigious Nobel Peace Prize—has taken place only in the last century. So has the evolution of Oxfam and the World Health Organization (WHO).

For the last one hundred years the Olympic games have provided an inspiring example of how empathic mammalian play can trump the too often divisive efforts of political scientists to create world peace. The glory of the Olympics is that deep reverence for national flags and pride in sacred tribal anthems can be preserved without danger to others. Through empirical, if largely unconscious, experimentation over a century, not by scientists or theologians but by people who like games, a cultural formula has evolved in which compassionate competition can coexist side by side with "religious" and "national" identity.

On the first day of the Olympic games, in a reptilian zero-sum battle for a very limited number of gold medals, nationalistic tribes march into the stadium in military formation. Each tribe is clad in distinctive uniforms and proudly holds its sacred totemic flag aloft. For days on end the tribes battle. But, as with mammalian play between wolves, such battle is nontoxic. For the admiring world, through a miracle of positive emotion, Olympic athletes are just playing intertribal games—something reptiles and sometimes even some enlightened eighteenth-century humans were unable to do.

Even in the 1956 Melbourne Olympics' water polo finals between Hungary and the Soviet Union—a match in which the negative emotions could not have been more intense—the rules were observed and nobody was really hurt, let alone killed. The watching world could cheer on the under-dog Hungarian water polo team with joy instead of with the horror with which it had watched Soviet tanks crush the Budapest freedom fighters and Russian tank crews burned alive by the freedom fighters' Molotov cocktails.

At the end of the Olympic games, at the grand closing, the center of the stadium is no longer filled with competing regiments but instead with a polyglot congregation of milling humanity hugging each other, sharing each other's uniforms, and exchanging intercontinental addresses. Winners cannot be distinguished from losers. When nobody takes themselves too damned seriously, everybody is a winner. Allahu Akbar; God be praised. Positive emotions do not make all the evil in the world go away, but they are certainly the most powerful anodynes that we have.

Social Darwinists, take notice. At least in the Olympics, Franciscan "peace" is a survival strategy superior to war. Conceivably, those who win the medals might have more progeny than those who finish last, but I doubt it. Just to have marched into that stadium at all provides community for a lifetime. Everyone in the Olympic village is an alpha male or female. With similar safeguards of dialogue and play, diplomats might also learn how not to be a danger to humanity. Perhaps play, humor, and not taking ourselves too damned seriously should be added to our lexicon of "theological," or at least diplomatic, virtues.

۞

Over the past three thousand years, Asian sages across the five thousand miles that separate Jerusalem and Tarsus from the early capitals of China have given to the other five continents their eight (or eleven, depending on who's counting) great religions. All of these religions shared the common theme of compassion. The fact that the world's surviving great religions, despite their enormously different geographic and cultural contexts, all came up with similar solutions suggests that they discovered an enormously important principle of human nature. No, the Dalai Lama, himself something of a scientist, did not lie to Professor Anne Harrington when he called basic human nature compassionate.

As Karen Armstrong explains, "It was not a question of discovering your belief in 'God' first and then living a compassionate life. The practice of disciplined sympathy [I would prefer that she had used the word 'empathy'] would itself yield intimations of transcendence."[15] We need further scientific investigation of the neurobiological basis of the compassion that lies at the core of all our great faith traditions.

10

Awe and Mystical Illumination

𑁍

The brain is wider than the sky,
For, put them side by side,
The one the other will include
With ease, and you beside . . .

The brain is just the weight of God.
For, lift them, pound for pound,
And they will differ, if they do,
As syllable from sound.

—EMILY DICKINSON

𑁍

Awe and the sense of the sacred are dismissed as superstitious and infantile by both the new evolutionary humanists like Daniel Dennett and Richard Dawkins and the older psychoanalytic humanists like Sigmund Freud. Yet awe is the most "spiritual" of the positive emotions. The distinguished French academician and philosopher René Girard, in *Violence and the Sa-*

cred, reminds us that spirituality is not primarily about God but about the sacred.[1] The experience of mystical illumination, awe, the sacred, call it what you will, is hardwired in the human brain. Awe can be suppressed, ignored, and even desecrated (the tribute paid to awe by humanism gone berserk), but never destroyed.

The last thirty years have seen a number of studies that place awe and the experience of spiritual illumination firmly in the limbic system. But before I discuss the relationship of spiritual inner illumination and positive limbic emotion, let me make one point clear: the brain is a coordinated whole. To be conscious of inner illumination requires cognition, and thus our communitarian ideas and beliefs shape our inner illumination even as our inner illumination adds passion and survival value to our communitarian beliefs.

To many readers, my association of spirituality with community building and the six emotions of the "Peace Prayer" of St. Francis may have seemed off the mark. For up to now I have ignored the emotion of awe. In the minds of many, spirituality refers to awe and the search for the sacred.[2] Many acute spiritual experiences involve a sense of inner illumination and awe.

Nevertheless, in order to communicate our awe and spirituality to others, it helps if we replace our spoken words not only with drumming and music but also with loving behaviors. As Case Western bioethicist Stephen Post counsels, "All true virtue and meaningful spirituality is shaped by love, and any spiritual transformation that is not a migration toward love is suspect."[3] One difficulty, however, is that our spirituality embraces not just others but also subjective inner illumination. It is not easy to keep disparate concepts like awe and love or self and other simultaneously in mind. Defining spirituality, after all, is a little like defining Shakespeare's genius. Everybody agrees that it exists, but no two observers use the same words or even similar metaphors to capture it. Consensus statements like those created by the Fetzer Institute are helpful to researchers but do not resolve the problem.[4] Words fail to capture spirituality just as words fail to capture the aroma of perfume, the "nose" of great wine, or the cuteness of puppies. In a blind wine tasting, I recall a brilliant woman, soon to become a major university president, describing a distinguished first-growth Bordeaux as "nummy!"

A physician friend of mine, Maren Batalden, defined spirituality as follows:

> Spirituality is derived from spirit, which is from the Latin "breath." Spirituality, like breathing, is a participation in this animating energy that cycles through time and space to create and sustain all life. Through spiritual practice we come to know ourselves in interdependent relation to the universe. We learn to live as radically responsive to the needs and desires of others as we come to see ourselves as integrally connected. Through this discipline of understanding our connectedness to all life and the source of all life, we grow in humility, reverence and openness. Inevitably, a deep and abiding gratitude awakens.[5]

Batalden's metaphor, of course, makes tangible the concept of the spirit becoming flesh. No metaphysics here, just the facts. Like faith, the air is the evidence of things unseen. We can neither smell air nor taste it. Air, like faith, becomes manifest only in action. Its substance is blowing in the wind. We all take air for granted, but we can only notice its absence. Then, like Albert Camus's Dr. Rieux, and not like Father Paneloux, we gasp for breath. In Batalden's definition, inner illumination and being "radically responsive to the needs and desires of others" are of equal importance—the inside and the outside of a single experience of spirituality. Batalden also reminds us that the "Peace Prayer" of St. Francis omitted two very important positive emotions, gratitude and awe. They belong, however, in any "paint box" of spiritual emotions.

The heart and the brain, science and spirituality, the limbic and the neocortical, are all, of course, inextricably linked. Similarly, with the exception of their differing religious beliefs, the great spiritual exemplars of history have shared much in common in terms of their outward behavior: Albert Schweitzer, the Lutheran; Mother Teresa, the Catholic; Viktor Frankl, the Jew; Martin Luther King Jr., the Baptist; Mohandas Gandhi, the Hindu; the Dalai Lama, the Buddhist; Leo Tolstoy, the Russian Orthodox—

all have left lasting spiritual impressions upon billions. All these men and women modeled the triumph of positive over negative emotion; none was a theologian. They may have differed enormously in their core beliefs and in the amount of time each spent in prayer and meditation. Nevertheless, they all were brilliant; all used their highly evolved neocortices to focus, channel, and transmute their limbic passion for the betterment of others. The moral compass of their inner lives produced awe in their admirers. Of note, however, is that none of them were just humanists. They all believed in a power greater than themselves.

Let me now examine the scientific evidence linking the emotion of awe to survival. For instance, consider the link between inner illumination and community involvement. A devout Tibetan Buddhist being studied while in deep meditation reported, "There's a sense of timelessness and infinity. It feels like I am part of everyone and everything in existence."[6] Intense Buddhist, Hindu, Native American, and Catholic devotional exercises all lead toward such connection. At times both mystics and scientists appreciate this "reality." Indeed, this sense of loving mystical union is echoed even by a committed atheist, the astrophysicist and popular writer Carl Sagan. Ellie Arroway, the heroine in the film version of his novel *Contact*, exults, "I had an experience I can't prove. . . . I was part of something wonderful, something that changed me forever; a vision of the universe that tells us undeniably how tiny and insignificant and how rare and precious we all are. A vision that tells us we belong to something that is greater than ourselves. That we are not, that none of us is, alone."[7]

The same intellectual rocket technology that created Hitler's short-lived vengeance weapons has also brought us, for the last half-century, beautiful, awe-invoking photographs of our fragile blue-and-white earth. These images have helped to make tangible the spiritual reality that "we are all one planet." The Hubble telescope put into space by rational, mechanical minds provides us with inspirational visions of nebulae and awe-inducing glimpses of the origin of our universe. Of course, such spiritual recognition of unity was evident to many illiterate but deeply spiritual nomadic peoples, like the Plains Indians and the Australian Aboriginals, long before it was painfully rediscovered by literate, left-brain rocket scientists.

In any case, I believe that our genetically derived, visceral awe for the unity of humanity helps us to survive just as effectively as do our more scientifically respectable "selfish" genes—and rather more effectively than our intercontinental rockets.

For example, geneticist and psychiatrist Robert Cloninger of Washington University in St. Louis developed a questionnaire to identify "self-transcendence" (spirituality) as a core dimension of character.[8]

Items from Robert Cloninger's Scale of Self-Transcendence (1994)

5. I sometimes feel so connected to nature that everything seems to be part of one living organism.

7. Sometimes I have felt like I was part of something with no limits or boundaries in time and space.

11. I often feel a strong spiritual or emotional connection with all the people around me.

16. I have had moments of great joy in which I suddenly had a clear deep feeling of oneness with all that exists.

Not only have the items in this list been used to quantify spirituality in neurobiological studies, but they also reflect the positive emotions and inner illumination described by the mystics.[9] In addition, the statements reflect the communitarian spirit that I have already suggested has been so important to human evolution. Responses to these "spiritual" statements are only minimally correlated with formal religious denomination. Rather, studies of identical twins separated at birth suggest that our responses to these statements are under the control of our genes.[10] Although only about one person in four will answer "true of me" to all four items in the list, that does not mean that the remaining 75 percent are lacking in spirituality. Few of us would respond "never true of me" to all of the statements. Only some people are six feet tall, but we all are tall enough to have stature; we are all spiritual enough to have experienced profound awe at some point in our lives, if only on mountaintops and in art museums.

Spirituality embraces both mystical experience and communitarian responsibility. For example, twelve-step groups correctly regard themselves as highly spiritual. On the one hand, such groups are libertarian: they do "not wish to impose anything on anyone," and they advocate trusting your own life experience. On the other hand, they also believe deeply in being of service to others, "letting go and letting God," and recognizing that the universe is not just about me. In short, spirituality, like a successful life, is a judicious balance between obedience and desire, and both are important.

Nevertheless, at the end of the day, service to the community usually trumps meditative bliss. Our biologic need to provide care to others cannot be ignored. Let me offer an analogy. At times, raising children can feel like being subjected to slavery, whereas solitary meditation or fishing alone on a pristine mountain lake can bring utter bliss. Nevertheless, on their deathbeds more people probably rejoice in having raised children than in having achieved precious moments of meditational Nirvana. We profit from both an inner quest for the sacred and altruistic service to others, but the latter is more closely linked to survival.

Nevertheless, I need to justify my assertion that spirituality seeks a fusion of the soul both with "God" *and* with some external secular community. Did not "spirituality" create the dispossession (unworldliness) of the great Spanish mystics? Is not dispossession what is sought by the Zen Buddhist, the Amazonian shaman, and the yogi master? Was not inner, not outer, illumination the goal of the spiritual exercises of Saint Ignatius of Loyola? Did not John of the Cross tell us that "the mysterious and sweet tasting wisdom comes home so clearly to the inmost parts of our soul. . . . The soul then feels as if placed . . . in an immense and boundless desert, a desert the more delicious the more solitary it is"?[11] Yes, those are the words of the mystics—their talk.

How, then, can I refer to spirituality as "community building" as well as a private search for the sacred? The answer is that I must pay attention not to the "talk" of John of the Cross but to his "walk." I must pay attention to how he spent his working life. Though the poetry of spirituality is about inner illumination, the behavior of those who "do faith" is about loving and community building. If we wish to understand fully the spirituality of mystics like John of the Cross, we may wish to avoid the hundreds of thousands of words written in exegesis trying to understand their poetry and theology.

Instead, we may wish to pay attention to the loving behaviors engendered by their mystical meditations. Like so many of the mystics, John of the Cross was a community builder. He minded priories, convents, and monasteries throughout Spain. Though platonic, the love between the two thirteenth-century mystics Saint Teresa of Avila and John of the Cross was very deep. Good community builder that Saint Teresa was, she wrote to John of the Cross, with perhaps an undercurrent of big-sister criticism, "God deliver us from people who are so spiritual that they want to turn everything into perfect contemplation."[12] The positive emotion—the joy— that so enriches the inner illumination of meditation also leads one outward to share that comfort with others.

William James wrote of the author of *Spiritual Exercises*, "Saint Ignatius was a mystic, but his mysticism made him assuredly one of the most powerfully practical human engines that ever lived."[13] The great legacies of the spiritual exercises of Saint Ignatius of Loyola were not just individual dispossession and self-forgetfulness, but a legacy of founding innumerable, and surprisingly tolerant, Jesuit universities that eventually spread throughout the world.

Nor is the synthesis of inner illumination and community building foreign to the Hindu and Buddhist traditions. The spirituality of Hinduism occurs in two steps. The looking inward serves to produce an outward selfless love for all creation. In his autobiography, Mohandas Gandhi observed, "Such power as I possess in the political field has derived from my experiences in the spiritual field."[14] And at the heart of Buddhist enlightenment is a commitment to seek the welfare of all humanity. As the Buddhist Pali Canon observes, "One act of pure love in saving a life is greater than spending the whole of one's time in religious offerings to the Gods." The Buddha ordered his first sixty disciples: "Go forth, O Monks, and travel for the welfare and happiness of the multitude, out of compassion for the world, for the good, welfare and happiness of gods and men."[15] In short, human spirituality, like human welfare, is deeply rooted in relationship. Spirituality is rarely just about solitary gurus on mountaintops—not in the West, not in the East. Not anywhere.

᪥

Mystical illumination does not emanate from the ether or, like Athena, spring fully developed from the head of Zeus. Mystical experience is firmly rooted in the limbic system. In the early nineteenth century the pioneering French psychiatrist Étienne Esquirol recognized the association of mysticism with temporal lobe epilepsy. (Other names for this disorder are complex partial seizures, temporal lobe epilepsy [TLE], and psychomotor epilepsy.) During these seizures that affect the limbic system there may be increased emotionality, anger, sadness, elation, and guilt.[16] Temporal lobe epilepsy involving the limbic system is also associated with awe, an enhanced sense of personal destiny, sensations of unity, déjà vu experience, "enlightenment," white light, and the sudden recognition of hidden meanings and causation. Common behavioral alterations associated with TLE include increased philosophical and religious concerns, increased likelihood of religious conversion, illusions of familiarity, and a "characteristic deepening of the emotional life."[17] These are similar to the traits noted in individuals considered to be high in Robert Cloninger's genetically based "spiritual transcendence." However, in contrast to most spiritual experiences, TLE can also induce negative emotion and paranoid delusions.

The Russian novelist Fyodor Dostoyevsky's temporal lobe seizures began with a sense of rapture and awe and then plunged him into guilt for some terrible unknown crime. The fact that Dostoyevsky went on to give the world the deeply spiritual novel *The Brothers Karamazov* is probably no coincidence. Nor is it coincidence that if his novel embraces the tenderest love, it also embraces the most selfish negative emotions. Dostoyevsky himself was wracked by guilt and was a pathological gambler. In short, the limbic system and its inner illumination create emotion of all shades and stripes, not just sweetness and light.

Dostoyevsky identified with Muhammad, whom he deemed a fellow epileptic, but he especially identified with the founder of Islam's ineffable joy.[18] In Dostoyevsky's words, "During a few moments I felt such a happi-ness . . . an extraordinary light that flooded the soul."[19] On another occa-sion, prior to a seizure, Dostoyevsky told a friend, "I felt that heaven was going down upon the earth and that it had engulfed me. I have really touched God."[20]

In his partly autobiographical novel *The Idiot*, Dostoyevsky imbues Prince Myshkin, the novel's epileptic protagonist, with a pre-epileptic aura in which "the sense of life, the consciousness of self, were multiplied almost tenfold at these moments, which passed like a flash of lightning." Then Prince Myshkin reflects, "What of it, if it is a disease? . . . What does it mat-ter that this intensity is abnormal, if the result, if the minute of sensation, remembered and analyzed afterward in a healthy state, turns out to be the acme of harmony and beauty . . . of reconciliation, and of ecstatic worship-ful fusion with the highest synthesis of life?"[21]

Prince Myshkin noted an important distinction. Namely, these mo-ments of spiritual joy were qualitatively different—more real—than the ec-stasy from hashish, opium, or wine. In other words, for Dostoyevsky, as for many modern marijuana users, in retrospect the ecstasy of drug-induced spirituality seemed bogus, while moments of sober, if epileptic, spiritual joy might well have been the truest moments of his whole life. The key to dis-tinguishing inner illumination from both madness and intoxication is the way "the minute of sensation" is "remembered and analyzed afterwards in a healthy state." More than a century later Dostoyevsky's Prince Myshkin is remembered less as a neurological cripple than as a loving, almost saintly man whose spiritual mantra was that "compassion was the chief and per-haps the only law of human existence." What did it matter that Dos-toyevsky had epilepsy if the insights of his epilepsy helped him to become one of the greatest novelists who ever lived? Never underestimate the spir-itual power of the limbic system.

Admittedly, for every long-remembered Dostoyevsky and Prince Mysh-kin, there are many "divinely inspired" epileptics who are more rapidly for-gotten. Always the critical distinction between benign illumination and "evil" illumination is the distinction between empathy and projection, be-tween responsibility and paranoia. Anything that improves brain function or contributes to the evolution of humankind or the maturation of the individual also increases empathy. Anything that damages the brain—stroke, intoxication, and fatigue—increases projection and narcissism.

Two weeks after a TLE seizure, a twenty-three-year-old British airman, while walking alone, suddenly felt God's reality and his own insignificance.[22] From that moment on, he was determined to live in a "Christian" manner. Over the next eleven years his conversion experience faded. Then, at age thirty-four, he experienced two seizures in one day. Several hours later he had a sudden, dreamlike feeling, saw a flash of light, and exclaimed, "I have seen the light." He suddenly knew that God was behind the sun. An electroencephalogram (EEG) identified a left anterior temporal lobe, and a surgical lobectomy was performed. His seizures were cured, but he continued to believe that the message was from God and that he had been specially singled out. The aberrant brain tissue was removed, but his conviction of a spiritual mission remained.

The "spiritual" insights from a joint smoked on a moonlit beach are soon forgotten. In contrast, Saul of Tarsus (later known as Saint Paul) was a Roman citizen, a devout and highly educated Jewish Pharisee, a relentless persecutor of Christians, and an accomplice in the murder of the first Christian martyr, Saint Stephen. In 34 CE, while accompanied by a physician, Luke, who also became his biographer (Acts 3–6, 8–9), Paul had an experience (quite possibly a temporal lobe seizure) on the road to Damascus that changed his life. "Suddenly a light from heaven flashed round him; he dropped to the ground and heard a voice saying to him, 'Saul, Saul, why do you persecute me?' " Later Paul spoke of the recurrence of such spells as a "thorn" and an affliction sent by "an angel of Satan to rack me." But it makes greater sense to classify the consequences of Paul's possible temporal lobe disturbance as creative rather than pathological, for his positive emotions—the faith, hope, and love expressed in his subsequent writings—continue to inspire people two thousand years later.

⚶

Some theologians see near-death experiences as having much in common with the deepest religious illuminations. Like TLE, near-death experiences seem unusually real. They are never forgotten; they increase altruistic concerns; and they show persistent positive aftereffects. As one of William James's near-death experience informants put it, "I was very selfish . . . now I desire the welfare of all mankind."[23] Almost always the emotions associated with near-death experiences are awe, love, and joy.

Although the term "near-death experience" was not coined until 1975 by Raymond Moody, similar accounts had been described around the world for centuries.[24] In 1865 a British surgeon told of a sailor who was rescued from near drowning and claimed that he had been in heaven. The surgeon wrote that prior to his drowning the sailor had been a "worthless fellow," and yet afterwards he became one of the best-behaved sailors on the ship. To risk being too fanciful, it is as if the near-death and mystical experience had enhanced the very part of the sailor's brain that the dynamite-tamping rod destroyed in Phineas Gage.

Another near-death experience comes from a study of such experiences during childbirth.[25] A new mother recollected, "So I went to this light, got crossed over into this light. It was huge, it was bright, it was every place. . . . If you can imagine absolutes—it was absolute peace and love." In such mothers the fruits of the experience seemed to have been a deep attachment to their children, a greater ability to comprehend paradox, and a more relaxed, less self-centered attitude toward life in general.

Near-death experiences, perhaps owing to modern methods of resuscitation, are relatively common. Bruce Greyson, the Chester F. Carlson Professor of Psychiatry at the University of Virginia, has for thirty years been a sophisticated observer of these phenomena and has examined them from multiple scientific perspectives.[26] Such experiences are characterized by the five criteria that William James used to define a mystical experience: (1) difficult to express in words but provides evocative insights; (2) experienced as new depths of truth; (3) involving a sense of being controlled by or belonging to a power outside of the self; (4) rarely sustained beyond an hour or two; and (5) often accompanied by a sense of bright light.[27] A more recent "mystical experience questionnaire" includes additional facets that would have seemed by no means foreign to William James, John of the Cross, the Buddha, or Fyodor Dostoyevsky.[28] These facets include "transcendence of time and space," "a sense of sacredness," and "a deeply-felt positive mood." Indeed, a major difference between TLE and near-death experiences is that in the latter case positive emotions are consistently dominant. Perhaps in part this difference is due to the exogenous opioid drugs often administered during cardiac resuscitations and to the endogenous endorphins released during the agonal near-fatal event. For example, studies have shown that dogs subjected to cardiac arrest have a sudden increase in beta-endorphin in brain tissue and cerebro-spinal fluid.[29]

Whatever their explanation, secular or divine, near-death experiences are profoundly spiritual. For example, after open-heart surgery a thirty-one-year-old woman explained, "But I wasn't afraid. . . . I felt this feeling of love. It was like all of a sudden I could feel this whole feeling of love and joy. It was all around me. . . . I saw this circle of light off in the distance. I'll never forget it. And I could feel this love just coming from that light . . . it's a true love, a pure love, free of earthly worries. Absolute pure love!"[30] Note that in her mystical experience there is no mention of God—just "absolute pure love!"

In my opinion, the most thorough study of the near-death experience was conducted by a Dutch cardiologist, Pim van Lommel, and his colleagues. It was recently published in an authoritative medical journal, The Lancet.[31] Their study was prospective and adequately controlled and had an eight-year follow-up. They studied 344 consecutive patients who required cardiac resuscitation in the hospital. Sixty-two patients (18 percent) in this series had at least a suggestive near-death experience, and twenty-three (7 percent) had most of the hallmarks of such an experience. Of the sixty-two patients with near-death experiences, 56 percent experienced positive emotions, 23 percent felt communion with a bright light, 31 percent experienced moving through a tunnel, and 13 percent engaged in life reviews. The occurrence of near-death experiences was not associated with either the duration of cardiac "death" or the severity of the resulting hypoxia.

Eight years later van Lommel's patients could recall the near-death events almost exactly. (Just think of an event eight years ago that you could describe today as vividly as you might have recorded it in a diary at the time.) To a significant degree when compared to the other 282 patients with stopped hearts who did not report near-death experiences, the patients with such experiences believed they had become better at sharing their feelings. They believed that they had become more loving, more empathic, and more aware of the meaning of life and that they had become more involved with their families. The van Lommel research was unusual in that these researchers employed external observers to confirm the patients' alleged increase in prosocial concerns. In contrast to the controls who after eight years believed their spirituality had declined, the near-death experience patients claimed a significant increase in spirituality. Finally, the changes induced by these transformative spiritual experiences appeared more marked at eight years than at the two-year follow-up. Both PTSD (post-traumatic stress disorder) and the experience of awe are limbic experiences that natural selection has "chosen" to be remembered forever.

ئۇ

There is an important difference between voluntary and involuntary spiritual illumination. Moses, Saint Paul, and Muhammad had no control over their mystical illumination. The Buddha and Saint Ignatius of Loyola did. Through drugs, ritual, drumming, fasting, and meditation, shamans can induce inner illumination voluntarily—from without, as it were. For thousands of years shamans, through drumming and sometimes with the aid of serotonergic "magic mushrooms," have induced a mystical state in which, through a dark tunnel, he or she reaches a brightly lit world of ancestors and totemic power animals. In both the West and the East, "holy" men and women achieve mystical experience through meditation and fasting. A study was made of psychologically normal Carmelite nuns who in youth, through voluntary meditation, had had intense mystical religious experiences.[32] As one sister put it, "It is more than a feeling. It is more intense than feeling, but you sense God is physically there. It brings intense happiness, even bliss." Or as another nun described her experience, "I have never felt so loved."

Through brain imaging, radiologist Andrew Newberg has studied brain function in Tibetan Buddhist meditation.[33] He has identified two patches of parietal neocortex located in the upper rear of the brain—above and behind the ears. This region, called the orientation association area, keeps track of our physical boundaries and locates us in space. When meditators achieve a state of mystical union, the activities of those parts of the neocortical brain are functionally cut off from the rest of the brain. At the same time, both the limbic hippocampus and amygdala are more active.[34] Epinephrine and cortisol levels (associated with the fight-or-flight response) are diminished, and dopaminergic (pleasure) and serotonergic (contentment) pathways are enhanced. This increase of positive emotion is experienced as spiritual. Thus, the meditator feels an expansion of the self into space—an oceanic merging with something greater than the self. (Consider the item on Robert Cloninger's spiritual transcendence scale: "I have had moments of great joy in which I suddenly had a clear deep feeling of oneness with all that exists.")[35]

Newberg's study has revealed that

> the altered states of consciousness described by mystics and saints are not the involuntary results of the delusional fanatics [such as described by Jon Krakauer and Anthony Storr][36] or the chemical misfiring of a neurologically damaged brain [such as described by Dostoyevsky's Prince Myshkin][37]. Instead, the psychic alterations of the Buddhist meditator are brought about when the meditator voluntarily focuses his attention on a sacred image or mantra or on the mood of loving-kindness; thereby the meditator liberates his limbic brain from the constraining effects of attention to external reality by the "orientation association area."

Again, the meditative state is very different from ordinary dreaming or waking. The EEG of the person who is dreaming manifests a theta rhythm

twice as rapid as the delta rhythm of deep sleep, half as fast as the alpha
rhythm of drowsiness, and one-quarter as fast as the beta rhythm of full
wakefulness. Deep meditation combines alpha, theta, and beta rhythms.[38]
There is increased activity in the orbital prefrontal and anterior cingulate
cortices.

In general the "spiritual" experiences induced by voluntary ingestion of psychedelic drugs are as short-lived as the conversion experiences induced in
the tents of itinerant nineteenth-century evangelists. Like the fleeting insights produced by our nocturnal dreams, when we "waken" from psychedelic reverie, the drug-induced inspiration becomes rapidly unreal. Thus,
great shamans often prefer to enter their mystical worlds through drumming
and fasting alone.

Nevertheless, like a few of the reports of lasting effects of TLE, under
special circumstances the effects of psilocybin ("magic mushrooms") can
last a lifetime. Like most psychedelic drugs, psilocybin is thought to exert
its effect by mimicking serotonin at selected (5-HT2 a/c) receptors.[39] The
cell bodies affecting these receptors are concentrated in midline brain structures integrating input from the five senses, thus perhaps accounting for the
oceanic feeling of merger that accompanies psilocybin-induced and other
mystical experiences.

Convinced that "a classic means of evaluating mystical experiences is
by their fruits," Rich Doblin carried out a twenty-five-year follow-up of one
of the best scientific studies of the spiritual effects of psilocybin ever conducted.[40] In many ways, the design of his study anticipated the already mentioned study of near-death experiences conducted by van Lommel. The
original study by a Harvard graduate student, Walter Pahnke, was a double-
blind controlled study of divinity students conducted in a Good Friday service at Boston University's School of Theology and led by the inspirational
professor and preacher Howard Thurman.[41] At Pahnke's six-month follow-
up and again at Doblin's twenty-five-year mark, the students who received

thirty milligrams of psilocybin reported a significant spiritual change. Many of the divinity students regarded the well-remembered psilocybin experience as a high point of their spiritual life. As one student summarized, "I got very involved with civil rights after that." After twenty-five years, the controls who had received a placebo could barely even remember the experiment. As an aside, if you stimulate the limbic amygdala and hippocampus by unbearable trauma, by LSD-induced "bad trips," and sometimes by epilepsy, you can produce equally long-lasting but infinitely more painful memories and flashbacks.[42] We remember the terror of severe trauma and the awe of "mountaintop" epiphanies all of our lives.

Admittedly, the results of psychedelic-induced awe experiences, especially when conducted with less communitarian group support, have been unimpressive. In general, lasting spiritual change comes from disciplined regimens of group-supported worship in combination with emotional but drug-free experiences enhanced by meditation, fasting, drumming, and sensory deprivation.

Recently, a still more elegant experiment with psilocybin has been conducted.[43] In a double-blind crossover designed study of psychologically screened, hallucinogen-naive volunteers, the effects of psilocybin were compared to the effects of Ritalin (an amphetamine-like stimulant used in the treatment of attention deficit disorder). Half the subjects received first psilocybin and then, on another day, the mind-altering Ritalin control; half received the control drug first and then the psilocybin. Neither experimenter nor subject knew which drug was administered. When given thirty milligrams of psilocybin, individuals reported at least twice as much "joy," "peace," "distance from ordinary reality," "oceanic boundlessness," "sacredness," and "deeply felt positive mood" as those receiving the stimulant drug. They scored almost twice as high on a scale assessing "mysticism."[44] Two months after receiving the two drugs, sixteen out of twenty-four subjects described the state following psilocybin as among the top five most "personally meaningful" experiences of their lives. Only two of the same twenty-four individuals categorized the experience with the active control drug Ritalin as particularly meaningful.

Dean Hamer, a geneticist at the National Institutes of Health, identified a "God gene" that "codes for a monoamine transporter—a protein that controls the amount of crucial brain signaling chemicals" (norepinephrine and serotonin) that are released by drugs like LSD and psilocybin.[45] Hamer's so-called God gene appears to affect individuals' scores on Cloninger's scale of self-transcendence, or what in this chapter has been called awe or mystical illumination. Although the finding that a specific gene can affect heightened spirituality is exciting, caution is called for. Hamer's findings, while "statistically significant," explain only 1 percent of the variability in assessed spirituality.[46] Put differently, a clarinet is a significant musical instrument, but by itself a clarinet does not produce a symphony. Computers run on electricity; brains run on chemicals, but it is the programming, not the power source, that makes them interesting.

❧

The point of this detour into neurophysiology is to illustrate that the evolution of the limbic system has given us all a path to life-affirming spirituality. As Emily Dickinson reminds us, "The brain is wider than the sky." The principal value of focusing on a relatively uncommon experience, temporal lobe epilepsy, and an ingestion of psilocybin, a brain poison, is that they suggest where in the brain spiritual experiences are located—the same areas associated with positive emotion. The same spiritual transformations that I have described in epileptics are also seen in individuals without pathology. The problem is that we have no means of localizing such spontaneous spiritual transformations in the brain.

A New Mexico research psychologist, William Miller, has referred to such experiences as "quantum change."[47] He collected a series of such "everyday life" spiritual experiences by placing an advertisement in an Albuquerque newspaper asking for volunteers "who have been transformed in a relatively short period of time—who have had a deep shift in core values, feelings, attitudes or actions." Fifty-five people responded to his advertisement. Their spiritual experiences had usually occurred independent of epilepsy, psychopathology, chemicals, or known direct religious influence. Miller defines such "quantum change" as a vivid, surprising, benevolent, and enduring personal transformation. Profound awe, a sense of bright light, and a feeling of love were all usually present. Such experiences were often kept "secret" and not shared until years later. In summarizing these fifty-five experiences, Miller and his colleague Janet C'de Baca reported that more than half of their informants said "true" to statements like "I felt at one or connected to everything around me," "I felt like I was in the hands of a power much greater than myself," and "I felt loved and cared for."

Retrospectively, Miller's subjects were asked to note priority shifts in fifty values. The values that had increased the most were positive emotions like personal peace, forgiveness, spirituality, humility, and generosity. After the experience, men reported that they became less macho and less materialistic; they reported major drops in the importance of achievement, adventure, comfort, fame, fun, and power (values that women rated low to begin with). Women's postchange priorities also placed the positive emotions higher, with lessened emphasis on traditional "feminine" values like fitting in, safety, and self-control. William Miller has likened such experiences to the spiritual transformation of Ebenezer Scrooge in Charles Dickens's *A Christmas Carol*. Real life offers similar examples of spontaneous, sudden, life-changing spiritual experiences in the lives of Joseph Smith, Bill Wilson, Martin Luther, John Wesley, Florence Nightingale, and Malcolm X. In all these examples, awe and mystical illumination led to community building.

Miller believes that such "quantum change" reflects a broader and more enduring phenomenon than the transient experience of religious conversion at revival meetings. He suggests that the suddenness of such transformative experience is analogous to finally recalling the combination of a locked safe after a period of increasing frustration and anxiety. Suddenly, all the tumblers fall into place—and the ensuing emotional experience is a mixture of relief and joy. The individual is changed forever. It becomes better to give than to receive.

To be "reborn" may be only a mystic's metaphor for the occasionally lasting effects of the emotion of awe, which is hardwired in us all. The neurobiological purpose of awe appears to be linked to appreciation of beauty, of nature, of the wonder induced by childbirth, and of courageous acts of compassion—all survival skills of the first rank.

Sometimes awe does not happen mysteriously but is inspired by the unambiguously momentous. In *Moondust*, journalist Andrew Smith describes the transformative experiences induced by literally flying to the moon.[48] Only twelve men have enjoyed the extraordinary experience of setting foot on the lunar surface. All these men had begun adult life as unflappable, unimaginative engineers and right-stuff test pilots; all had been trained to be Cold War military combatants. Once on the moon, most of the astronauts perceived the earth as a beautiful but seemingly fragile blue-and-white globe very much alone in the universe. Such a view was not evident to most of the astronauts who had just orbited the earth and not journeyed to deep space. Perhaps six of the twelve moon walkers were changed forever by their experience and became preoccupied with a concern for the earth as a whole.

After viewing the Genesis Rock, a four-and-a-half-billion-year-old boulder formed just after the solar system was born, one moon walker, James Irwin, heard God's voice. After returning to earth, Colonel Irwin quit NASA and founded the High Flight Ministry, a religious organization. His wife agreed that his awe-filled moon walk had changed him forever. After his trip, another astronaut, Alan Bean, who had experienced an "epiphany," eventually quit NASA to become a full-time artist of the cosmos; as he explained, "I think really of the whole earth as the Garden of Eden."[49]

The most dramatic example of life-altering awe came from Captain Edgar Mitchell—a Ph.D. from MIT and the Apollo 14 lunar module pilot—who recollected that "the intricate beauty of Earth overwhelmed the senses."[50] He reported that he had experienced "this exhilaration every time I looked out the [lunar module] window. . . . These states of mind can be naturally derived. You don't need psychedelics to do it."[51] When he returned to earth, Captain Mitchell left NASA to found the Institute of Noetic Sciences, a new-age organization wishing to integrate science and religion. In 2007 the institute was still sponsoring conferences.

Findings like those recounted in William Miller's book raise important questions: Is human spirituality evolving? Does natural selection favor a brain with capacity for a deepening spiritual life? Since humans have learned to induce involuntary excitation of the limbic system—from within through sacred drugs and fasting or from without by voluntarily reducing cortical inhibition of the limbic system through meditation and sensory deprivation—some have wondered whether such experiences are not an effort to move toward a new evolutionary level: the accessing of a recently evolved facet of the brain.[52] Others believe that such experiences are mere illusions produced by an adaptive reordering of abnormal brain function, as in Oliver Sacks's famous example of the brain-damaged man who mistook his wife for his hat. Since the jury is still out, neuroradiologist Andrew Newberg offers a middle ground. He suggests that, for meditating nuns, "while in prayer, their sense of God became physiologically real," and that meditating Buddhists caught a glimpse of what for them was "an absolute reality."[53]

Christians may call the union of mystical illumination and community building "God and church"; twelve-step groups may call it "higher power" and "home group"; humanists may call it "love and family"; anthropologists may call it "animism and tribe." But whatever language we choose to speak, by paying attention to the music, we can begin to understand why awe and group cohesion go hand in hand.

ॐ

In closing this chapter, I must acknowledge that I tread on treacherous ground. As e. e. cummings trumpeted in an undated manuscript:

> While you and i have lips and voices which
> are for kissing and to sing with
> who cares if some oneeyed son of a bitch
> invents an instrument to measure Spring with?[54]

As soon as my writing becomes proscriptive, as soon as I suggest that I *know* how or why spiritual enlightenment and mystical experiences develop, I have lost my way. To suggest as I have done in this book that our spirituality lives in the limbic system, or that spirituality is more mature than religion, or that religion reflects only metaphor and not divine truth, I risk substituting my cognitive belief for another's emotional trust. What is sacred about science is what is sacred about religion—both reflect honest seeking, and neither owns a proprietary stranglehold on truth. Always, butterflies see real colors to which scientists are blind; bats hear real noise to which scientists are deaf; and much that science teaches us as truth will in the future prove untrue. Always, faith remains "the evidence of things not seen, the substance of things hoped for." Thank God!

11

The Difference Between
Religion and Spirituality

છ્જ

He is forever free who has broken
Out of the ego-cage of I and Mine
To be united with the Lord of Love.
This is the supreme state. Attain thou this
And pass from death to immortality.

—BHAGAVAD GITA, *chapter 2, translated by Mohandas Gandhi*[1]

ૌૌ

The past seven chapters have shown us the survival value of the positive emotions. We've seen their roots in mammalian group bonding and their role in recent centuries in powering a cultural movement toward transcending tribal rivalry and enlarging our definition of community. In this chapter, I reach for the conclusion that I hope has come to seem inevitable: that the human capacity for positive emotions is what makes us spiritual, and that to focus on the positive emotions is the best and safest route to spirituality that we are likely to find.

In his spirited critique of religion, *Breaking the Spell*, Tufts University philosopher Daniel Dennett reminds us that there was a time when there was no religion on this earth and now there is lots of it. He wonders why some religions spread while others fade into obscurity.[2] Why? Because organized religion is what Daniel Dennett would call "a Good Trick."

To put too much emphasis on "selfish" genes is to miss the influential evolution of a loving culture. I believe that the survival of the world's great religions, relatively unchanged, for the last two thousand years has been due as much to their ritual emphasis on the positive emotions of faith, forgiveness, hope, joy, love, and compassion as to "guns, germs, and steel" or cancerlike memes.

Over the past twenty thousand years, the forward march of spiritual development, artistic skill, and culturally mandated, unselfish care of the weak, supported by organized religion, has been inexorable. The concepts of "group evolution" and "unselfish" genes were ideas that in the 1960s and 1970s were regarded by geneticists as at worst heresy and at best quaint blasts from the past. In 1994 Antonio Damasio broke ranks when he wrote, "Suprainstinctual survival strategies generate something probably unique to humans: a moral point of view that, on occasion, can transcend the interest of the immediate group and even the species."[3] More recently, evolutionary biologist David Sloan Wilson and evolutionary psychologist Mark Hauser have also suggested that "maturity" and empathy have been positively selected for in the evolution of *Homo sapiens*.[4] The biology of *Homo sapiens* has hardwired our brains to feel joy in communal efforts with strangers—but only under special circumstances. Admittedly, the United Nations, the Olympic games, the Nobel Peace Prizes, and the world's response to the 2004 tsunami in southern Asia all reflect cultural evolution that has occurred only over the last century.

In *Anna Karenina*, Leo Tolstoy's alter ego, Constantine Levin, asks what the spirituality that undergirds the world's great religions is really about. Then he asks, "And this [spiritual] knowledge I did not acquire. It was given to me, like all the rest, given. Did I get it from reason? But would reason ever have proved to me that I ought to love my neighbor, instead of choking him? I was taught that in my childhood, but I believed it gladly because it already existed in my soul."[5] A neuroscientist might substitute the less mystical term "limbic system" for Tolstoy's term "soul," but the music would not change.

To be made safe our emotional life must always be tempered by reason and obedience. That is where sacred cognitive rituals come in. They help our limbic systems serve our future rather than the "right now!" of our reptilian impulses. A few years ago a Philippine mob achieved victory by placing flowers lovingly in the barrels of soldiers' rifles. In a prior century they would have given vent to the delicious satisfaction of impulsive, angry, homicidal, but ultimately suicidal riot. We have Leo Tolstoy, Mohandas Gandhi, and Martin Luther King Jr. to thank for the alternative. Religion provided a framework for the spirituality of the three world leaders and for the Philippine mob. But how can we separate the spirituality of religion from its dangerous dogmatic baggage?

At first the idea of distinguishing spirituality from religion may seem impossible. Is not our spirituality often expressed using the language, metaphors, and rituals of religion? Do not virtually all religions arise from humankind's innate spirituality? Is not the mystical longing for subjective connection with the divine at the heart of all spirituality and the essence of all religions?[6] Of course.

How, then, are cults and religions different from spirituality? Let me count the ways—while acknowledging that many readers will equate their own faith tradition with spirituality.

The first difference is that religion refers to the interpersonal and institutional aspects of religiosity/spirituality that are derived from engaging with a formal religious group's doctrines, values, traditions, and co-members. By contrast, spirituality refers to the psychological experiences of religiosity/spirituality that relate to an individual's sense of connection with something transcendent (be it a defined deity, truth, beauty, or anything else considered to be greater than self) and are manifested by the emotions of awe, gratitude, love, compassion, and forgiveness. Second, religion arises from culture; spirituality arises from biology. Religion and cults are as different from spirituality as environment is from genes. Like culture and language, religious faith traditions bind us to our own community and isolate us from the communities of others. Like breathing, our spirituality is common to us all. On the one hand, religion asks us to learn from the experience of our tribe; spirituality urges us to savor our own experience. On the other hand, religion helps us to mistrust the experience of other tribes; spirituality helps us to regard the experience of the foreigner as valuable too. Over the short term, fear of strangers and xenophobia are social virtues. Over the long term, avoiding inbreeding by embracing strangers is a genetic necessity.

Much of religion and culture is accidental—without either universality or survival value. B. F. Skinner found that if you randomly reinforced pigeons with food, they developed inflexible rituals around the food tray. Religion, too, can happen by chance. Today in Micronesia there are tribes that engage in colorful but obsessional cargo cults, constructing bush airports instead of temples in hopes that "iron birds" will again fly in food and machinery as DC-3s did during World War II. To survive, the brains of children are wired to believe without question what their parents tell them; when they grow up, these cognitive beliefs, although outgrown, are sometimes hard to change. Catholic priests could marry until the twelfth century; popes were not infallible until 1879. Had the group vote gone the other way, these now immutable memes might not exist.

In contrast, the intensity of spiritual inner illumination is a genetically based trait, analogous to the traits of introversion and extroversion. Although individual differences exist, all humans are spiritual. Assessments of subjective spirituality are far more similar in identical twins raised apart than they are among siblings raised in the same family.[7] In contrast, church attendance and religion, for example, are far more congruent among unrelated stepsiblings raised in the same family than among identical twins raised apart.[8]

The third difference between religion and spirituality is that religion is more cognitive and spirituality is more emotional. Thus, cognitive religious schisms over belief divide the world, and at the same time limbic commonalities toward "melody" bind the world together. Spirituality and religion are both about love, but too often, in different religions, the lovers dispute, "I say *tomahto* and you say *tomayto*—let's call the whole thing off." Religion involves belief; spirituality involves trust.

When put into psychological terms, the distinction between religious belief and spiritual trust brings us to the distinction between projection and empathy. In both projection and empathy the speaker's words tell us, "I know what you are feeling." However, trying to thrust your religious beliefs upon other people is like telling them too much about your political beliefs: you must first convert them or you will annoy them with your prejudices. However, if you empathize with *their* religious and political beliefs, you have a friend for life. When we browbeat another person with our cognitive, oh so intelligent, missionary zeal, they may regard us as paranoid zealots, or they may abandon their own identities and become our all too loyal followers, as in a folie à deux. In contrast, when we pay attention to the emotions of another with our own limbic mirror neurons, they feel "seen" and in attunement with us. Always, the capacity for empathy increases with maturity. Mothers are more empathic than toddlers, and wise elders are more empathic than soccer moms. Always, with brain damage empathy recedes and is replaced with projection and paranoid belief. Of course, the problem is that sometimes the most paranoid leaders exhibit an intuitive gift for reading and manipulating the emotions of their followers. A dangerous paradox.

A fourth difference between religion and spirituality is that cults and religions tend to be authoritarian and imposed from without, while spirituality is more likely to be democratic and arise from within. As a child, my very agnostic and independent son adamantly refused to learn the Lord's Prayer from his father. But at age fourteen, when he stepped into Paris's Notre Dame Cathedral for the first time, he burst out with "Wow!" and then invoked his favorite term of endearment, "What a turn-on!" For one shining moment his search for the sacred was fulfilled. Within the loving embrace of the cathedral whose name freely translated means "Our mother who art in Heaven," my son still believed nothing, yet he trusted everything.

Both cults and religion ask you to learn from the experience of others.

Not only do they demand obedience to an external power infinitely greater than yourself, but they often involve deference to an intermediary "instructor" who is elevated above you through *his* fancy robes, education, and sacred ordination. He is a superior who will tell you how to find God or "the Way." Religious education can become as authoritarian and as unilateral as a military academy.

Spirituality encourages you to learn from your own experience. God, if one exists, lives within. As in a Montessori school, spiritual enablers, pastoral counselors, and life coaches, not didacts, listen and lovingly suggest how to find your own way. Understandably, many fear that the populist search for God, embodied in modern spirituality, will lead to anarchy. But remember that the authors of the U.S. Constitution feared that giving the vote to the unpropertied masses could be equally dangerous. Thomas Jefferson thought differently. He helped the world trust universal suffrage at the same time that he helped governments emancipate themselves from religious dogma.

A fifth difference often cited by Western critics of religion is that spirituality is tolerant and religion is intolerant. We are all spiritual beings, but as my college social science professor Crane Brinton explained to us, "If you don't believe your religion is the only religion, you have no religion." In contrast, both the Baptist Martin Luther King Jr. and the Hindu Mohandas Gandhi could adopt Russian Orthodox Leo Tolstoy as a spiritual mentor.

Most mystics and too few religious leaders understand that deep spirituality is facilitated by humility rather than by dogmatic certainty. I remember Harvard Medical School dean George Packer Berry addressing my first-year medical school class. We students all shared an abiding "religious" faith that medical science was the best path to our ultimate concern—the caring preservation of human life. Yet, in acknowledging that he shared our ultimate concern and our faith in medical science, our dean reminded us to remain self-critical and humble. "The bad news," he confessed, "is that half of everything we teach you may be proved wrong in the future . . . and we don't know which half."

﷽

While it is not controversial to suggest that the positive emotions of spirituality are valuable, many popular authors, like Christopher Hitchens, Richard Dawkins, and Sam Harris—and let us not forget Karl Marx and Sigmund Freud—have called religion dangerous. So what is religion good for?

My answer is that the rituals and cultural formats of the world's great religions form the surest way to pull our positive emotions into conscious reflection. Until the day he died, Gandhi remained faithful to the religion of his birth, Hinduism, but he modeled wise humility for us all. As a religious leader, Gandhi was insignificant; as a spiritual leader, he was hard to surpass. "I prefer to retain the label of my forefathers as long as it does not cramp my growth and does not debar me from assimilating all that is good anywhere else," he acknowledged. ". . . We must have innate respect for other religions as we have for our own. Mind you, not mutual tolerance, but equal respect. . . . After long study and experience I have come to the conclusion that (1) all religions are true; (2) all religions have some errors in them."⁹ Gandhi's ideal for religion was to retain the spiritual baby and to detoxify the religious bathwater.

Neuroscience, like cultural anthropology, has affirmed the relevance of religious ritual to connect with the limbic world of emotion. As we have seen, the disciplined and rigidly formatted rites of meditation prescribed by many of the world's great religions are designed as a gateway to spiritual "enlightenment." Through brain imaging, neuroscientist Andrew Newberg has observed that intense devotional meditation inhibits some higher neocortical brain centers; by excluding the mundane outside world, we can attend to the reality of the inner, more "spiritual" world. He summarizes: "The transcendence of the self and the blending of the self into some larger reality, is a major goal of ritualized behavior."¹⁰ Today we still are seeking the healing ingredients and proper dosages of religion. Science can help.

Always, to discover the truth of spiritual revelation, both science and religion need to remember that sometimes the message is not concrete but metaphorical. Part of Einstein's greatness was that he could conceptualize the universe in metaphor as well as in terms of cognitive science. He believed that the marriage between science and religion should endure and that "if religion without science is blind, science without religion is lame."[11] On the one hand, wise science appreciates that the emotional certainty that "faith can move mountains" can mean either that highly motivated bulldozer operators can remove a hill or that love can soften a hardened heart. On the other hand, wise religion, like science, must also distinguish metaphor from dogma; the saying does not mean that prayer alone is likely to level the Matterhorn.

༝

The wonderful virtue of science is that it can often distinguish delusion from reality, and of equal importance, science can help us distinguish empathy from projection. Science makes this distinction by holding both the passion and the prose in abeyance while it looks through the "telescope" of long-term follow-up. The answer to the Beatles' chorus "Will you still need me, will you still feed me, when I'm sixty-four?" can be answered only by the passage of time. Only science and long-term follow-up allows us to determine whether the comfort we get from our guru/doctor/lover is for them an unempathic get-rich scheme or for us a safe and long-lasting form of comfort. Only by their fruits shall ye know them.

A friend of mine once told me that she hated the word "spirituality" because of the "hoke" that went with it. I asked her to define hoke. She explained that hoke was "the promise of cure never delivered." Spirituality, like religion, becomes hoke when its practitioners try to explain its effects too concretely, or overcharge for their services, or confuse comfort with healing. The eagle feathers and power animals of the shaman, the twelve meridians and five elements of the Chinese acupuncturist, the arcane mantras and lotus position of the Buddhist, the Trinity and holy water of the Catholic, or the specificity of dream interpretation by Freudian psycho-analysts (like me)—all distract us from what is common to these religious modes of comfort: the positive emotions of forgiveness, faith, hope, love, and the compassionate witness of another's pain.

On the one hand, it is widely believed and it has been statistically demonstrated that churchgoing "improves" health. Recently, however, more careful epidemiological studies have shown that the putative causal link between church attendance and health, although supported by a vast "scientific" literature, may be due to other factors, like healthy lifestyle.[12] In other words, good health is *associated* with religious involvement; it is not *caused* by religious involvement. My own research has come to similar con-clusions. For the majority of the members of the Study of Adult Develop-ment, it made no difference to psychological well-being or to physical health whether between ages forty-five and seventy-five they had mani-fested intense religious and spiritual involvement or no involvement at all.[13] Admittedly, the two study members mentioned in previous chapters, Bill Graham and Tom Merton, reflect dramatic exceptions.

On the other hand, a young Air Force psychiatrist who returned from duty in Vietnam to a position in a community drug clinic came to a different con-clusion. He told us, "I embarked on a little informal research. I identified a few people who seemed to have overcome serious addictions to alcohol and other drugs, and I asked them what had helped them turn their lives around. . . . They kindly acknowledged their appreciation for the professional help they had received but . . . what had healed them was something spiritual. . . . I re-laxed a little. I honestly considered there might be some power greater than myself involved in healing."[14] Thus, sometimes the theological virtues of faith, hope, and love do more than just comfort; they heal. My own research has come to similar conclusions. The men who had suffered major depression and/or severely traumatic life events beyond their control were more likely over time to have become religiously and spiritually involved.[15] Their need for healing may have led them to an institutional source of positive emotion, and they lived longer than those who did not seek religious involvement.

꿍

So when is spirituality (and religion) for real and when does it resemble hoke? I believe that Alcoholics Anonymous provides a concrete example of spirituality being made safe for human consumption. No, I am not an alcoholic. I am not a member of Alcoholics Anonymous. But for thirty-five years, as a family member, a clinician, and a research scientist, I have marveled at how alcoholics, by giving empathic comfort to others and focusing daily "on a power greater than themselves" and on the positive emotions in general, heal themselves. The Peace Prayer of Francis, the epigraph for chapter 1, is an integral part of the eleventh step of AA's twelve-step program. For men in my study who developed alcoholism, Alcoholics Anonymous worked far better than psychiatric care.[16] Yet for fifty years many have regarded AA as a cult.[17] How shall we discover the truth?

If I am to frame my question in empirical terms and if I am to suggest that the AA program is more like penicillin than it is like the Moonies' Unification Church, I must respect the rules of empiricism. I must first elucidate spirituality's mechanism of action. Next, I must offer empirical evidence that it works better than a placebo. Finally, I must address any allegedly dangerous side effects. I must rely on the scientific method and long-term follow-up, not on intuition and divinely revealed truth.

By way of introduction, alcoholism, if not interrupted, is a cunning, baffling, and persistent foe that kills 100,000 Americans a year.[18] In the United States alcoholism kills far more people than breast cancer does. Over the long term, however, professional medicine can do little to halt alcoholism.

Certainly, up to now the medical and psychological professions do not have a good record of curing alcoholism. Much of what has been done to treat alcoholism scientifically has been at best placebo and at worst hoke.[19] For example, cognitive behavior therapy works less well than we would like. And I can say this after having been codirector of an alcohol clinic for ten years. Thirty years ago, Linda and Mark Sobell's study of training alcoholics to return to controlled drinking was famous worldwide—until their patients were followed up at the ten-year mark and found to have fared no better than controls.[20]

One reason for the failure of professional therapy to alter the natural history of alcoholism is that drug addiction's hold on human beings does not rest in our neocortex. The hold of addiction on our minds lies in what has been called our reptile brain. The hold comes from cellular changes in midbrain nuclei with esoteric names like the nucleus accumbens and the superior tegmentum. Eventually these changes move abstinence beyond the reach of willpower, beyond the reach of conditioning, and beyond the reach of psychoanalytic insight. Alligators do not come when they are called.

Modern medicine can detoxify alcoholics, save lives, and delay relapse. But all too often alcoholics treated by modern medical science eventually relapse. In contrast, Alcoholics Anonymous heals. Indeed, about 40 percent of all of the stably abstinent alcoholics I have known in my personal, in my clinical, and in my research life have achieved their stable ten years or more of abstinence in AA.[21]

What is the mechanism of action of Alcoholics Anonymous? For example, the mechanism of action of insulin is that insulin permits the cells of diabetics to utilize blood sugar. The mechanism by which AA "cures" alcoholism is relapse prevention. Professional treatment fails to prevent relapse in alcoholism for the same reason that lifesaving hospitalization fails to cure diabetes, another chronic disease. Hospitalization does not prevent relapse. Change in clinical course in both alcoholism and diabetes can be achieved only by relapse prevention, and to quote Lady Macbeth's physician, "Therein the patient must minister to herself." But often we can minister to ourselves only by turning ourselves over to a power greater than ourselves. We are quite incapable of tickling or cuddling ourselves. But how easily we can perform these tasks for someone else!

AA achieves relapse prevention by providing a loving community. Often Alcoholics Anonymous is referred to as a "self-help" group. Nothing could be further from the truth. Self-help is very limited. How often have you read a diet book that kept its reader slim for five years? Why so seldom? Because such books depend on "the ego-cage of I and mine," not on human communion. Wishes and self-help books are autistic and isolate us. In sharp contrast, so-called self-help groups like Alcoholics Anonymous are as communal as a barn-raising.

There are four factors that are commonly present in relapse prevention in addiction, and it does not matter if the addiction is to alcohol, smoking, compulsive eating, gambling, or opiates.[22] The four factors that prevent relapse are external supervision, ritualized dependency on a competing behavior, new love relationships, and deepened spirituality. (This list sounds a little like religious membership.)

Usually, two or more factors must be present for relapse prevention to occur. In other words, recovery from alcoholism is anything but spontaneous or "miraculous." The reason these four factors are effective is because, unlike most professional treatments, they do not work to create temporary abstinence or reduced drinking. They work to effect relapse prevention. All but external supervision depend on positive emotions.

First, *external supervision* in the recovery process is necessary because, surprisingly, conscious motivation and willpower are *not* associated with recovery. To repeat, alligators do not come when they are called. Some kind of leash to control the reptile brain is necessary.

AA, religions, and most personal trainers provide external supervision. They do not trust free will. They suggest that clients return again and again. In AA members are encouraged to find a sponsor to telephone and to visit often. The sponsor in turn encourages new members to "work the steps," attend frequent meetings, and engage in service to other alcoholics. Each of these activities provides a daily involuntary reminder that alcohol is enemy, not friend. However, AA also understands that compulsory supervision works best if it has been freely chosen. We willingly suffer under the strict rules of our athletic coach, but we sometimes evade traffic regulations and parental supervision of which we do not approve.

Second, it is important to find a *competing behavior* for the addiction. You cannot easily give up a habit without having something else enjoyable to do. AA understands what all behaviorists know and what many doctors, priests, and parents forget: bad habits yield to substitutes, not prohibition. Punishments and negative emotion alone do not change deeply ingrained habits. Thus, AA and most religions provide a gratifying schedule of social and service activities in the presence of supportive, and now healed, former "sinners," especially at times of high risk, like holidays. Consider that on the holidays, when all you can get is your physician's voice mail, most religious organizations make themselves especially available. In addition, unlike some places of worship, weekly AA home group meetings focus only on positive emotions. Ritually, criticism is replaced by "loving suggestions" and unconditional positive regard. AA meetings are filled with celebrations of anniversaries of sobriety, unlimited coffee, and hugs—and humor.

Critics sometimes complain that AA, like cults, is addicting. But so are puppies. Like heroin and puppies, positive emotion has a sneaky way of making us come back for more. As we shall see, the brain chemistry of both addiction and attachment is the same.

Third, *new love relationships* are important to recovery. It seems important for ex-addicts to bond with people whom they have not hurt in the past and to whom they are not deeply emotionally in debt. Indeed, it helps for them to bond with people to whom they can offer compassionate help.[23] Remember that my two examples of spiritual transformation, Bill Graham and Dr. Tom Merton, recovered not just by taking love and compassion in but also by giving it away.

Perhaps it is not an accident that maternal-infant bonding and endorphin (our brain's natural "morphine") release go hand in hand.[24] Love trumps drugs, as Cole Porter, that great student of positive emotions, understood. He croons to us, "I get no kick from cocaine. I get a kick out of you." And "I'd even give up coffee for Sanka, even Sanka, Bianca, for you." As in the evolution of the mammalian limbic system, in drug addiction love can tame the reptile brain. In the nineteenth century, when opium smoking was a luxury of the rich, Karl Marx quipped, "Religion is the opiate of the masses." Turning Marx on his head, wealthy Victorians may have found in opium pipes a bogus sense of oceanic peace that deeply spiritual common folk achieved through private prayer, meditation, and daily readings. As we saw in the life of Eugene O'Neill's mother, opiates may serve as an ersatz religion for those who have lost faith, hope, and love. An AA member's "home group" becomes a deeply trusted, nonjudgmental family. AA calls such a forgiving fellowship "the language of the heart." Moreover, in any close-knit congregation, as in any healing dyad, there is shared responsibility for pain.

The fourth common feature in recovery from addiction is the discovery or rediscovery of *spirituality*. Inspirational, altruistic group membership and faith in a power greater than "me" seems important to recovery from addiction. In *The Varieties of Religious Experience*, William James first articulated the close relationship between religious conversion and recovery from intractable alcoholism.[25] Three decades later Carl Jung gave to the founder of AA, Bill Wilson, the mantra "Spiritus contra spiritu" (use spirituality as an antidote for addiction to alcoholic spirits).[26]

Since it is doubtful that our prehistoric ancestors shot dope or fermented grapes, the limbic brain circuitry underlying addiction may have evolved originally to facilitate the human attachment, social cohesion, and spiritual community so necessary to survival over the past two million years. Brain opiates are released during the attachment behaviors of social grooming and during the social bonding of mother rat-pup reunions.[27]

As Thomas Insel, current director of the National Institute of Mental Health, summed up this hypothesis, "It is also possible that neural mechanisms that we associate with drug abuse and addiction might have evolved for social recognition, reward and euphoria—critical elements in the process of attachment."[28]

Let me provide further evidence for this armchair speculation. Dopaminergic brain tracts can be shown to underlie addictive behavior in mammals and reptiles. Alcohol stimulates dopamine release in the previously mentioned nucleus accumbens, a core region of the brain reward system. Alcohol also decreases amygdala excitation and thus decreases fear and—better yet—guilt. Experimental evidence suggests that secure attachment as extrapolated from brain imaging studies of mother-child attachment is also associated with reduction in amygdala firing and increases in nucleus accumbens activity.[29] Oxytocin release, another accompaniment of loving attachment, inhibits tolerance to (and thereby dependence on) alcohol.[30]

Having illustrated its mechanism of action, I must now show that AA is better than a placebo. Unfortunately, empirical information on the efficacy of AA is hard to come by. First, like most spiritual organizations, AA is uninterested in research. Second, owing to ideological differences and, I suspect, unconscious rivalry, medical researchers sometimes have difficulties assessing AA without negative bias. Finally, in the course of their long and chronic disorder, alcoholics encounter many different kinds of interventions, often simultaneously. Therefore, unlike most formal drug trials, a truly controlled study of the efficacy of AA is not possible. Until very recently, it remained unclear whether AA attendance *caused* abstinence or whether AA attendance was merely a *correlate* of abstinence and of greater compliance with professional therapy.

Despite such difficulties, the overall evidence that AA works as a scientific "cure" has become quite convincing. Multiple studies that in combination involved thousands of individuals suggest that good clinical outcomes are significantly correlated with frequency of AA attendance, with having a sponsor, with leading meetings, and with engaging in altruistic step-twelve work, defined as reaching out to still-suffering alcoholics.[31]

At Stanford, research psychologists Keith Humphreys and Rudolf Moos carried out a long-term study that contrasted AA attendance to compliance with professional treatment.[32] By eight years the two goals of less drinking and more abstinence were only weakly related to days of professional treatment but were robustly related to frequency of AA attendance.[33] In addition, alcoholics who received professional treatment *and* attended AA had almost twice the rate of abstinence as those who only received professional treatment.[34] In short, the effect of AA does not just rest on compliance with treatment.

For thirty-five years I have been director of the Study of Adult Development. For sixty-five years this community study has followed two cohorts of men, 268 so-called college men and 456 socially disadvantaged inner-city men.[35] In that study, 76 men continued abusing alcohol all their lives. In their lifetimes, the 76 men in this poor-outcome group reported attending an average of five AA meetings each. In the same study, 66 men with an average past history of twenty years of severe alcoholism more recently had achieved an average of nineteen years of continuous sobriety. These men reported attending an average of 142 AA meetings each.[36] In other words, the men who recovered from alcoholism attended almost *thirty times* as many AA meetings as those men who remained alcoholics for a lifetime.

The third "scientific" question I must answer is: what are the side effects of AA? It is well known that whatever the benefits of cults and religions, like potent medications and automobiles, they often have serious side effects. Even if Alcoholics Anonymous does cure alcoholism, is it safe? Certainly, AA has its detractors. The rhetoric and the emotional language of AA is designed to penetrate the reptile brain, and it can enrage journalists and social scientists who understandably fear demagogues and cults.[37] Sam Harris and Richard Dawkins deem all faith-based organizations dangerous. Individual alcoholics who have attended incompatible AA groups or aligned themselves with unempathic sponsors tell horror stories about the fellowship. But in my experience these are exceptions. Alcoholics have often suffered even worse in the hands of well-meaning but ignorant physicians who prescribed either blame or booze in pill form like Xanax, sleeping pills, and, in the 1950s American South, morphine.

So what are the safeguards that protect AA from becoming a dogmatic cult? I earlier suggested that long-term follow-up was the best way to judge the safety of controversial spiritual "cults" like AA and Scientology. After twenty years, Scientology was put on the cover of *Time* with the title "The Cult of Greed."[38] After twenty years, Alcoholics Anonymous received the Lasker Award—America's only "Nobel Prize" for medical science. AA's founder, however, refused to be put on the cover of *Time*. It would have violated AA's twelfth tradition: "Anonymity is the spiritual foundation of all our traditions, ever reminding us to place principles before personalities."

True, cults and AA both take advantage of the fact that people experience relief from emotional distress when they feel held by what Marc Galanter calls a "social cocoon."[39] But healing through intense affiliation is hardly confined to cults. Families, sororities, and soccer teams also provide social cocoons. Indeed, in the evolution of *Homo sapiens* natural selection has favored our capacity to create social cocoons.

Nevertheless, AA has been accused of a suspiciously high level of social cohesion. It is true that besides recovery and service, the third cornerstone of AA membership is unity. But the dogmatic unity of AA is based on the same principles that drove the thirteen original colonies to achieve social cohesion as the United States. In the words of Ben Franklin, "If we don't all hang together, we will all hang separately."

Unlike membership in an Islamic mosque, a Hassidic synagogue, or a Roman Catholic church, following the rigidly sequential rules of AA is like following the rigidly numbered steps of a Nautilus exercise regimen—your participation is voluntary, and it is always your turn. When it was first introduced, coronary bypass surgery did not lengthen patients' lives; rather, patients' lives were extended by the rigid exercise regimens imposed on postcoronary patients—with their consent. The purpose of the rigidity of both postcoronary and AA step programs is not, as is the case with cults, to take away your autonomy, but only to provide a disciplined program of relapse prevention so that you won't revert to bad habits and die. I too have a profound mistrust of Puritanism, jogging, and diets with too many vegetables. But if such rigid behavior would keep me from dying from heart disease, I just might become more tolerant.

I have acknowledged that religions have serious side effects, but AA insists that it is not a religion, and furthermore that it is different from religion in the same way that spirituality is different from religion. First, it is hard to belong to two religions at the same time. However, devout religious convictions do not prevent AA membership. Over the last twenty years, AA membership has increased tenfold in Hindu India, in Buddhist Japan, and in Catholic Spain. AA membership has risen exponentially in atheistic Russia.

Worth noting are some of the ways in which AA has avoided becoming a religion or a cult. The spiritual foundation of AA evolved from the intellectual experience of three men deeply mistrustful of all organized religions. Instead, these three men, William James with his *Varieties of Religious Experience*, Carl Jung with his prescription "Spiritus contra spiritu," and Dr. Robert Smith, cofounder of AA, were all devout students of what was truly healing among all religions. Thus, the editors of the Twelve Steps consciously tried to balance their language so that neither atheists nor those who believed deeply in God would be turned away. Indeed, AA is not about religion at all. As one member put it, "We don't affiliate with any particular church, but we sure like to meet in their basements."

Another difference between AA and many healing cults is that the spirituality of AA does not compete with medical science. AA literature is very clear that it is "wrong to deprive any alcoholic of medication which can alleviate or control other disabling physical and/or emotional problems" and that "no AA member plays doctor."[40]

Except in its insistence on abstinence rather than moderation, AA tries to avoid black-and-white thinking. AA has no written dogma or rules. In the words of cofounder Dr. Robert Smith, the famous Twelve Steps are "suggestions not dogma."[41] AA believes instead in the limbic language of the heart.

From the beginning, AA has made no clear distinction between God and "the fellowship of AA." There has always been a tacit, if not explicit, permission to replace the concept of God with Jung's other antidote for alcoholism, the "protective wall of human community"—by definition a power greater than ourselves.[42] Rather than demand that its members believe in God, AA asks each member to reflect: can I admit that the universe is not just about me?

Indeed, the evolution of Alcoholics Anonymous has mimicked the evolution of science rather than that of cults. To identify what is wheat and what is chaff, AA, like science, has proceeded by trial and error. Admittedly, unlike religions, AA has possessed an objective measuring stick of outcome—sustained abstinence. In point of fact, we have no way of knowing who goes to heaven, but we do know who stays sober. Its objectivity has helped AA avoid the fate of most religions where sooner or later prejudice, personalities, and superstitions seem to distract members from basic principles.

Another major difference between religions and AA is their governing structure. Charismatic leaders with infallible powers and an autocratic governing structure characterize cults and many religions. In AA, "our leaders are trusted servants; they do not govern." Most of the service positions in AA are unpaid, and all jobs are frequently rotated so that power cannot be consolidated. At AA meetings charismatic speakers are often replaced by shyer, newer members.

A fundamental principle of AA is that "it's dangerous to impose any-thing on anybody." Thus, the organizational chart of AA that has evolved is a pyramid on its head. Positions of responsibility within AA are defined as "service without authority," and the legislative processes of AA are dem-ocratic to a fault. In its conferences, "roundups," and assemblies of elected delegates, the critical issues before AA are discussed, not debated, for the goal is consensus, not victory. Politics, of course, exist in AA, but less so than in any other organization with which I am familiar. A fundamental tradition of AA—and of no other organization of which I have heard ex-cept the best judiciaries—is "Don't put personalities over principles." In AA, but not in cults or religion, dissident opinions are respected. Just as the American founding fathers gave as many senators to Delaware and Rhode Island as to the more populated states of New York and Virginia, just so AA in its organizational deliberations pays particular attention to minority opinions.

In all democratic spiritual communities, the playing field is level. Part of the beauty of the early Christian church was that, like the democratic Greek city-states in which it grew up, the early church was free of past rab-binical or future papal authority. Today part of the appeal of "alternative" medicine is that it is often more democratic than "scientific" medicine. In AA the egalitarian definition of a "pigeon" (a new member) is "someone who comes along just in time to keep her sponsor sober."

A criticism of both AA and monotheistic religions is that in contrast to spiritual programs like Buddhism, AA encourages dependence. Many ob-servers worry that AA members become as needy of their 8:00 P.M. meet-ings as they once were of alcohol itself. However, the dependence engendered by AA differs from the dependence engendered by cults. De-pendence can weaken us or strengthen us. We are weakened by dependence on cigarettes, slot machines, and junk food. We are strengthened by de-pendence on exercise, vitamins, and our families. A common nickname for an AA member's home group is "family."

Another feature that distinguishes AA from most religions is that AA has a sense of humor. Every meeting of AA that I have ever attended has been filled with laughter. Dictators, cult leaders, mullahs, bishops, and training analysts often fail to observe AA's venerable rule number sixty-two: "Don't take yourself too damn seriously." (*Nota bene*: the other sixty-one rules do not exist.)

Finally, AA's Twelve Traditions reflect founder Bill W's twenty-year conscious effort to embrace humility, awe, and reverence for a power greater than himself.[43] This embrace distinguishes spirituality from humanism and yet at the same time protects AA from becoming a cult or a religion. Several of AA's traditions would go a long way to helping many religions become more mature and spiritual. One such tradition is corporate poverty. AA, like the early monastic orders, successfully strives to stay poor. Unlike cults, universities, major charities, and religious denominations, AA owns no property. As Saint Francis understood as well as anyone, possessions often interfere with spirituality. Only members can give AA money, and even then, they can leave no more than $2,000 to AA in their wills.

∻

Where do we go from here? Alcoholics Anonymous has simply served as a concrete illustration of safe spirituality at work. Obviously, AA's principles of inclusiveness, service, equality, corporate poverty, and humility exist outside of AA. My point is that spirituality at its best replaces the exclusionary, omnipotent, and often painful facets of religion with a more open, vulnerable, and trusting stance. Dr. Bob suggested that the spiritual principles of even the allegedly inviolate Twelve Steps of AA could be boiled down to three words: "love and service."[44] His summary of the Twelve Steps differs little from Rabbi Hillel's famous synopsis of Jewish Law while standing on one leg: "Do not do unto others as you would not have done to you. That is the Torah; the rest is commentary." The Golden Rule and "love and service" reflect safe credos for all of our planet's six billion inhabitants.

Certainly, we must remain open to experience, and we must remain open to the dimension of time. To understand the role of faith, hope, and well-intentioned compassion in our lives, we must focus on long-term results, not sentiment. On the one hand, two hundred years ago the good citizens of Boston rioted against "false" medical prophets who insisted that cowpox inoculations would immunize human beings against smallpox. Today the prophets stand vindicated. Thanks to "religious" adherence to cowpox inoculation, the scourge of smallpox has been eradicated from the entire planet. On the other hand, I have already noted that just fifty years ago medical science had faith (supported by seven hundred scientific papers) that insulin coma alleviated schizophrenia. Today medical science acknowledges its mistake. Insulin coma therapy was only a powerful placebo, and as a therapy insulin coma is as extinct as smallpox. Thus, a major reason that many prefer science to religion is that the former is more ready to admit error. But the abandonment of faith is not the answer.

The mistrust that both psychoanalysis and science entertain toward spirituality reminds me of the fable of a miner who was a heavy drinker. He pawned his furniture. He beat his wife. He abused his children. Then, through the efforts of a local priest, he became a fervent member of his local church. Down in the pits his fellow miners ribbed him about "getting religion." One day they asked him if he really believed the miracle of Christ turning water into wine. "I don't understand anything about miracles or how they work," he replied. "I am a simple man. But I do know that in my house liquor has been turned into furniture, despair into hope, and hatred into love. And that's miracle enough for me." Any program that fosters positive emotion is worth taking seriously. Honey catches more flies than vinegar.

Historian Karen Armstrong suggests:

The one and only test of a valid religious idea, doctrinal statement, spiritual experience, or devotional practice was that it must lead directly to practical compassion. If your understanding of the divine made you kinder, more empathic, and impelled you to express this sympathy in concrete acts of loving-kindness, this was good theology. But if your notion of God made you unkind, belligerent, cruel, or self-righteous, or if it led you to kill in God's name, it was bad theology. Compassion was the litmus test for the prophets of Israel, for the rabbis of the Talmud, for Jesus, for Paul, and for Muhammad, not to mention Confucius, Lao-tzu, the Buddha.[45]

Skeptical academic minds have tended not to accept the universal importance of spirituality in human life. Too often the mere mention of spirituality leads academics to roll their eyes with the same disbelief—dare I say disgust—with which Skinner treated emotion. Academics have wished to keep scientific and spiritual truths separate, insisting that the scientific is truer than the spiritual. I believe that is a mistake. Once again, sociobiologist Edward O. Wilson comes to our rescue: "The essence of humanity's spiritual dilemma is that we evolved genetically to accept one truth and discovered another."[46] Humanity evolved to accept the truth that the highest values of humanity could be expressed through limbic awe for the beautiful and through the enduring guidance of positive emotions. The science that humanity has discovered allows dispassionate reflection in order to validate—and when necessary invalidate—the perceptions of our five senses. Science reflects our cognitive urge to analyze the world and render it both conscious and predictable. Our task in the future is to integrate Wilson's two truths. For example, a hundred $1 bills are worth more than a hundred love letters. And yet a single love letter is worth more than $100.

In part, a person's maturity reflects his or her capacity to tolerate, integrate, and learn from paradox. For example, on a global basis automobiles account for more than 100,000 deaths a year, but many hundreds of millions regard the automobile as a blessing. On a global basis, religion "causes" many thousands of deaths a year, but for literally billions of people religion provides a conduit for the positive emotions to enter and remain in consciousness. Thus, I do not wish to suggest that Sam Harris, Christopher Hitchens, and Richard Dawkins are wrong in their view of evolution. However, I *do* wish to suggest that over the long term, having love for all people and compassion for all religious beliefs will reflect a cultural evolutionary advance.

NOTES

ঞ৯

Chapter 1

1. Jack Kornfield, *After the Ecstasy, the Laundry* (New York: Bantam Books, 2000), pp. 235–36.

2. Antonio Damasio, *Descartes' Error* (New York: Putnam, 1994), p. 267.

3. Dacher Keltner and Jonathan Haidt, "Approaching Awe as Moral Aesthetic and Spiritual Emotions," *Cognition and Emotion* 17 (2003): 297–314.

4. Michael E. McCullough et al., "Gratitude as Moral Affect," *Psychological Bulletin* 127 (2001): 249–66.

5. Barbara L. Fredrickson, "The Role of Positive Emotions in Positive Psychology?" *American Psychologist* 56 (2001): 218–26.

6. Barbara L. Fredrickson, "The Broaden and Build Theory of Positive Emotions," *Philosophical Transactions of the Royal Society of London* 359 (2004): 1367–77.

7. Alice M. Isen, Andrew S. Rosenzweig, and Mark J. Young, "The Influence of Positive Affect on Clinical Problem Solving," *Medical Decision Making*, 11 (1991): 221–27; Sonya Lyubomirsky, Laura King, and Ed Diener, "The Benefits of Frequent Positive Affect: Does Happiness Lead to Success?" *Psychological Bulletin* 131 (2005): 803–55.

8. Herbert Benson, *Timeless Healing* (New York: Scribner's, 1996).

9. Andrew Newberg and Jeremy Iversen, "The Neural Basis of the Complex Mental Task of Meditation: Neurotransmitter and Neurochemical Considerations," *Medical Hypothesis* 8 (2003): 282–91.

10. Robert Emmons, *Thanks!: How the New Science of Gratitude Can Make You Happier* (Boston: Houghton Mifflin, 2007), p. 4.

11. Barbara Kantrowitz, "In Search of the Sacred," *Newsweek*, November 28, 1994, pp. 52–62.

12. Herbert Benson, *Timeless Healing* (New York: Scribner's, 1996).

13. Richard J. Davidson and Anne Harrington, *Visions of Compassion* (Oxford: Oxford University Press, 2002), p. 17.

14. Antonio Damasio, *The Feeling of What Happens: Body and Emotion in the Making of Consciousness* (New York: Harvest Books, 2000), p. 54.

15. Gerald Edelman, *Bright Air, Brilliant Fire: On the Matter of Mind* (New York: Basic Books, 1992).

16. Damasio, *Descartes' Error*; Jaak Panksepp, *Affective Neuroscience: The Foundations of Human and Animal Emotion* (New York: Oxford University Press, 1998).

17. David S. Wilson, *Darwin's Cathedral: Evolution, Religion, and the Nature of Society* (Chicago: University of Chicago Press, 2002).

18. Lyubomirsky, King, and Diener, "The Benefits of Frequent Positive Affect."

19. Albert Schweitzer, *The Spiritual Life: Selected Writings of Albert Schweitzer* (Boston: Beacon Press, 1947).

20. Harris B. Ackner and A. J. Oldham, "Insulin Treatment of Schizophrenia: A Controlled Study," *Lancet* i (1957): 607–11; W. A. Cramand, "Lessons from the Insulin Story in Psychiatry," *Australia and New Zealand Journal of Psychiatry* 21 (1987): 320–26.

21. George E. Vaillant, *Adaptation to Life* (Boston: Little, Brown, 1977); George E. Vaillant, *Wisdom of the Ego* (Cambridge, Mass.: Harvard University Press, 1993); George E. Vaillant, *Aging Well* (Boston: Little, Brown, 2002).

22. Louis Sheaffer, *O'Neill: Son and Playwright* (Boston: Little, Brown, 1968).

23. Gail Ironson, "The Ironson-Woods Spirituality/Religiousness Index Is Associated with Long Survival, Health Behaviors, Less Distress, and Low Cortisol in People with HIV/AIDS," *Annals of Behavioral Medicine* (2002): 24, 34–38.

24. George E. Vaillant, Janice A. Templeton, Stephanie Meyer, and Monika Ardelt, "Natural History of Male Mental Health XVI: What Is Spirituality Good For?" *Social Science and Medicine*, 66 (2008): 221–31.

25. Christopher Peterson and Martin Seligman, "Character Strengths Before and After September 11," *Psychological Science* 14 (2003): 381–84.

26. Barbara Fredrickson et al., "What Good Are Positive Emotions in Crises?" *Journal of Personality and Social Psychology* 84 (2003): 365–76.

27. Karen Armstrong, *The Great Transformation* (New York: Knopf, 2006), p. 396.

Chapter 2

1. Russell D'Souza and Kuruvilla George, "Spirituality, Religion, and Psychiatry: Its Application to Clinical Practice," *Australian Psychiatry* 14 (2006): 408–12.

2. George P. Murdock, "The Common Denominators of Cultures," in *The Science of Man in the World Crisis*, ed. Ralph Linton (New York: Columbia University Press, 1945).

3. Wilhelm Wundt, *Lectures on Human and Animal Psychology* (New York: Macmillan, 1896); William James, *The Principles of Psychology* (New York: Henry Holt, 1890).

4. Max F. Meyer, "The Whale Among the Fishes: The Theory of Emotions," *Psychological Review* 40 (1933): 292–300.

5. Burrhus F. Skinner, *Science and Human Behavior* (New York: Macmillan, 1953), 137–208.

6. Harry Harlow, "The Nature of Love," *American Psychologist* 13 (1958): 673–85; Deborah Blum, *Love at Goon Park* (Cambridge, Mass.: Perseus Books, 2002).

7. Jane Goodall, *In the Shadow of Man* (Boston: Houghton Mifflin, 1971).

8. Paul Ekman, *Emotions Revealed* (London: Weidenfeld & Nicholson, 2003).

9. Benjamin J. Sadock and Virginia A. Sadock, *Comprehensive Textbook of Psychiatry* (Philadelphia: Lippincott, Williams & Wilkins, 2004).

10. William James, *The Varieties of Religious Experience* (London: Longmans, Green & Co., 1902), pp. 486, 498, 501.

11. Michael S. Gazzaniga et al., "Collaboration Between the Hemispheres of a Callostomy Patient: Emerging Right Hemisphere Speech and the Left-Brain Interpreter," *Brain* 119 (1996): 1255–62.

12. Antonio Damasio, *Descartes' Error* (New York: Penguin, 1994); Eric R. Kandel, James H. Schwartz, and Thomas M. Jessell, *Principles of Neural Science*, 4th ed. (New York: McGraw-Hill, 2000); Antonio Damasio, "Neuroscience and Ethics: Intersections," *American Journal of Bioethics* 7 (2007): 3–6.

13. Harold W. Gordon and Joseph E. Bogen, "Hemispheric Lateralization of Singing After Intracarotid Sodium Amylbarbitone," *Journal of Neurology, Neurosurgery and Psychiatry* 37 (1974): 727–39.

14. Steven Mithen, *The Singing Neanderthals* (Cambridge, Mass.: Harvard University Press, 2006).

15. Charles Darwin, *The Expression of the Emotions in Men and in Animals* (New York: D. Appleton & Co., 1899).

16. Paul Broca, "Anatomie comparée des circonvolutions cérébrales: Le grand lobe limbique," *Revue Anthropologique* 1 (1878): 385–498.

17. Antoine de Saint-Exupéry, *The Little Prince* (New York: Harcourt, Brace and World, 1943), p. 68.

18. Joan B. Silk, Susan C. Alberts, and Jeanne Altmann, "Social Bonds of Female Baboons Enhance Infant Survival," *Science* 302 (2003): 1231–34.

19. James Olds, "Physiological Mechanisms of Reward," in *Nebraska Symposium on Motivation*, ed. M. R. Jones, (Lincoln: University of Nebraska Press, 1955), 73–139.

20. Paul MacLean, *The Triune Brain in Evolution* (New York: Plenum, 1990).

21. Antonio R. Damasio et al., "Subcortical and Cortical Brain Activity During the Feeling of Self-Generated Emotions," *Nature Neuroscience* 3 (2000): 1049–56.

22. Jaak Panksepp, *Affective Neuroscience: The Foundations of Human and Animal Emotion* (New York: Oxford University Press, 1998); Jeffrey Burgdorf and Jaak Panksepp, "The Neurobiology of Positive Emotions," *Neuroscience and Biobehavioral Reviews* 30 (2006): 173–87.

23. Jon-Kar Zubietta et al., "Regulation of Human Affective Responses by Anterior Cingulate on Limbic Mu-opioid Neurotransmission," *Archives of General Psychiatry* 60 (2003): 1145–53.

24. See, for example, Burgdorf and Panksepp, "The Neurobiology of Positive Emotions."

25. Joseph LeDoux, *The Emotional Brain* (New York: Simon & Schuster, 1998), p. 101.

26. Paul MacLean, "Psychosomatic Disease and the 'Visceral Brain': Recent Developments Bearing on the Papez Theory of Emotion," *Psychosomatic Medicine* 11 (1949): 338–53, 52.

27. Martin Luther, *The Table Talk of Martin Luther* (1569), ed. Thomas Kepler (New York: Dover Publications, 2005), p. 79.

28. E. M. Forster, *Howard's End* (1910) (New York: Edward Arnold, 1973), pp. 183–84.

29. Sylvan S. Tomkins, *Affect Imagery Consciousness*, vol. 1, *The Positive Affects* (New York: Springer Publishing, 1962), p. 112.

30. Jaak Panksepp, Eric Nelson, and Marni Berkkedal, "Brain Systems for the Mediation of Social Separation-Distress and Social Reward: Evolutionary Antecedents and Neuropeptide Intermediaries," *Annals of the New York Academy of Science* 807 (1997): 78–100.

31. Michael S. Mega et al., *The Limbic System in the Neuropsychiatry of Limbic*

and Subcortical Disorders (Washington, D.C.: American Psychiatric Press, 1997), pp. 3–18.

32. Andrew Newberg and Jeremy Iversen, "The Neural Basis of the Complex Mental Task of Meditation: Neurotransmitter and Neurochemical Considerations," *Medical Hypothesis* 8 (2003): 282–91.

33. Myron Hofer, "Early Social Relationships: A Psychobiologist's View," *Child Development* 59 (1987): 192–207.

34. John M. Allman et al., "The Anterior Cingulate Cortex: The Evolution of an Interface Between Emotion and Cognition," *Annals of the New York Academy of Science* 935 (2001): 107–17.

35. Fredrich Sanides, "Functional Architecture of Motor and Sensory Cortices in Primates in the Light: A New Concept of Neocortex Evolution," in *The Primate Brain*, ed. Charles R. Noback and William Montagna (New York: Appleton Century Crofts, 1970).

36. Guido Gainotti, "Emotional Behavior and Hemispheric Side of the Lesion," *Cortex* 8 (1972): 41–55.

37. Allman et al., "The Anterior Cingulate Cortex."

38. Walle J. Nauta, "The Problem of the Frontal Lobe: A Reinterpretation," *Journal of Psychiatric Research* 8 (1971): 167–87.

39. John K. Fulton, ed., *The Frontal Lobes* (Baltimore: Williams & Wilkins, 1948).

40. Melvin Konner, *The Tangled Wing*, 2nd ed. (New York: Henry Holt, 2002), p. 251.

41. Antonio Damasio, "Neuroscience and Ethics: Intersections," *American Journal of Bioethics* 7 (2007): 3–6.

42. P. Thomas Schoenemann, Michael J. Sheehan, and L. D. Glotzer, "Prefrontal White Matter Volume Is Disproportionately Larger in Humans Than in Other Primates," *Natural Neuroscience* 8 (2005): 242–52.

43. Damasio, *Descartes' Error.*

44. Konner, *The Tangled Wing.*

45. Damasio, *Descartes' Error.*

46. Robert D. Hare, "Electrodermal and Cardiovascular Correlates of Psychopathy," in *Psychopathic Behavior: Approaches to Research*, ed. Robert D. Hare and D. Scharing (Chichester, England: John Wiley, 1978), 107–43; Antonio R. Damasio and D. Tranel, "Individuals with Sociopathic Behavior Caused by Frontal Damage Fail to Respond Autonomically to Social Stimuli," *Behavioral Brain Research* 41 (1990): 81–94.

47. Richard Davidson, "Well-being and Affective Style: Neural Substrates and

Biobehavioral Correlates," *Philosophical Transactions of the Royal Society, London,* B, 359 (2004): 1395–1411.

48. Richard Davidson and Anne Harrington, *Visions of Compassion* (London: Oxford University Press, 2002).

49. Richard Davidson, "Affective Style, Psychopathology, and Resilience: Brain Mechanisms and Plasticity," *American Psychologist* 55 (2000): 1196–1214.

50. Herbert Benson, *Timeless Healing* (New York: Scribner's, 1996); J. L. Kristeller, "Mindfulness Meditation," in *Principles and Practice of Stress Management,* ed. Paul M. Lehrer, Robert L. Woolfolk, and Wesley E. Sime (New York: Guilford Press, 2007).

51. John M. Allman et al., "Intuition and Autism: A Possible Role for Von Economo Neurons," *Trends in Cognitive Science* 9 (2005): 367–73.

52. Sandra Blakeslee, "Humanity? Maybe It's in the Wiring," *New York Times,* December 7, 2003, D1 and D4.

53. Laurie Carr et al., "Neural Mechanisms of Empathy in Humans: A Relay from Neural Systems for Imitation to Limbic Areas," *Proceedings of the National Academy of Science USA* 100 (2003): 5497–5502; Giacomo Rizzolatti, "The Mirror Neuron System and Its Function in Humans," *Anatomy and Embryology* 210 (2005): 419–21.

54. Sara W. Lazar et al., "Meditation Experience Is Associated with Increased Cortical Thickness," *Neuro Report* 16 (2005): 1893–97.

55. Francine M. Benes et al., "Myelinization of a Key Relay Zone in the Hippocampal Formarien Occurs in the Human Brain During Childhood, Adolescence, and Adulthood," *Archives of General Psychiatry* 51 (1994): 477–84.

Chapter 3

1. Adam Sedgwick, letter to Charles Darwin, in *The Darwin Collection* (London: British Museum, 1859).

2. Richard Dawkins, "Is Science a Religion?" *The Humanist* (January–February 1997): 26.

3. Jaak Panksepp, *Affective Neuroscience: The Foundations of Human and Animal Emotion* (New York: Oxford University Press, 1998).

4. Christopher B. Stringer and Robin McKie, *African Exodus: The Origins of Modern Humanity* (New York: Henry Holt & Co, 1997).

5. Michael J. Raleigh and Gary L. Brammer, "Individual Differences in Sero-

tonin-2 Receptors and Social Behavior in Monkeys," *Society for Neuroscience Abstracts* 19 (1993): 592.

6. Thomas R. Insel and Larry J. Young, "The Neurobiology of Attachment," *Nature Reviews Neuroscience* 2 (2002): 129–36.

7. John M. Allman et al., *Evolving Brains* (New York: Scientific American Library, 1998).

8. Yves Coppens, "Brain Locomotion, Diet, and Culture: How a Primate by Chance, Became a Man," in *Origins of the Human Brain*, ed. Pierre Changeux and Jean Chavaillon (Oxford: Clarendon Press, 1995), 104–12.

9. John E. Pfeiffer, *The Creative Explosion: An Inquiry into the Origins of Art and Religion* (New York: Harper & Row, 1986).

10. Steven Mithen, *The Singing Neanderthals* (Cambridge, Mass.: Harvard University Press, 2006).

11. On the fossil record, see Christopher B. Stringer, "Out of Ethiopia," *Nature* 423 (2003): 92–95; on the mitochondrial evidence, see Max Ingman et al., "Mitochondrial Genome Variation and the Origin of Modern Humans," *Nature* 408 (2000): 708–13.

12. Wolfgang Enard et al., "Molecular Evolution of FOXP2, a Gene Involved in Speech and Language," *Nature* 418 (2002): 869–72.

13. Michael Balter, "Speech Gene Tied to Modern Humans," *Science* 297 (2002): 1105.

14. Michael Balter, "Are Human Brains Still Evolving? Brain Genes Show Signs of Selection," *Science* 309 (2005): 1662–63; Patrick D. Evans et al., "Microcephalin: A Gene Regulating Brain Size Continues to Evolve Adaptively in Humans," *Science* 309 (2005): 1717–20.

15. Nitzan Mekel-Bobrov et al., "Ongoing Adaptive Evolution of ASPM: A Brain Size Determined in Homo Sapiens," *Science* 309 (2005): 1720–22.

16. Joan B. Silk and Susan C. Alberts, "Social Bonds of Female Baboons Enhance Infant Survival," *Science* 302 (2003): 1231–34; Elliot Sober and David S. Wilson, *Unto Others: The Evolution and Psychology of Unselfish Behavior* (Cambridge, Mass.: Harvard University Press, 1998).

17. Richard G. Klein, *The Dawn of Human Culture* (New York: John Wiley, 2002).

18. Derek Bickerton, *Language and Human Behavior* (Seattle: University of Washington Press, 1995).

19. Grahame L. Walsh, *Bradshaw Art of the Kimberley* (Toowong, Queensland, Aust.: Takarakka Nowan Kas Publications, 2000).

20. Steven D. Levitt and Stephen J. Dubner, *Freakonomics* (New York: Morrow, 2005).

21. Karen Armstrong, *Holy War: The Crusades and Their Impact on Today's World* (New York: Doubleday, 1991).
22. Karen Armstrong, *The Great Transformation* (New York: Knopf, 2006), p. xii.
23. Ibid., p. 130.
24. Julian Jaynes, *The Origin of Consciousness in the Breakdown of the Bicameral Mind* (Boston: Houghton Mifflin, 1990).
25. Robert Potter, trans. *The Persians by Aeschylus* (New York: Players, 1998), p. 47.
26. Armstrong, *The Great Transformation*, p. 227.
27. Ibid., p. 271.
28. Arthur Waley, ed. and trans., *The Analects of Confucius* (New York: Harper Collins, 1922), p. 68.
29. Armstrong, *The Great Transformation*, p. 277.
30. Walsh, *Bradshaw Art of the Kimberley*.
31. Pierre Teilhard de Chardin, *The Phenomenon of Man* (London: Collins, 1959).
32. Khalil H. N. Khalil, "Evolutionary Humanism: A Foundation for a Theory of Education," Ph.D. diss., University of Massachusetts (1975).
33. William R. Miller and Carl E. Thoresen, "Spirituality, Religion, and Health," *American Psychologist* 58 (2003): 24–35.
34. Leon Neyfakh, "The Science of Smiling" *The Harvard Crimson*, February 15, 2006.
35. Pierre Teilhard de Chardin, *Toward the Future* (New York: Harcourt Brace Jovanovich, 1975).
36. Francine M. Benes, "Development of the Cortical-Limbic System," in *Human Behavior and the Developing Brain*, ed. Geraldine Dawson and Kurt W. Fischer (New York: Guilford Press, 1994).
37. William E. Phipps, *Amazing Grace in John Newton* (Macon, Ga.: Mercy University Press, 2001).
38. Ana Maria Rizzuto, *The Birth of the Living God* (Chicago: University of Chicago Press, 1979), p. 44.
39. Ibid., p. 47.
40. Else Frenkel-Brunswik, "Studies in Biographical Psychology," *Character and Personality* 5 (1936): 1–34.
41. Carol Gilligan, *In a Different Voice* (Cambridge, Mass.: Harvard University Press, 1982).
42. Jean Piaget, *The Moral Judgment of the Child* (London: Kegan Paul, 1932).

43. On neural brain structure, see Walle J. H. Nauta, "The Problem of the Frontal Lobe: A Reinterpretation," *Psychiatric Research* 8 (1971): 167–87; on neural brain function, see Antonio Damasio, *Descartes' Error* (New York: Penguin, 1994).

44. Benes, "Development of the Cortical-Limbic System."

45. Dawkins, "Is Science a Religion?"

46. Jane Loevinger, *Ego Development* (San Francisco: Jossey-Bass, 1976); James Fowler, *Stages of Faith* (New York: Harper & Row, 1981).

47. Michael Commons, Francis Richards, and Cheryl Armon, eds., *Beyond Formal Operations: Late Adolescent and Adult Cognitive Development* (New York: Praeger, 1984).

Chapter 4

1. Ajai Singh and Shakurtala Singh, "Gandhi on Religion, Faith, and Conversion," *Mens Sana Monographs II* (Mumbai, India, 2004): 79–87, 84.

2. Gregory L. Fricchione, unpublished manuscript.

3. Michael Kosfeld et al., "Oxytocin Increased Trust in Humans," *Nature* 435 (2005): 673–76.

4. Dines Anderson and Helmer Smith, eds., *Sutta-Nipata* (1913) (London: Oxford University Press for the Pali Text Society, 1948), p. 26.

5. Albert Camus, *The Plague*, trans. Stuart Gilbert (New York: Knopf, 1950), pp. 196–97.

6. Antoine de Saint-Exupéry, *The Little Prince* (New York: Harcourt Brace and World, 1943), p. 68.

7. Ibid., p. 67.

8. Herbert Benson and Marg Stark, *Timeless Healing: The Power and Biology of Belief* (New York: Scribner's, 1996).

9. Wilford C. Smith, *Faith and Belief: The Difference Between Them* (Princeton, N.J.: Princeton University Press, 1979).

10. Donald Corcoran, "Spiritual Guidance," in *Christian Spirituality*, ed. Bernard McGinn and John Meyendorff (New York: Crossroad Publishing, 1985), p. 447.

11. George Johnson, *Fire in the Mind* (New York: Knopf, 1995), p. 6.

12. Kenneth S. Kendler, C. O. Gardner, and C. A. Prescott, "Religion, Psychopathology, and Substance Use and Abuse: A Multi-Measure, Genetic-Epidemiological Study," *American Journal of Psychiatry* 154 (1997): 322–29.

13. Jon Krakauer, *Under the Banner of Heaven* (New York: Doubleday, 2003).

14. Anthony Storr, *Feet of Clay* (New York: Harper Collins, 1996), p. 15.

15. Sam Harris, *The End of Faith* (New York: Norton, 2004), pp. 131, 126.

16. Jeffrey Saver and John Rabin, "The Neural Substrates of Religious Experience," in *The Neuropsychiatry of Limbic and Subcortical Disorders*, ed. Stephen Salloway, Paul Malloy, and Jeffrey L. Cummings (Washington, D.C.: American Psychiatric Press, 1997).

17. Hugh Milne, *Bhagwan: The God That Failed* (London: Sphere Books, 1983); Storr, *Feet of Clay*.

18. Harris, *The End of Faith*, p. 64.

19. Barbara L. Fredrickson, "The Role of Positive Emotions in Positive Psychology?" *American Psychologist* 56 (2001): 218–26.

20. Rudolf Otto, *The Idea of the Holy* (1917) (New York: Oxford University Press, 1958).

Chapter 5

1. Anthony Walsh, *The Science of Love* (Amherst, N.Y.: Prometheus Books, 1996), p. 31; Erich Fromm, *The Art of Loving* (New York: Basic Books, 1956), p. 7; 1 Corinthians 13:13.

2. Richard Hack, *Hughes* (Beverly Hills, Calif.: New Millennium Press, 2001).

3. Ibid.

4. *Great Soviet Encyclopedia*, vol. 15, 3rd ed., English ed., ed. Jean Paradise (New York: Macmillan, 1973/1997), p. 153.

5. Ali Shari Ati, *Hajj*, trans. Laleh Bakhtian (Teheran: Islamic Publications International, 1988), pp. 54–56.

6. Stephen G. Post, *Unlimited Love* (Philadelphia: Templeton Foundation Press, 2003), p. 3.

7. Helen Fisher, Arthur Aron, and Lucy L. Brown, "Romantic Love: An fMRI Study of a Neural Mechanism for Mate Choice," *Journal of Comparative Neurology* 493 (2005): 58–62; Arthur Aron, "Reward Motivation and Emotion Systems Associated with Early-Stage Intense Romantic Love," *Journal of Neurophysiology* 94 (2005): 327–37.

8. Harry Harlow, "The Nature of Love," *American Psychologist* 13 (1958): 673–85, 673.

9. Thomas Lewis, Fari Amini, and Richard Lannon, *A General Theory of Love* (New York: Random House, 2000), p. 84.

10. Robert C. Solomon, *Love: Emotion, Myth, and Metaphor* (New York: Anchor Press, 1981), p. 276.

11. Howard Miller and Paul S. Siegel, *Loving: A Psychological Approach* (New York: Wiley, 1972).

12. Bernard L. Murstein, "A Taxonomy of Love," in *The Psychology of Love*, ed. Robert J. Sternberg and Michael L. Barnes (New Haven, Conn.: Yale University Press, 1988), p. 26.

13. John Bowlby, *The Making and Breaking of Affectional Bonds* (London: Tavistock, 1979; Deborah Blum, *Love at Goon Park* (Cambridge, Mass.: Perseus Books, 2002), p. 59.

14. Blum, *Love at Goon Park*, p. 57.

15. Myron Hofer, "Early Social Relationships: A Psychobiologist's View," *Child Development* 59 (1987): 192–207; Thomas Lewis, Fari Amini, and Richard Lannon, *A General Theory of Love* (New York: Random House, 2000), p. 84.

16. David Spiegel, "Healing Words," *Journal of the American Medical Association* 281 (1999): 1328–29.

17. Frans B. M. de Waal, *Peacemaking Among Primates* (Cambridge, Mass.: Harvard University Press, 1990).

18. Lawrence Shapiro and Thomas R. Insel, "Infants' Response to Social Separation Reflects Adult Differences in Affinitive Behavior: A Comparative Developmental Study in Prairie and Mountain Voles," *Development Psychobiology* 23 (1990): 375–93; Thomas R. Insel and Larry J. Young, "The Neurobiology of Attachment," *Nature Reviews Neuroscience* 2 (2002): 129–36.

19. Richard J. Davidson and Anne Harrington, *Visions of Compassion* (Oxford: Oxford University Press, 2002), p. 116.

20. Griffith Edwards, *Matters of Substance* (London: Penguin Books, 2004), p. 138.

21. Jonathan Haidt, *The Happiness Hypothesis* (New York: Basic Books, 2006).

22. Judith Herman, *Trauma and Recovery* (New York: Basic Books, 1997).

23. Kerstin Uvnas-Moberg, *The Oxytocin Factor* (Cambridge, Mass.: Da Capo Press, 2003).

24. Marcus Heinrichs, "Social Support and Oxytocin Interact to Suppress Cortisol and Subjective Responses to Psychosocial Stress," *Biological Psychiatry* 24 (2003): 153–72.

25. David Quinton, Michael Rutter, and Christopher Liddle, "Institutional Rearing, Parenting Difficulties, and Marital Support," *Psychological Medicine* 14 (1984): 102–24.

26. George E. Vaillant, *Wisdom of the Ego* (Cambridge, Mass.: Harvard University Press, 1993).

Chapter 6

1. Alta May Coleman, "Personality Portrait: Eugene O'Neill," *Theatre Magazine* 31 (1920): 302.

2. Eugene O'Neill, *Long Day's Journey into Night* (New Haven, Conn.: Yale University Press, 1955), p. 69; all subsequent quotations are from this edition.

3. Louis Sheaffer, *O'Neill: Son and Playwright* (Boston: Little, Brown, 1968); Arthur Gelb and Barbara Gelb, *O'Neill* (New York: Harper & Row, 1962), p. 78.

4. Sheaffer, *O'Neill: Son and Playwright*, p. 4.

5. Gelb and Gelb, *O'Neill*, p. 434.

6. Karl Menninger, "Hope," *American Journal of Psychiatry* 115 (1959): 481–91.

7. Karl Menninger, *Love Against Hate* (New York: Viking, 1942), pp. 216–18.

8. Thomas Oxman, Daniel H. Freeman, and Eric Manheimer, eds., "Lack of Social Participation or Religious Strength and Comfort as Risk Factors for Death After Cardiac Surgery in the Elderly," *Psychosomatic Medicine* 57 (1995): 5–15.

9. Menninger, "Hope."

10. Madeline Visintainer, Joseph Volpicelli, and Martin Seligman, "Tumor Rejection in Rats After Inescapable or Escapable Shock," *Science* 216 (1982): 437–39.

11. George E. Vaillant and Kenneth Mukamal, "Successful Aging," *American Journal of Psychiatry* 158 (2001): 839–47.

12. Erik Erikson, *Insight and Responsibility* (New York: Norton, 1964).

13. Menninger, *Love Against Hate*, pp. 216–18.

14. Sigmund Freud, "Jokes and Their Relation to the Unconscious," *Complete Works of Sigmund Freud* (1905), vol. 8 (London: Hogarth Press, 1960), pp. 225, 233.

15. Reginald Pound, *Scott of the Antarctic* (New York: Coward-McCann, 1966), p. 300.

16. Jean Anouilh, *Antigone* (London: George G. Harrap, 1954), p. 84.

17. Benjamin Franklin, *Report of Dr. Benjamin Franklin and other commissioners charged by the King of France with the examination of the animal magnetism, as now practiced in Paris* (London: J. Johnson, 1785), pp. 100, 102.

18. Lee C. Park and Lino Covi, "Nonblind Placebo Trial," *Archives of General Psychiatry* 12 (1965): 336–45.

19. Jerome D. Frank, *Persuasion and Healing: A Comparative Study of Psychotherapy* (Baltimore: Johns Hopkins University Press, 1961), p. 63.

20. Howard Spiro, *The Power of Hope* (New Haven, Conn.: Yale University Press, 1998).

21. Ibid., p. 707.

22. Coretta Scott King, *My Life with Martin Luther King Jr.* (New York: Holt, Rinehart, Winston, 1969), p. 78.

Chapter 7

1. Antonio Damasio, *Looking for Spinoza* (New York: Harcourt, 2003), p. 85.

2. Michael Harner, *The Way of a Shaman* (San Francisco: Harper San Francisco, 1990), p. 22.

3. William R. Miller and Janet C'de Baca, *Quantum Change* (New York: Guilford Press, 2001), pp. 98–100.

4. Joseph M. Jones, *Affects as Process* (London: Analytic Press, 1995), p. 87.

5. Melvin Konner, *The Tangled Wing: Biological Constraints of the Human Spirit*, 2nd ed. (New York: Henry Holt, 2003).

6. André Comte-Sponville, *A Small Treatise on the Great Virtues* (New York: Henry Holt, 1996), p. 253.

7. Jones, *Affects as Process*, p. 85.

8. Robert N. Emde et al., "Emotional Expression in Infancy: A Bio-behavioral Study," *Psychology Issues* 10 (1976): 1–200.

9. Jaak Panksepp, *Affective Neuroscience: The Foundations of Human and Animal Emotion* (New York: Oxford University Press, 1998).

10. Ibid.

11. Sigmund Freud, *Beyond the Pleasure Principle*, vol. 18, *Standard Edition of the Complete Psychological Works of Sigmund Freud* (London: Hogarth Press), pp. 75–76.

12. Sigmund Freud, *Civilization and Its Discontents*, vol. 21, *Standard Edition of the Complete Psychological Works of Sigmund Freud* (London: Hogarth Press), pp. 64–65.

13. Jones, *Affects as Process*, p. 89.

14. Sylvan S. Tomkins, *Affect Imagery Consciousness*, vol. 1, *The Positive Affect* (New York: Springer Publishing, 1962).

15. Ibid., p. 356.

16. Karen Armstrong, *The Spiral Staircase: My Climb Out of Darkness* (New York: Knopf, 2003), pp. 272, 298.

17. C. S. Lewis, *Surprised by Joy* (New York: Harcourt Brace, 1966), p. 18.

18. Tomkins, *Affect Imagery Consciousness*, p. 421.

Chapter 8

1. Robert Enright et al., "The Psychology of Interpersonal Forgiveness," in *Exploring Forgiveness*, ed. Robert D. Enright and Joanna North (Madison: University of Wisconsin Press, 1998), pp. 46–47.

2. Robert R. Palmer, *A History of the Modern World* (New York: Knopf, 1951), p. 698.

3. Joseph Sandler and Anna Freud, *The Analysis of Defense: The Ego and the Mechanisms of Defense Revisited* (New York: International University Press, 1985), p. 185.

4. Andrew B. Newberg et al., "The Neuropsychological Correlates of Forgiveness," in *Forgiveness: Theory, Research, and Practice*, ed. Michael E. McCullough, Kenneth I. Pargament, and Carl E. Thoresen (New York: Guilford, 2000), p. 298.

5. Giacomo Bono and Michael E. McCullough, "Religion, Forgiveness, and Adjustment in Older Adulthood," in *Religious Influences on Health and Well-being in the Elderly*, ed. K. Warner Schaie, Neal Krause, and Alan Booth (New York: Springer Publishing, 2005).

6. Shin-Tseng Huang and Robert Enright, "Forgiveness and Anger-Related Emotions in Taiwan: Implications for Therapy," *Psychotherapy* 37 (2000): 71–79.

7. Charlotte VanOyen Witvliet et al., "Granting Forgiveness or Harboring Grudges," *Psychological Science* 12 (2001): 117–23.

8. Michael E. McCullough, Kenneth I. Pargament, and Carl E. Thoresen, eds., *Forgiveness: Theory, Research, and Practice* (New York: Guilford, 2000).

9. Ibid., p. 21.

10. Luigi Accattoli, *When a Pope Asks Forgiveness* (Boston: Pauline Books and Media, 1998).

11. Michelle Girard and Étienne Mullet, "Propensity to Forgive in Adolescents, Young Adults, Older Adults, and Elderly People," *Journal of Adult Development* 4 (1997): 209–20; Michael J. Subkoviak et al., "Measuring Interpersonal Forgiveness in Late Adolescence and Middle Adulthood," *Journal of Adolescence* 18 (1995): 641–55.

12. Nelson Mandela, *Long Walk to Freedom* (Boston: Little, Brown, 1994).

13. Girard and Mullet, "Propensity to Forgive"; Loren Toussaint et al., "Forgiveness and Health: Age Differences in a U.S. Probability Sample," *Journal of Adult Development* 8 (2001): 249–57.

14. Malcolm Fraser, *Common Ground* (Camberwell, Aust.: Viking, 2002), p. 206.

15. Melanie A. Greenberg and Arthur A. Stone, "Emotional Disclosure About Traumas and Its Relation to Health Effects of Previous Disclosure and Trauma Activity," *Journal of Personality and Social Psychology* 63 (1992): 75–84.
16. Michael Henderson, *Forgiveness* (London: Grosvenor Books, 2002).
17. Coretta Scott King, *My Life with Martin Luther King Jr.* (New York: Holt, Rinehart, Winston, 1969), pp. 129–30.
18. Newberg et al., "The Neuropsychological Correlates of Forgiveness."
19. Henderson, *Forgiveness*, p. 170.
20. Judith Herman, *Trauma and Recovery* (New York: Basic Books, 1997).
21. Louis Sheaffer, *O'Neill: Son and Playwright* (Boston: Little, Brown, 1968).
22. Arthur Gelb and Barbara Gelb, *O'Neill* (New York: Harper & Row, 1962), p. 836.
23. Eugene O'Neill, *Long Day's Journey into Night* (New Haven, Conn.: Yale University Press, 1955), p. 69.
24. John Patton, *Is Human Forgiveness Possible? A Pastoral Care Perspective* (Nashville, Tenn.: Abington Press, 1985).
25. Robert Wuthnow, "How Religious Groups Promote Forgiving: A National Study," *Journal for the Scientific Study of Religion* 39 (2000): 125–39.
26. Henderson, *Forgiveness*, p. 159.

Chapter 9

1. Richard Davidson and Anne Harrington, *Visions of Compassion* (London: Oxford University Press, 2002), p. 52.
2. Richard Warren, *The Purpose-Driven Life* (Grand Rapids, Mich.: Zondervan, 2002), p. 12.
3. Tania Singer et al., "Empathy for Pain Involves the Affective but Not Sensory Components of Pain," *Science* 303 (2004): 1157–62.
4. Janas T. Kaplan and Marco Iacoboni, "Getting a Grip on the Other Minds: Mirror Neurons, Intention Understanding, and Cognitive Empathy," *Social Neuroscience* 1 (2006): 175–83.
5. George E. Vaillant, *Adaptation to Life* (Boston: Little, Brown, 1977).
6. Ibid.; George E. Vaillant, *Wisdom of the Ego* (Cambridge, Mass.: Harvard University Press, 1993).
7. Vaillant, *Wisdom of the Ego*.
8. Anne Colby and William Damon, *Some Do Care* (New York: Free Press, 1994).

9. Howard Spiro, *The Power of Hope* (New Haven, Conn.: Yale University Press, 1998), p. 225.

10. Raul de la Fuente-Fernandez et al., "Expectation and Dopamine Release: Mechanism of the Placebo Effect in Parkinson's Disease," *Science* 293 (2001): 1164–66.

11. Rachel Bachner-Melman et al., "Dopaminergic Polymorphisms Associated with Self-Report Measures of Human Altruism: A Fresh Phenotype for the Dopamine D4 Receptor," *Molecular Psychiatry* 10 (2005): 333–35.

12. Jorge Moll et al., "Human Frontal-Mesolimbic Networks Guide Decisions About Charitable Donation," *Proceedings of the National Academy of Sciences* 103 (2006): 15623–28.

13. Antonio Damasio, "Neuroscience and Ethics: Intersections," *American Journal of Bioethics* 7 (2007): 3–6.

14. Moll et al., "Human Frontal-Mesolimbic Networks," p. 15626.

15. Karen Armstrong, *The Great Transformation* (New York: Knopf, 2006), p. 391.

Chapter 10

1. René Girard, *Violence and the Sacred* (Baltimore: Johns Hopkins University Press, 1977).

2. Kenneth I. Pargament, "The Psychology of Religion and Spirituality? Yes and No," *International Journal for the Psychology of Religion* 6 (1999): 3–16.

3. Stephen G. Post, *Unlimited Love* (Philadelphia: Templeton Foundation Press, 2003), p. 41.

4. Fetzer Institute, "Multidimensional Measurement of Religiousness/Spirituality," for use in health research (Kalamazoo, Mich.: John E. Fetzer Institute, 2003).

5. Maren Batalden, personal communication.

6. Andrew Newberg and Eugene D'Aquili, *Why God Won't Go Away: Brain Science and the Biology of Belief* (New York: Ballantine Books, 2001), p. 2.

7. Carl Sagan, *Contact* (New York: Pocket Books, 1986), p. 372.

8. C. Robert Cloninger, *Feeling Good: The Science of Well-being* (New York: Oxford University Press, 2004); "Is God in Our Genes?" *Time*, October 25, 2004, p. 70.

9. Dean Hamer, *The God Gene* (New York: Doubleday, 2004); Katherine M. Kirk, Lindon J. Eaves, and Nicholas G. Martin, "Self-Transcendence as a Measure of Spirituality in a Sample of Older Australian Twins," *Twin Research* 2 (1999): 81–87.

10. Kirk, Eaves, and Martin, "Self-transcendence as a Measure of Spirituality."

11. John of the Cross, *The Dark Night of the Soul*, book ii, ch. xvii.

12. Gerald Brenan, *St. John of the Cross* (Cambridge: Cambridge University Press, 1973), p. 23.

13. William James, *The Varieties of Religious Experience* (London: Longmans, Green & Co., 1902), p. 143.

14. John Templeton, *Agape Love* (Philadelphia: Templeton Foundation Press, 1999), p. 44.

15. Lawrence-Khantipalo Mills, *Buddhism Explained* (Bangkok: Silkworm Books, 1999), p. 144.

16. David M. Bear and Paul Fedio, "Quantitative Analysis of Interictal Behavior in Temporal Lobe Epilepsy," *Archives of Neurology* 34 (1977): 454–67.

17. Norman Geschwind, "Changes in Epilepsy," *Epilepsia* 24 (supp. 1, 1983): S23–30.

18. Frank R. Freemon, "A Differential Diagnosis of the Inspirational Spells of Muhammad the Prophet of Islam," *Epilepsia* 17 (1976): 423–27.

19. Norman Geschwind, "Dostoevsky's Epilepsy," in *Psychiatric Aspects of Epilepsy*, ed. Dietrich Blumer (Washington, D.C.: American Psychiatric Press, 1984), pp. 325–34.

20. Theophile Alajouanine, "Dostoyevsky's Epilepsy," *Brain* 86 (1963): 209–18.

21. Fyodor Dostoyevsky, *The Idiot* (1872), trans. Anna Brailovsky (New York: Modern Library, 2003), p. 244.

22. Kenneth Dewhorst and A. W. Beard, "Sudden Religious Conversion in Temporal Epilepsy" (1970), *Epilepsy and Behavior* 4 (2003): 80.

23. James, *The Varieties of Religious Experience*, p. 157.

24. Kenneth Ring, "Religiousness and Near-Death Experience: An Empirical Study," *Theta* 8 (1980): 3–5.

25. Anne L. Vaillant, "Women's Response to Near-Death Experience During Childbirth," unpublished thesis, Massachusetts General Hospital, Boston (1994), p. 30.

26. Bruce Greyson, "Near-Death Experiences and Spirituality," *Zygon* 41 (2006): 393–414.

27. James, *The Varieties of Religious Experience*.

28. Walter N. Pahnke and William A. Richards, "Implications of LSD and Experimental Mysticism," *Journal of Religion and Health* 25 (1966): 64–72.

29. Radamés Perez et al., "Changes in Brain Plasma and Cerebro-spinal Fluid Contents of Beta-endorphin in Dogs at the Moment of Death," *Neurological Research* 17 (1995): 223–25.

30. Greyson, "Near-Death Experiences and Spirituality," p. 395.

31. Pim van Lommel et al., "Near-Death Experience in Survivors of Cardiac Arrest: A Prospective Study in the Netherlands," *Lancet* 358 (2001): 2039–45.

32. Anne McIlroy, "Hardwired for God," *Globe and Mail* (Canada), December 6, 2003, F-1 and F-5.

33. Andrew Newberg and M. R. Waldman, *Why We Believe What We Believe* (New York: Free Press, 2006).

34. Andrew Newberg and Jeffrey Iversen, "The Neural Basis of the Complex Mental Task of Meditation: Neurotransmitter and Neurochemical Considerations," *Medical Hypothesis* 8 (2003): 282–91.

35. C. Robert Cloninger et al., "The Temperament and Character Inventory (TCI): A Guide to Its Development and Use" (St. Louis: Washington University, Center for Psychobiology and Personality, 1994).

36. Jon Krakauer, *Under the Banner of Heaven: A Story of Violent Faith* (New York: Doubleday, 2003); Anthony Storr, *Feet of Clay* (New York: Harper Collins, 1996).

37. Dostoyevsky, *The Idiot*, p. 181.

38. Cloninger et al., "The Temperament and Character Inventory."

39. Solomon H. Snyder, "Commentary on Paper by Griffiths et al.," *Psychopharmacology* 187 (2006): 287–88.

40. Rich Doblin, "Pahnke's 'Good Friday Experiment': A Long-Term Follow-up and Methodological Critique," *Journal of Transpersonal Psychology* 23 (1991): 1–28.

41. Walter N. Pahnke and William A. Richards, "Implications of LSD and Experimental Mysticism," *Journal of Religion and Health* 25 (1966): 64–72.

42. Joseph E. LeDoux, *The Emotional Brain: The Mysterious Underpinnings of Emotional Life* (New York: Simon & Schuster, 1998).

43. R. R. Griffiths et al., "Psilocybin Can on Occasion Cause Mystical-Type Experiences Having Substantial and Sustained Personal Meaning and Spiritual Significance," *Psychopharmacology* 187 (2006): 268–83.

44. Pahnke and Richards, "Implications of LSD and Experimental Mysticism."

45. Hamer, *The God Gene*, p. 11.

46. Ibid., p. 77.

47. William R. Miller and Janet C'de Baca, *Quantum Change* (New York: Guilford Press, 2001).

48. Andrew Smith, *Moondust: In Search of the Men Who Fell to Earth* (New York: Harper Collins, 2005).

49. Ibid., p. 197.
50. Ibid., p. 46.
51. Ibid., pp. 58–59.
52. Pierre Teilhard de Chardin, *Toward the Future* (New York: Harcourt Brace Jovanovich, 1975).
53. Newberg and Waldman, *Why We Believe What We Believe*, p. 191.
54. Edward E. Cummings, "voices to voices, lip to lip," unpublished manuscript, Harvard University (BMS AM 1823.5 [392]), Houghton Library typescript.

Chapter 11

1. James Fowler, *Becoming Adult, Becoming Christian* (San Francisco: Harper & Row, 1984), p. 71; the translation of the Bhagavad Gita, chapter 2, is attributed to Gandhi, and the last eighteen verses of Gandhi's version are from Eknath Easwaran, *Gandhi the Man* (Petaluma, Calif.: Nilgiri Press, 1978).
2. Daniel C. Dennett, *Breaking the Spell* (New York: Viking, 2006).
3. Antonio Damasio, *Descartes' Error* (New York: Putnam, 1994), p. 126.
4. David S. Wilson, *Darwin's Cathedral: Evolution, Religion, and the Nature of Society* (Chicago: University of Chicago Press, 2002); Mark Hauser, *Moral Minds: How Nature Designed Our Universal Sense of Right and Wrong* (New York: HarperCollins, 2006).
5. Leo Tolstoy, *Anna Karenina* (1877), vol. 3 (New York: Scribner, 1904), pp. 371–72.
6. Wayne Teasdale, *The Mystic Heart* (Novato, Calif.: New World Library, 1999).
7. Lindon J. Eaves et al., "Comparing the Biological and Cultural Inheritance of Personality and Social Attitudes in the Virginia 20,000 Study of Twins and Their Relatives," *Twin Research* 2 (1999): 62–80.
8. Thomas J. Bouchard et al., "Intrinsic and Extrinsic Religiousness: Genetic and Environmental Influences and Personality Correlates," *Twin Research* 2 (1999): 88–98.
9. Ajai R. Singh and Shakuntala A. Singh, "Gandhi on Religion, Faith, and Conversion," *Mens Sana Monographs* 2 (2004): 79–87.
10. Andrew Newberg and Eugene D'Aquili, *Why God Won't Go Away: Brain Science and the Biology of Belief* (New York: Ballantine Books, 2001), p. 80.
11. Albert Einstein, "A Symposium in Science, Philosophy, and Religion," unpublished paper, 1941.

12. Richard P. Sloan et al., "Should Physicians Prescribe Religious Activities?" *New England Journal of Medicine* 342 (2000): 1913–16; Emilia Bagiella, Victor Hong, and Richard P. Sloan, "Religious Attendance as a Predictor of Survival in the EPESE Cohorts," *International Journal of Epidemiology* 34 (2005): 443–51.

13. George E. Vaillant, "A Sixty-Year Follow-up of Male Alcoholism," *Addiction* 98 (2003): 1043–51.

14. Gerald G. May, *Addiction and Grace* (San Francisco: Harper San Francisco, 1991), pp. 6–7.

15. George E. Vaillant, Janice A. Templeton, Stephanie Meyer, and Monika Ardelt, "Natural History of Male Mental Health: What Is Spirituality Good For?" *Social Science and Medicine* 66 (2008): 221–31.

16. George E. Vaillant, *Natural History of Alcoholism Revisited* (Cambridge, Mass.: Harvard University Press, 1995).

17. Arthur H. Cain, "Alcoholics Anonymous: Cult or Cure?" *Harper's* (February 1963): 48–52; Nancy Shute, "What AA Won't Tell You," *U.S. News and World Report*, September 8, 1997, 55–65.

18. J. Michael McGinnis and William H. Foege, "Actual Causes of Death in the United States," *Journal of the American Medical Association* 270 (1993): 2207–12.

19. Lars Lindstrom, *Managing Alcoholism* (Oxford: Oxford University Press, 1992).

20. Mark B. Sobell and Linda C. Sobell, "Alcoholics Treated by Individualized Behavior Therapy: One-Year Treatment Outcome," *Behavior Research and Therapy* 1 (1973): 599–618; Mary L. Pendery et al., "Controlled Drinking by Alcoholics? New Findings and a Reevaluation of a Major Affirmative Study," *Science* 217 (1982): 169–75.

21. Vaillant, *Natural History of Alcoholism Revisited.*

22. Kelly D. Brownell et al., "Understanding and Preventing Relapse," *American Psychologist* 41 (1986): 765–82; Robert Stall and Paul Biernacki, "Spontaneous Remission from the Problematic Use of Substances: An Inductive Model Derived from a Comparative Analysis of the Alcohol, Opiate, Tobacco, and Food/Obesity Literature," *International Journal of Addictions* 21 (1986): 1–23; George E. Vaillant, "What Can Long-Term Follow-up Teach Us About Relapse and Prevention of Relapse in Addiction?" *British Journal of Addiction* 83 (1988): 1147–57.

23. George E. Vaillant, "A Twelve-Year Follow-up of New York Narcotic Addicts IV: Some Characteristics and Determinants of Abstinence," *American Journal of Psychiatry* 123 (1966): 573–84.

24. Jaak Panksepp, Eric Nelson, and S. M. Sivity, "Brain Opiates and Mother-Infant Bonding Motivation," *Aota Paediatrica Supplement* 397 (1994): 40–46.

25. William James, *The Varieties of Religious Experience* (London: Longmans, Green & Co., 1902).

26. Carl Jung, letter to Bill Wilson (1961), reprinted in *Alcoholics Anonymous Grapevine* (January 1963): 30–31.

27. Jaak Panksepp, Eric Nelson, and Marni Bekkedal, "Brain Systems for the Mediation of Social Separation-Distress and Social-Reward," *Annals of the New York Academy of Science* 807 (1997): 78–100.

28. Thomas R. Insel and Larry J. Young, "The Neurobiology of Attachment," *Nature Reviews Neuroscience* 2 (2002): 135.

29. Andrea Bartels and Semir Zeki, "The Neural Correlates of Maternal and Romantic Love," *Neuroimage* 21 (2004): 1155–66.

30. George L. Kovacs, Z. Sarnyai, and G. Szaba, "Oxytocin and Addiction: A Review," *Psychoneuroendocrinology* 23 (1998): 945–62.

31. J. C. D. Emrick et al., "Alcoholics Anonymous: What Is Currently Known?" in *Research in Alcoholics Anonymous: Opportunities and Alternatives*, ed. B. S. McCready and W. R. Miller (Piscataway, N.J.: Rutgers Center for Alcohol Studies, 1993), pp. 41–76.

32. Keith Humphreys and Rudolf H. Moos, "Reduced Substance Abuse–Related Health Care Costs Among Voluntary Participants in Alcoholics Anonymous," *Journal of Studies on Alcohol* 58 (1996): 231–38; Keith Humphreys, Rudolf H. Moos, and Caryn Cohen, "Social and Community Resources and Long-Term Recovery from Treated and Undirected Alcoholism," *Psychiatrist Services* 47 (1997): 709–13.

33. Christine Timko et al., "Long-Term Treatment Careers and Outcomes of Previously Untreated Alcoholics," *Journal Study of Alcohol* 60 (1999): 437–47.

34. Christine Timko et al., "Long-Term Outcomes of Alcoholic Use Disorders Comparing Untreated Individuals with Those in Alcoholics Anonymous and Formal Treatment," *Journal of Studies in Alcohol* 61 (2000): 529–40.

35. George E. Vaillant, *Natural History of Alcoholism Revisited* (Cambridge, Mass.: Harvard University Press, 1995).

36. George E. Vaillant, "A Sixty-Year Follow-up of Male Alcoholism," *Addiction* 98 (2003): 1043–51.

37. Stanton Peele, *The Diseasing of America* (Lexington, Mass.: Lexington Books, 1989).

38. Richard Behar, "Scientology, the Cult of Greed," *Time*, May 6, 1991.

39. Marc Galanter, "Cults and Zealous Self-Help Movements: A Psychiatric Perspective," *American Journal of Psychiatry* 147 (1990): 543–51.

40. Alcoholics Anonymous, "The AA Member, Medications, and Other Drugs" (medical pamphlet) (New York: AA World Services, n.d.), p. 11.

41. Robert Smith, "Dr. Bob and the Good Old Timers" (New York: AA World Services, 1950, 1980).

42. Ernest Kurtz, *Not God: A History of Alcoholics Anonymous* (Center City, Minn.: Hazelden, 1977).

43. Alcoholics Anonymous, *Twelve Steps and Twelve Traditions* (New York: AA World Services, 1953).

44. Robert Smith, brief remarks at the First International AA Convention, Cleveland, Ohio, July 3, 1950.

45. Karen Armstrong, *The Spiral Staircase: My Climb Out of Darkness* (New York: Knopf, 2003), p. 293.

46. Edward O. Wilson, *Consilience* (New York: Knopf, 1998), p. 264.

PERMISSIONS

INDEX

&

Schweitzer, Albert, 10, 12, 39, 50, 89
  spirituality and, 166–67
Scott, Robert, 112–13
Sedgwick, Adam, 40–41, 161
Seligman, Martin, 14–15, 108
septal area, 33, 39, 124–25
September 11, 2001, 15–16, 152–53
sex, sexuality, 35, 74, 121, 129–32, 152,
  159–60
  evolution and, 58–59, 63
  joy and, 124–25, 129–30, 132
  love and, 83, 90–91, 94–95, 98–99
Shakespeare, William, 165, 195
  love and, 89, 93, 101
Sharon, Ariel, 145
Skinner, B. F., 21, 23, 26, 32, 188, 206
slaves, slavery, 10, 57, 124, 139
Smith, Robert, 201–2, 204
Smith, Walter Chalmers, 81
Smith, Wilford Cantwell, 65
Sobell, Linda and Mark, 194–95
Sound of Music, The, 65–66
South Africa, 148–49
South Pacific, 94, 98, 108, 123
Soviet Union, 161–62, 201
Spain, 9, 66, 74, 79, 169–70, 201
Sperry, Roger, 24
spindle cells, 38, 88, 160
Spinoza, Baruch, 26
spirituality, 1, 3–8, 12–17, 32–33, 161,
  175–206
  AA and, 14, 194, 196, 198–204
  awe and, 5, 164–73, 175–84, 187, 192
  brain and, 6, 16, 19, 24, 26, 33, 36, 42,
    109, 172–73, 180, 183–84
  communality in, 16–17, 168–70, 187–88,
    198
  defining of, 4–5, 104, 165–66
  evolution and, 7–8, 10, 14, 46, 48,
    50–57, 64, 74, 83–87, 206
  faith and, 4–6, 67, 71–72, 74–76, 78–80,
    198
  forgiveness and, 4–5, 137, 149, 187
  healing and, 13, 72, 193–96
  hope and, 5, 117
  joy and, 5, 120–24, 126–27, 129, 132–33,
    172, 177
  love and, 5–6, 16, 83–88, 92, 165, 170,
    187, 189, 197

meditation and, 6, 191
metaphor vs. dogma in, 192, 194
psychobiological basis of, 6–7
religion and, 14, 16, 165–70, 184–94,
  196, 201, 204–5
science and, 19, 51, 206
Spiro, Howard, 116, 158
Stanford family, 111–12
Storr, Anthony, 77, 177

Teilhard de Chardin, Pierre, vii, 53–54,
  56, 119
temporal lobe epilepsy (TLE), 171–75,
  178, 180
Teresa of Avila, Saint, 170
terror, terrorists, terrorism, 15–16, 22, 26,
  61, 75, 78
  compassion and, 152–53
  forgiveness and, 137, 141–42, 147
"To His Coy Mistress" (Marvell), 96–97
Tolstoy, Leo, 99, 166–67, 186–87, 190
Tomkins, Sylvan, 33, 131–32
Traviata, La (Verdi), 130
Tutu, Desmond, 135
Twelfth Night (Shakespeare), 93

United Nations, 50, 53–55, 62, 186

van Lommel, Pim, 175–76, 178
Varieties of Religious Experience, The (James),
  23, 198, 201
ventromedial (orbitofrontal) prefrontal cor-
  tex, 31, 33, 35–39, 43, 61, 159
Verdi, Giuseppe, 24, 130
Versailles peace treaties, 135–36, 144–45
Visintainer, Madeline, 108
Visions of Compassion (Dalai Lama), 82

Warren, Rick, 152
West Side Story, 109
Whitman, Walt, 97
Wilson, Bill, 181, 198, 204
Wilson, David Sloan, 7, 186
Wilson, Edward O., 18, 206
World War I, 10, 152
  forgiveness and, 135–36, 142–45
World War II, 63, 109, 152, 188
  forgiveness and, 136, 142–45

ABOUT THE AUTHOR

George E. Vaillant, M.D., is the director of the Study of Adult Development at Harvard University. He is the author of *Aging Well* and *Adaptation to Life*, a classic text in adult development. He lives in Cambridge, Massachusetts, and Melbourne, Australia.